The Forgotten Edwards:

A New Examination of the Life and Thought of Jonathan Edwards Junior

The Forgotten Edwards:

A New Examination of the Life and Thought of Jonathan Edwards Junior

John S. Banks

Volume 3
A Series of Treatises on Jonathan Edwards

JESociety Press

WWW.JESOCIETY.ORG

Softcover Edition October 13, 2021
ISBN 978-1-7379026-1-4
© 2021 John S. Banks

A publication of JESociety Press
Visit https://www.jesociety.org

All rights reserved. No part of this publication may be reproduced, distributed, or transmitted in any form or by any means, including photocopying, recording, or other electronic or mechanical methods, without the prior written permission of the author/publisher, except in the case of brief quotations embodied in critical reviews and certain other noncommercial uses permitted by copyright law.

For permission requests and inquiries,
Email: info@jesociety.org
Web: www.jesociety.org

A Series of Treatises on Jonathan Edwards

JESociety Press is pleased to announce *A Series of Treatises on Jonathan Edwards*, an all new series given exclusively to the select publication of cutting-edge research related to America's greatest theologian. The series provides authors with a venue for publishing original, concise, authoritative and peer-reviewed manuscripts. The series provides readers with lively, assessable and in-depth treatments of Edwards-specific subject matter. For more information about the series or with questions about JESociety Press, please visit our website at: www.jesociety.org or contact us directly at: info@jesociety.org.

PRAISE FOR THIS VOLUME

The "other" Jonathan Edwards has never received the attention his work as New Haven pastor, dedicated theologian, and interpreter of his famous father's legacy deserves. With especially fruitful use of the younger Edwards' manuscript sermons, this carefully researched book goes a long way to redress that undeserved neglect.

Mark Noll
author of
In the Beginning Was the Word: The Bible in American Public Life, 1492-1783

Jonathan Edwards, Jr. played a crucial but still largely unappreciated role as a conduit of his father's varied legacies. In this fine study by an up-and-coming scholar, that role is paid respect and Edwards Jr.'s own honor and legacy are defended against their critics, past and present. Many thanks to John Banks for coloring in our understanding of the Edwardsean tradition in Revolutionary America.

Douglas A. Sweeney
Dean, Beeson Divinity School
Samford University

This study offers an engaging account of a pastor and divine whose career included an early exposure to missions among Mohican and Mohawks, public debates about the culture of reason and Calvinism, the American Revolution, contestations over the abolition of slavery, and changes in the practice of collegiate education in New England. Based on deep original archival research and a solid grasp on current scholarship, it brings to life the complications and tensions in the career of the namesake son of Jonathan Edwards. In so doing, it gives us a humane and lucid narrative of theology and its relation to social life when America became a nation.

Mark Valeri
The Reverend Priscilla Wood Neaves Distinguished Professor
John C. Danforth Center on Religion and Politics
Washington University in St. Louis

Jonathan Edwards Jr. has remained entirely in his father's shadow. Moreover, there are also negative prejudices regarding his person and preaching. He is seen as a spiritless preacher under whom the spiritual life in the church was decreasing. Often he is only known for his moral government theory of atonement. Is this justified? Who was Jonathan Edwards Jr who lost his father at the age of thirteen? John Banks has done us a great service by researching the life, theology and spirituality of the young Edwards. It turns out that he made an impression as a preacher in his day and that - like his father - he lived by the vital piety of the work of the Holy Spirit in the heart. In his strength of thought he was not inferior to his father. His public significance in regard to the American Revolution and the advocacy of the abolition of slavery was great. A new world opens up to us in this study.

Willem van Vlastuin
Chair of Theology and Spirituality of Reformed
Protestantism in the Faculty of Religion and Theology
Vrije Universiteit Amsterdam

Through skillful archival work and in-depth research, John Banks dispels a common caricature of Jonathan Edwards Jr. *The Forgotten Edwards* presents the Younger Edwards as, rather than representing a significant deviation from his father's theology, in numerous respects, being a faithful disciple and developer of it. Banks chronicles several cases where Edwards Jr. augmented and extended areas where his father was silent. A case in point is the issue of slavery. Historians like to speculate counterfactually: "What if Edwards Sr. lived long enough to see the budding of the movement that eventually ended slavery?" His son's teachings on abolitionism and activism may be the key to such an inquiry. This new biographical sketch of Edwards Jr. rightly underscores his father's growing uneasiness towards the slave trade and demonstrates how his son's advocacy for abolition was actually underpinned by his father's thoughts.

Chris Chun
Director of Jonathan Edwards Center
Professor of Church History
Gateway Seminary

This fresh interpretation of Jonathan Edwards Jr. is situated deep in primary sources and archival work. Banks's work points the way to a new appreciation of Edwards Jr., and provides a standard for stripping away the tired, old interpretations of the New

Divinity as impersonal metaphysicians who cared more about doctrinal coherence than piety, revival, and pastoral care. While recognizing minor differences between Edwards Jr. and his famous father, Banks shows us that they shared far more in common than is generally recognized.

Robert W. Caldwell III
Professor of Church History
Southwestern Baptist Theological Seminary

Will we ever see a resurgence of interest in the history of New England Theology? If we see more works like this one, we may. Banks' treatment of Jonathan Edwards Jr. is wind in the sails to those of us who continue to explore the darker corners of the development of the New England mind. A healthy deposit on what will doubtless be a profitable future in Christian scholarship, Banks' *The Forgotten Edwards* offers readers a detailed blend of historical and theological inquiry wrapped up in an artful prose.

S. Mark Hamilton
Research Associate, JESociety

With an array of letters, sermon notes, diary entries, and other primary sources, John Banks offers a compelling alternative to the prevailing narrative of the "disconnect and decline" between Jonathan Edwards Sr. and Jr. Wiping away some of the historiographical haze, Banks presents a theologian and philosopher whose thinking was consistent with, not counter to, his legendary father's. Since Joseph Haroutunian's biting critique of the New Divinity and even long before, the exact relationship between Edwards and the Edwardseans has long been scrutinized. This book takes us a step closer to understanding that complex relationship, as Edwards Jr. can be easily caricaturized and may not have been the "spiritless" and unintelligible preacher that so many have painted him to be.

Obbie Tyler Todd
Pastor of Third Baptist Church of Marion, Illinois and
Adjunct Faculty at Luther Rice College & Seminary

It has long been assumed that discontinuity existed between "America's Theologian," Jonathan Edwards, and his son, Jonathan Edwards, Jr. Grappling with troves of new manuscripts, John Banks offers a new perspective on their relationship that was both Edwards, Jr.'s theological and intellectual inheritance from his father. With a new, collective sum of Edwards, Jr.'s work, Banks showcases a new account of Edwards, Jr.'s thought as one of equal prowess to his father within the realms of philosophy and theology. Likewise, Banks argues for a consistency between the two Edwards men which has thought to be contrary to this point. With a host of fresh primary source material, Banks propels Edwards, Jr. into new light, and brings clarity to the complex relationship Edwards had with his father. Therefore, Banks has righted the ship from old vestiges into a clearer understanding of Edwards' legacy and the narratives of the New England Theological tradition.

John T. Lowe
PhD Candidate, Vrije Universiteit Amsterdam
Adjunct Professor, University of Louisville

John S. Banks's *The Forgotten Edwards* is a model study of unpublished and largely unknown manuscripts, in the case of Jonathan Edwards, Jr., over 1200 works. Readers of American religious history will be interested in Banks's argument that the younger Edwards sought to be a spirited preacher, not, as he has often been portrayed, a logician of American Calvinism. Students of American abolitionism will benefit from Banks's demonstration that the younger Edwards's best known publication, his attack on the slave trade and the institution of slavery, was not only a reflection of am antislavery consensus among a core of Edwards's heirs but also a part of a cycle of sermons preached on the Sermon on the Mount, casting this important pamphlet in a new light for historians. Scholars of early American literature will learn from Banks's careful reconstruction of the textual history of the younger Edwards's sermons for condemned men Joseph Mountain and Moses Paul. All these advances, which are qualitatively different from rehashing old debates, were possible because Banks worked in the archives on a corpus of rarely studied manuscripts. Bravo!

John Saillant
Professor of English and History
Chair of the Department of English
Western Michigan University

For the

glory of God,

my dear wife,

Abigail Joy,

who is a constant source of joy,

and our heritage from the Lord:

Adam, Noah, Jonah,

Seth, & Anna

List of Illustrations

A Gideon Hawley's Hand-Drawn Map of Onohquaughe 24

B Portrait of Jonathan Edwards Jr. 37

C Sketch, by Dr. Ezra Stiles, of the Invasion of New Haven 54

D Examples of partial and full note manuscripts 152

List of Abbreviations

AAP1   William B. Sprague, *Annals of the American Pulpit [...]*. Vol. 1. New York: Robert Carter and Brothers, 1857.

AAP2   William B. Sprague, *Annals of the American Pulpit [...]*. Vol. 2. New York: Robert Carter and Brothers, 1857.

LDES1   Ezra Stiles, *The Literary Diary of Ezra Stiles: January 1, 1769–March 13, 1776*. Vol. 1. Edited by Franklin Bowditch Dexter. New York: Charles Scribner's Sons, 1901.

LDES2   Ezra Stiles, *The Literary Diary of Ezra Stiles: March 14, 1776–December 31, 1781*. Vol. 2. Edited by Franklin Bowditch Dexter. New York: Charles Scribner's Sons, 1901.

LDES3   Ezra Stiles, *The Literary Diary of Ezra Stiles: January 1, 1782–May 6, 1795*. Vol. 3. Edited by Franklin Bowditch Dexter. New York: Charles Scribner's Sons, 1901.

JEW1   Jonathan Edwards, *The Works of Jonathan Edwards, D.D., Late President of Union College. With a Memoir [...]*. Vol. 1. Edited by Tryon Edwards. Andover, MA: Allen, Morril and Wardwell, 1842.

JEW2   Jonathan Edwards, *The Works of Jonathan Edwards, D.D., Late President of Union College. With a Memoir [...]*. Vol. 2. Edited by Tryon Edwards. Andover, MA: Allen, Morril and Wardwell, 1842.

Acknowledgements

I originally wanted to write about Joseph Bellamy because his biographers painted a more winsome character of him than his protégé Jonathan Edwards Jr. Yet while I had this alternative proposed in my mind, I am especially thankful for Dr. Michael A. G. Haykin, my research advisor, for encouraging me to give serious consideration to the "cornucopia" available to me in Edwards Jr. instead. After observing that Bellamy's handwriting was in fact microscopic, and much of it, on water-smudged manuscripts, I agreed to go with Edwards Jr. Yet, even from the foggy beginning, Dr. Haykin patiently listened to my first topic suggestion "the theological trigger which caused the rise of the cults after the second great awakening" and led me to simply: "Edwards Jr." Turning to the Edwards Jr. manuscripts I found that them to resonate with a sincere piety, which has profited me my own understanding of the third person of the Trinity. Further, I would like to mention my research fellow, Jonathan Swan, who provided kind words of encouragement at each mid-semester check-in.

I am also grateful to Edwards Jr., who wrote with a large script, and really, the only difficulty I experienced in my research was knowing how to narrow the great volume of his unpublished manuscripts located in four different libraries (Hartford Theological Seminary, Yale Divinity School, Beinecke Rare Book Library, and Princeton University). The staff at the Hartford Seminary Library provided me such hospitality and assistance—especially Marie Rovero who I've still not met in person. I would also like to thank Dr. Rev. Stephen Blackburn, the former Hartford Seminary Librarian, who graciously allowed me to visit him at the parsonage of Colebrook Congregational Church to review the records of the church when Edwards Jr. was the pastor in the late 1790s. I am grateful to Joan Duffy and Kenneth

Minkema of Yale Divinity School who assisted me in tracking down the Newton-Andover manuscripts en route to the Beinecke Rare Book Library.

In my research, I have also just begun to uncover the connection that Edwards Jr. had in the planting and watering of the Whitestown, NY settlement churches during the great migration years in the mid-1780s. I would like to express my appreciation for Midge (Margorie) Bakos, a spry lady of nearly ninety-years and the church historian of the Stone Presbyterian Church in Clinton, NY. Midge pointed me to an early faithful copy of church documents Jonathan Edwards Jr. had brought with him in the founding of the first three churches in the Mohawk Valley. She was proud to reveal to me her own interest in Jonathan Edwards Jr. as she is apparently a descendent of the illustrious Edwards family. Harry Young, the historian of the New Hartford Presbyterian Church in New Hartford, is to be thanked as he was very helpful in providing photos of early church documents. He is also provides a wonderful historical walk through the church.

Last, I am very grateful to Peter Flowers, who I met at a regional Evangelical Theology Society meeting at Gordon-Conwell Theological Seminary. He enthusiastically read each chapter I sent his way and then returned to me a copy with constructive red ink for my attention and revision. My wife would also like to thank him as it minimized her need to do so.

John S. Banks, Th.M.
Lake Ariel, Pennsylvania
December 2020

Foreword

Michael A.G. Haykin

The Presbyterian theologian B. B. Warfield maintained, on more than one occasion, that a special interest in pneumatology lay woven into the fabric of the Reformed tradition. He traced this prominent thread back to Calvin and postulated that it could be especially found, after Calvin, in the warp and woof of English Puritanism and its legacy in English Nonconformity. Yet, while Warfield was convinced that Jonathan Edwards, Sr. was "the one figure of real greatness in the intellectual life of colonial America," he does not seem to have noticed the way that Edwards's doctrine of the Spirit supported his thesis about Reformed pneumatology. Time and again Edwards stressed that the central fruit of the atoning work of Christ was the gift of his indwelling Holy Spirit. Moreover, Warfield was entirely dismissive of Edwards's heirs, the New Divinity as they have come to be called, which included Edwards's namesake, Jonathan Edwards, Jr. The thought of this body of New England theologians, in Warfield's estimation, was fundamentally at odds with the Reformed tradition. In fact, Warfield argued, their deficient pneumatology prepared the ground for "a new Pelagianizing system" in the hands of the New Haven theologian Nathaniel W. Taylor. John Sherwin Banks could not disagree more with this negative opinion of the New Divinity men—and rightly so. These theologians are far more in line with Reformed orthodoxy than Warfield realized or was prepared to admit. In this fresh study of one of the key figures in the New Divinity movement, Jonathan Edwards, Jr., Banks details the way in which the pneumatology of the younger Edwards was very much in line with that of his father. But this monograph entails more than a fresh examination of Edwards, Jr.'s pneumatology. It seeks to make a case for Edwards the Younger as a significant pastor-theologian in his own right and thus the need for rescuing him from the obscurity that has enveloped him and other New Divinity pastor-theologians since Warfield's day. And in the opinion of this writer, Banks needs to be heard.

Dundas, Ontario
September 7, 2021

Contents

List of Illustrations i

List of Abbreviations iii

Acknowledgements v

Foreword — *Michael A.G. Haykin* vii

Chapter 1 — Introduction: Spirit and Style 1
   A Tendency to Confuse Preaching Style with Spirituality 4
   A Nineteenth Century Caricature of Edwards Jr 7
   A Need to Review the Inherited Caricature 9

Chapter 2 — A Biographical Sketch 17
   Hardship and Spiritual Nurture 18
   A Traumatic Apprenticeship 21
   Loss of Family and Awakening 23
   Early Ministry and Marriage Tragedy 31
   Revolution and Benevolent Justice 38
      Advocating Justice 38
      Advocating Benevolence 45
      Advocating Abolition 47
      Patriotism and Revolution 48
   Defense of the Gospel and Displacement 55
   Second Great Awakening and Union 63

Chapter 3 — A Shared Relish for True Religion 67
   The Beatitudes (Matt 5:2–12) 71

Introduction (Matthew 5:13–20) 79
The Law of Christ (Matt 5:21–48) 84
The Lord's Prayer (Matt 6:10–13) 88
God's Superior Kingdom (Matt 6:19–33) 91
The Invitation and Warnings of Christ (Matt 7:12–28) 92
Conclusion 98

Chapter 4 — A Received Edwardsean Pneumatology   101
Jonathan Edwards's Pneumatological Legacy 105
The Younger Edwards's Common Bond 112
    Mentoring Preachers 112
    Published 'Occasional' Sermons 127
    Unpublished Weekly Sermons 134
Conclusion 143

Chapter 5 — Conclusion: In Step with the Spirit   145

Appendix 1 — The Nature of Edwards Jr.'s Sermon Manuscripts   149

Appendix 2 — Sermon 79 (Rev. 22:17): a Transcript   153

Appendix 3 — Two Sermons for Moses Paul   165
    Jonathan Edwards Jr., "Volume 225," *Jonathan Edwards Jr. Papers
        (Sermons),* Hartford Seminary Library (Box 166, Folder 2732) 166
    Jonathan Edwards Jr., "Volume 242," *Jonathan Edwards Jr. Papers
        (Sermons),* Hartford Seminary Library (Box 166, Folder 2732) 177

Appendix 4 — Sermon 412: For a Fast On Account of our Present
    Disputes with Great Britain   183

Appendix 5 — "Confession of Faith"   201

Appendix 6 — List of Theological Questions of Edwards Sr. and
    Edwards Jr. Relevant to the Holy Spirit   203

Appendix 7 — Oneida County, NY Church Documents   205
    Confession of Faith 205
    Covenant 206
    Rules for the Admission of Members 207

Appendix 8 — Jonathan Edwards Jr.'s Sermons Derived from the
   Sermon on the Mount   209

Bibliography   215
   Primary Sources 215
      Primary Published 215
      Primary Unpublished Manuscripts 221
      Primary Letters and Church Records 223
   Secondary Sources 226

Index   235

Chapter 1

Introduction: Spirit and Style

"The expectation, renown, and legacy of Jonathan Edwards (1703–1758) casts a shadow so great that even to this day the younger Edwards (1745–1801) is only now beginning to be measured—but even then—only slightly.[1] Tryon Edwards (1809–1895), the younger's grandson and nineteenth-century memoirist, had the vexing task of commending the natural abilities of Edwards Jr. without casting doubt upon the elder Edwards's widely acclaimed genius. Tryon advised his readers that

> the first President Edwards was a greater man than the second; but if the father had higher powers of invention, the son was perhaps the most acute and dexterous as a logician. If the former could dive deeper, and bring up more pearls from the bottom, he could not arrange them when procured with greater skill and advantage than the latter. If his eye was more excursive, it was not keener. If he could lift the telescope easier, we doubt whether he could manage the microscope so well.[2]

---

[1] Donald Weber does much to rehabilitate the image of Edwards Jr. as a capable revolutionary patriot in the pulpit with a thorough examination of his unpublished patriotic sermons at Harford Seminary to which I hope to bring additional insight into his sensitivity to the Spirit in his theology and pulpit work. Donald Weber, "The Edwardsean Legacy: The Example of Jonathan Edwards Jr. of White Haven," in *Rhetoric and History in Revolutionary New England* (New York: Oxford University Press, 1988), 72.

[2] *JEW1*, xxxviii.

The pressure placed upon the namesake[3] of a famous father often produces anxiety and insecurity in the successor to either plant their own flag or to hoist their parent's flag higher.[4] When Edwards Jr. came of age, he offered commentary on his father's "Improvements in Theology"[5] as well as engrossed himself in the transcribing and preparation for publication of his father's works.[6] Indeed, the pressure was transatlantic.

A decade after the death of the elder Edwards, William Gordon (1728–1807) expressed his hope in a letter to Joseph Bellamy (1719–1790), if not, a benediction over the "son of the late president Edwards" that "if possible a double portion of his father's spirit and abilities" might rest upon him.[7] While the younger Edwards seems to have succeeded at the latter, the former prayer request for the same spirit as his father is widely assumed to have been unanswered. While he may have received double the ability, often Edwards Jr. is presented as having none of the same spirit, when in actuality, he had at least as much, in spite of his difficult start.

---

[3] Jonathan was the second born boy (of three) in his parent's already large household of girls (eight). The oldest boy (July 25, 1738) was named for Edward's esteemed father, Rev. Timothy Edwards. Edwards Sr. named his youngest (April 8, 1750) in honor of the Pierrepont family's status at New Haven and perhaps a premonition that he was running out of time. Mr. Pierpont was a founder and trustee of Yale. This relationship would serve to advance the younger Edwards' future career in New Haven. On naming patterns in New England, see Daniel Scott Smith, "Child-Naming Practice, Kinship Ties, and Change in Family Attitudes in Hingham, Massachusetts, 1641 to 1880," *Journal of Social History* 18, no. 4 (Summer 1985): 554. Also see David D. Hall on naming practices in *Worlds of Wonder, Days of Judgment* (New York: Alfred A. Knopf, 1989), 10, 17.

[4] The honor of a namesake often creates the unintended consequence of overlooking the unique contributions of the heir who bears the memorial of the father. For example, in a trans-Atlantic letter to Jonathan Edwards Jr. from John Ryland Jr. of "Northampton in Old England" dated June 29, 1787, Ryland asks Edwards Jr. whether he has any children of his own, adding "I wish there might be a Jonathan Edwards the 3rd for my poor motherless boy to correspond with." *Jonathan Edwards Papers, Series V Edwards Family Correspondence, Jonathan Edwards 1745–1801 Incoming Letters.*, Beinecke Rare Book and Manuscript Library (Gen MSS 151, Box 26, Folder 1458).

[5] "Improvements" is a clever pun considering the typical structure of a sermon that ended with either an "Improvement" or an "Examination." *JEW1*, 481–92.

[6] Robert L. Ferm has a transcription of parishioner David Austin's letter to Roger Sherman (February 20, 1790) airing grievances over his pastor's (Edwards Jr.) misplaced time in preparing his father's sermons for publication in Hartford, and *The History of Redemption* to be sent to Scotland with an assortment of thirty-three other sermons. Austin felt that Edwards Jr. needed to spend more time so he might "win his people to the practice of virtue and religion." Robert L. Ferm, *A Colonial Pastor: Jonathan Edwards the Younger, 1745–1801* (Grand Rapids: Eerdmans Publishing, 1976), 141.

[7] William Gordon was a well-known dissenting pastor in London. He would later emigrate to America. William Gordon, letter sent to Joseph Bellamy, July 14, 1769, *Bellamy Papers*, Hartford Seminary Library (Box 188, Folder 2936, Item 81349).

INTRODUCTION: SPIRIT AND STYLE

Having lost his parents at the age of just thirteen, his father's pupils took him under their wing to preserve the integrity of the developing theological brand.[8] After graduation from the College of New Jersey in 1765, Joseph Bellamy in Bethlehem, Connecticut and Samuel Hopkins (1721–1803) in Great Barrington, Massachusetts[9] introduced him to the Edwardsean tradition in the haven of their respective homes. During the winter of 1765–1766, the younger Edwards had the privilege to spend time reading his father's manuscripts with Hopkins. Hopkin's biographer, William Patten, relates that the younger Edwards, in spite of his "amiable" disposition, demonstrated some youthful pride by objecting to his father's "leading doctrines."

However, after examining the arguments of his father, Edwards Jr. found he needed to more deeply examine his own theories. As the story goes, after just a night's reflection, the younger Edwards changed his tune in favor of the truth.[10] Robert L. Ferm also retells this moment but questions whether Patten's account is accurate in the portrayal of the younger, or that the account was an easy way of "building [up] the character of his subject [i.e., Hopkins]."[11] The apocryphal flavoring accorded to the story by Ferm dissipates when comparing a brief journal of resolutions penned by Edwards Jr. while he was still a student. In his journal, Edwards Jr. had pledged a willingness to acquiesce to the truth, at all times, regardless of its source.[12]

---

[8] Joseph A. Conforti describes how both Bellamy and Hopkins adopted the younger Edwards as a son to ensure that he followed in his father's footsteps. "When Hopkins sent Jonathan Edwards Jr., to study in Bethlehem, Connecticut, in 1766, he wrote Bellamy telling him the son of the great theologian 'will take it kindly if you converse with him particularly about his personal religion and act the part of a father to him, in freely giving him your best counsel and advice.'" Joseph A. Conforti, *Samuel Hopkins and The New Divinity Movement: Calvinism, the Congregational Ministry, and Reform in New England Between the Great Awakenings* (Grand Rapids: Christian University Press, 1981), 38.

[9] "[Edwards Jr.] ever retained a filial respect and affection for Mr. H. [Hopkins], and contributed to his support when he feared he might be in want, and Mr. H. felt a kind of pride in him as a son. In the hearing of the writer, when someone was highly praising Dr. E., Mr. H. said, 'Me make him;' alluding to an aged Indian minister who used this expression on hearing a younger Indian preacher commended who was very popular, and who had been brought up under his instruction." William Patten, *Reminiscences of the Late Rev. Samuel Hopkins, D. D. of Newport, RI [...]* (Providence, RI: I. H. Cady, 1843), 47.

[10] Patten, *Reminiscences*, 45–47.

[11] Ferm, *Edwards the Younger*, 22.

[12] "Always be open and attentive to receive truth from any, even from an adversary, or an inferior; however despicable. Let not pride, desire of mastery, shame of being taught, or anything blind the mind against truth." Jonathan Edwards Jr., "Observations and Rules for Conduct in Private Life" (n.d.), 2, in the *Jonathan Edwards Papers*, Beinecke Rare Book and Manuscript Library (Gen MSS 151, Box 24, Folder 1359).

While described by Patten as having an "amiable" disposition, no doubt Edwards Jr. must have exerted himself to create this effect. Edwards was conscious of the need to amend his tendency to be 'peevish.' In the same collection of resolutions, which he titled "Observations and Rules for Conduct in private life," he states,

> I observe it a common thing for men, especially men of close application to study, to be peevish and fretful, especially towards those of their own family, their wives, children and domestics, and that upon trivial occasions, upon very slight and [at the] same time no [real] provocations at all. Therefore, let it be a rule to guard against such a spirit as much as possible and never to indulge it; but calmly reprove and correct those things, which are amiss without spasms and peevishness.[13]

This irritability seems to have been a life-long struggle to overcome. Edwards's son-in-law, Calvin Chapin, gently describes him as self-aware of his innate "irritability," which he freely admitted to others as a "besetting infirmity of his nature."[14]

In contrast to Calvin Chapin, Rev. Timothy Mather Cooley's description was less gentle. Having known Edwards Jr. while "a member of Yale," Cooley recalled a less than flattering picture of his "impatient spirit" while on a visit together out-of-town. While on a northbound route, his horse's shoe needed emergency attention and Edwards Jr. "lost all patience with the blacksmith, who had either made a blundering job of it, or in some other way had him."[15] Cooley also had opportunity to hear Edwards Jr. preach, which he shared with the editors of the nine-volume *Annals of the American Pulpit*. This biographical set became a standard resource for modern dictionaries and nineteenth century novelists.

A Tendency to Confuse Preaching Style with Spirituality

In the *Annals of the American Pulpit,* Cooley elaborates at length on Edward Jr.'s preaching ministry as likely difficult to endure for the average parish-

---

[13] There are only four observations and rules. The fourth comprises just the top third of the page with plenty of room to add more. Jonathan Edwards Jr., "Observations and Rules" (n.d.), in the *Jonathan Edwards Papers, Series IV Edwards Family Writings,* Beinecke Rare Book and Manuscript Library (Gen MSS 151, Box 24, Folder 1359), 1.

[14] *AAP1,* 658.

[15] *AAP1,* 659.

ioner. According to Cooley, Edwards Jr. was "too profound to be interesting, or always intelligible [unintelligible] to ordinary minds. His own mind was so trained to philosophical disquisition that he seemed sometimes to forget that the multitude whom he was addressing were not also metaphysicians."[16] In what seems to be a feigned attempt to be gracious,[17] Cooley concedes that "a portion of his preaching, however, was highly practical, and sometimes it was irresistibly impressive and even terrible [that is, convicting]." Nevertheless, he returns to the unattractive details of Edwards's pulpit presence:

> His manner was the opposite of attractive. In his voice there was a nasal twang which diminished the effect of his utterance. He had little or no gesture, looked about but little upon his audience, and seemed like a man who was conscious that he was dealing in abstractions. Nevertheless, he was uttering great and profound thoughts; and those who were capable of estimating them, went away admiring the power of his genius, and edified by the striking and original views which had been presented to them.[18]

As noted above, Edwards Jr. was conscious of his own faults. In a private notebook, he noted several stylistic tendencies such as, speaking too fast on "too high a key" while "neglecting the spirit in preaching, preaching legally [...] preaching metaphysically [...] and having too much of a sameness in the argumentative part of the discourse and in the application."[19]

At one time Edwards Jr. asked Nathan Strong for advice while they were together at a revival in Hartford.[20] Edwards Jr. asked Strong,

---

[16] *AAP1*, 659.

[17] This detail is important to weigh when considering potential bias. Having matriculated into Yale at sixteen in 1788, Timothy Mather Cooley resided in town with some of the families of Dr. James Dana's congregation. During those years of residence, Edwards Jr. and James Dana were in sharp disagreement over a number of important New Divinity principles, such as, regenerate church membership and Edwards Jr.'s understanding of the will. Nathan Williams, John Smalley, and Benjamin Trumbull, eds., *The Congregational Quarterly*, vol. 2 (Boston: Edward L. Balch, 1860), 272–279.

[18] *AAP1*, 659–60.

[19] Edwards Jr.'s seven-point critique of self is recorded in an undated document titled "Corrigenda" in *Shephard Family Collection*, Beinecke Rare Book and Manuscript Library. Box and File are unavailable currently due to transfer of documents.

[20] Of significance is a similar account of Nathan Strong and Joseph Bellamy. At an event hosted by Strong in Harford, it was advised that perhaps Bellamy not preach as there were a number

> "Why does the influence of the Holy Spirit attend your preaching so much more than mine, when our congregations are so much alike, and we preach the same system of truth?" Strong replied, "The reason is that you present Gospel truth as a proposition to be proved, and go on to prove it; whereas I endeavor to exhibit it as something already admitted and to impress upon the hearts and conscience."[21]

While certainly not advocating an enthusiast approach, Strong was advising Edwards Jr. to switch from argumentation to assertion—a stylistic change—so as to see spiritual results.

A winsome preaching style was often considered a mark of spiritual endowment, especially by the separatists who put pressure upon the established Congregational churches.[22] C. C. Goen describes how these separatist preachers were often uneducated and self-trained in elocution. This lack of preparation increased their perceived spirituality. To the Separates, a spiritual preacher would depend on the Spirit, in the moment, without the use of any prepared notes, even increasing the pitch of their voice to sound spiritual.[23] A pleasing style, especially in an evangelical context, might at times be confused with spirituality, or in the case of Edwards Jr., the lack thereof.

Further, the mood of the nation was changing with regard to clergy. Feeling the economic effects of the rampant inflation as the Revolution was coming to an end, many young men went west looking for the lands they had seen while marching against the British. Eastern parishes became thinly populated. Nathan Hatch describes the era (1780s through 1820) as a time in which "ordinary folk came to distrust leaders of genius and talent and to

---

of people not pleased with his position on regeneration by the Holy Spirit, as that was "the great theological question at issue in that day" as some would see men as "regenerated by light." Bellamy instead preached on the millennium, but then baited his audience by suggesting they come back later in the afternoon, if they wanted to hear how a change of character might take place in a man. Joseph Bellamy, *The Works of Joseph Bellamy,* vol. 1 (Boston: Doctrinal Tract and Book Society, 1850), lxiii.

[21] Rev. Thomas Robbins reported this account. *AAP2,* 38.

[22] At about the mid-point of Edwards Jr.'s preaching career in New Haven, the Separates officially became a denomination in 1781. C. C. Goen, *Revivalism and Separatism in New England, 1740– 1800: Strict Congregationalists and Separate Baptists in the Great Awakening* (Hamden, CT: Archon Books, 1969), 172.

[23] C. C. Goen describes at length the characteristics of the Separates' preaching and worship including the peculiarities of the "holy whine," impressions, enthusiasm, and "improvement of spiritual gifts." Goen, *Revivalism and Separatism,* 174–84.

defend the right of common people to shape their own faith and submit to leaders of their own choosing."[24] During the Jacksonian era of the individualism, Charles Finney becomes the ministerial standard. This ministerial shift in style did not occur over night. The rhetoric of the revolution, of which Edwards Jr. was a part, contributed to the shifting of authority from a singular community pulpit to an outright anticlericalism.[25] With pressure to compete for parishioners in an increasingly mobile and economically constrained time, a nation with a penchant for popular preaching could cast an intellectual pastor as one bereft of the Spirit. Out of this new national mood, prior to the American Civil War, Edwards Jr.'s 'spiritless' caricature became crystalized.

A Nineteenth Century Caricature of Edwards Jr.

Both Cooley and Strong's account of Edwards Jr.'s preaching are contained in *The Annals of the American Pulpit*. This anthology of biography and anecdotes was published a decade before Harriet Beecher Stowe's *The Minister's Wooing*. In her novel comprised of New Divinity era pastors, Stowe depicts Edwards Jr. and Samuel Hopkins as more concerned with preaching abstractions to their congregations than the souls they were hurting by their abstractions.[26] Stowe's depiction is built upon a received perception of a difficult preaching style coupled with a natural irritability. Undoubtedly these elements would conspire to create a portrait of Edwards Jr. that is much less inviting than his father—even to the point of becoming a fixed narrative of austerity.[27]

---

[24]Nathan O. Hatch, *The Democratization of American Christianity* (New Haven, CT: Yale University Press, 1989), 14.

[25]"The fundamental religious quarrel of the late eighteenth century was not between Calvinist and Arminian, orthodox and Unitarian, evangelical and freethinker but between radically different conceptions of the Christian ministry. As respectable clergymen in these turbulent years reiterated their confidence in learning and civility, potent strains of anticlericalism welled up within the bounds of the church, challenging the right of any special order to mediate the gospel." Hatch, *Democratization of American Christianity*, 44.

[26]"Hopkins sends to Edwards the younger his scheme of the universe, in which he starts with the proposition, that God is infinitely above all obligations of any kind to his creatures. Edwards replies with the brusque comment,–"This is wrong; God has no more right to injure a creature than a creature has to injure God;" and each probably about that time preached a sermon on his own view, which was discussed by every farmer, in intervals of plough and hoe, by every woman and girl at loom, spinningwheel, or wash-tub. New England was one vast sea, surging from depths to heights with thought and discussion of the most insoluble of mysteries." Stowe, *The Minister's Wooing*, 334–35.

[27]William Breitenbach opines that "[t]he first, and still the most common [betrayal interpretation], characterizes the Edwardsians as arid metaphysicians and austere hyper-Calvinists who

Writing in the early twentieth century with this caricature in his rearview, Joseph Haroutunian paints Edwards Jr. as lacking any piety saying,

> Edwards the son had none of his father's glowing mysticism and natural piety. He was the arch-moralist among the Calvinists. In him that legalism which has previously been observed as creeping into Calvinism finds its supreme expression. His mind operates wholly in terms of crime and punishment, praise and blame, good and evil.[28]

Even in a more modern biography, *Dictionary of American Religious Biography* (1977), Edwards is described as losing his congregation of twenty-six years in New Haven to controversy over the Half-way Covenant and the preaching of

> dry, abstruse sermons ... dispensed on controverted points of Christian belief. Questions raised by deistic critiques occupied much of his attention, and he informed audiences of proper rebuttals in an exhibition of truth destitute of verbal adornment. His reasoning ways always closely confined to the topic, following rigid demonstrations that resembled pure mathematics, a subject which fascinated him avocationally throughout life.[29]

If Rev. Timothy Cooley or Nathan Strong's account had been the only record left, alongside Edwards Jr.'s own list of self-improvements, then a 'spiritless' caricature might be warranted.

---

systematized Edwards's thought, but in so doing drained it of its warm and vital piety." William Breitenbach, "Piety and Moralism: Edwards and the New Divinity," in *Jonathan Edwards and the American Experience,* ed. Nathan O. Hatch and Harry S. Stout (New York: Oxford University Press, 1988), 177.

[28] Jospeph Haroutunian, *Piety Versus Moralism: The Passing of the New England Theology,* 1932; reprint with "Introduction" by Sydney E. Ahlstrom (New York: Harper and Row, Publishers, 1970), 150.

[29] Henry Warner Bowden, *Dictionary of American Religious Biography,* ed. Edwin S. Gaustad (Westport, Conn: Greenwood Press, 1977), 143. Biographical dictionaries often provide handed-down characterizations without careful consideration. These dictionaries provide material for others who write on the period. For example, David Reynolds who wrote on John Brown, the abolitionist (and the terrorist of Harper's Ferry), describes Edwards Jr.'s religion as "perhaps even more severe than his father's, since he described the delights of salvation with less passion than had the elder Edwards, while he still emphasized sin and damnation." David S Reynolds, *John Brown, Abolitionist: The Man Who Killed Slavery, Sparked the Civil War, and Seeded Civil Rights* (New York: Vintage Books, 2005), 25.

Introduction: Spirit and Style

A Need to Review the Inherited Caricature

However, contrary to the inherited caricature, the younger Edwards was a much sought-after preacher for ordinations, convocations, college chapel, lectures before political bodies, and funerals for dignitaries.[30] Part of his popularity is likely a result of his printed disputations with elite theologians of the "Standing Order" in and around Boston like Charles Chauncey[31] and Stephen West[32]—and to a greater extent that his father was the venerable Jonathan Edwards of Stockbridge and Northampton. Had Jonathan Edwards's namesake received some of his esteemed father's mantle in the pulpit as William Gordon prayed? The younger Edwards's popularity as a public speaker alone challenges the inherited caricature that he was a legal, spiritless preacher *per se*.

Furthermore, while Ezra Stiles tended to be a critic of the New Divinity theology and pulpiteering,[33] he was not above giving compliment to whom

---

[30] In Edwards Jr.'s *published* sermons are two sermons preached before a joint session of both houses of the Connecticut Legislature and the Governor, five ordination sermons including the very successful second great awakening revivalist Edward Dorr Griffin, four sermons for the General Association of Congregational Churches in Connecticut in *JEW2*. In addition, he spoke for commencement at Yale. The Beinecke Rare Book and Manuscript Library holds an unpublished commencement address in the *Jonathan Edwards and Calvin Chapin Papers Collection* (Gen Mss 781, Box 1, Folder 5). Edwards Jr. also preached from time to time at the college chapel as noted by Ezra Stiles in *LDES2*: 544, 577; *LDES3*: 87, 141, 152, 197, 204, 400, 422, 439. Notably, when a Junior at Yale College died in a failed inoculation for smallpox Edwards Jr. was elected by the students to give the funeral sermon. *LDES3*, 27. Edwards also preached the funeral of the Mayor of New Haven on July 26, 1793 (*LDES3*, 500–501), as well as the funeral of US Senator, Constitutional Framer and signer of the Declaration of independence, Roger Sherman. *JEW2*, 173–184.

[31] Charles Chauncy's *The Mystery Hid From Ages and Generations, Made Manifest by the Gospel-Revelation: Or, the Salvation of All Men the Grand Thing Aimed at in the Scheme of God* (1784) drew the younger Edwards to respond with *The Salvation of All Men Strictly Examined; and the Endless Punishment of those Who Die Impenitent, Argued and Defended [...]* found in the *JEW1*, 1–294.

[32] Samuel West took exception to Edward Sr.'s position regarding the Sovereignty of God in Salvation in his work *The Freedom of the Will* and published the *Essays on Liberty and Necessity, in which the True Nature of Liberty is Stated and Defended; and the Principal Arguments used by Mr. Edwards and others, for Necessity are Considered* (1793). This drew Jonathan Edwards, Jr to publish a response which is found in, *JEW1*, 295–466. See also, Ferm, *Edwards the Younger*, 127–133.

[33] "Visited by Mr. Gemmil of Philadelphia. He tells me that New Divinity has got into those parts, and makes havoc in 2 or 3 churches." *LDES3*, 393; see also 273–74 for a full description of his ire for New Divinity theology. Stiles also believed that a "Coalition between New and old Divinity impracticable. After all the charitable Professions of the former they are determined to coalesce with none that are not in heart New." *LDES3*, 4–5. Stiles criticizes New Divinity theology and tendency toward "divisiveness" with the Old Divinity. *LDES3*, 4–5. In a later

compliment was due. As the President of Yale from 1778 to 1795, he patronized the local congregations with his presence, and expressed from time to time his appreciation for Edwards Jr.'s sermonic effort on particular themes in his diary. Stiles records dozens of visits to the White Haven Church in which he participated in sacramental services, even filling the pulpit for Edwards Jr. when ill or occupied with heavy pastoral duties. For example, on a memorably cold day on January 23, 1780 (at sunrise the temperature "stood on Cypher—at Noon 17 above"), he attended White Haven all day and took in Edwards on Romans 3:24. Stiles liked what he heard "on the Doctrine of Justification" and praised his effort saying that "he handled [it] well."[34] Two months later, on March 19th Stiles attended all day at "Mr. Edwards's [church]; he preached on 1 Pet. 1:12. Excellent Sermon!"[35] Then again a year later on June 24, 1781, he applauds, "Mr. Edwards preached an excellent sermon on Prov. 3:17."[36] He was also there to witness the admission into full communion of a woman on January 19, 1783,[37] and a man and woman on February 22, 1784. The woman giving public assent to an "Acknowledgment [of] fornication and then was baptized after admission into full Communion by votes of the Brethren."[38] Stiles noted in his diary

---

place he ridicules the younger stock of New Divinity including "Dr. Edwards, Mr. Trumbull, Mr. Judson, Mr. Smally, Mr. Spring, Mr. Robinson, Mr. Strong of Hartford, Mr. Dwight, Mr. Emmons, etc. They all want to be Luthers. But they will none of them be equal to those strong Reasoners President Edwards and Mr. Hopkins." *LDES3*, 274. In a very pungent critic of a Samuel Hopkins, Stiles lays out four scathing "remarks" concerning New Divinity teaching and preaching. *LDES2*, 504–505.

[34]*LDES2*, 407. Jonathan Edwards Jr., "No. 651 Jan. 23. 1780. Rom. 3.24," *Jonathan Edwards, Jr. Papers (Sermons)*, Hartford Seminary Library (Box 167, Folder 2740), 1–8.

[35]*LDES2*, 418. Jonathan Edwards Jr., "No. 659. March 19. 1780 1 Pet. 1.12," *Jonathan Edwards, Jr. Papers (Sermons)*, Hartford Seminary Library (Box 167, Folder 2740), 1–8.

[36]*LDES2*, 544. Sermon 648 was prepared on January 2, 1780 and preached in North Haven on April 30, 1780. This sermon was reused six times afterwards including at Yale in Ezra Stiles presence and also in Edwards Jr.'s second ministry at Colebrook on October 4, 1795. Jonathan Edwards Jr., "No. 648. Jan. 2. 1780 Prov. 3.17 Her ways are ways pleasant and all her paths are peace," *Andover Newton Miscellaneous Personal Papers Collection, Jonathan Edwards, Jr.*, Yale Divinity Library (Box 168, Folder 4), 1–8.

[37]*LDES3*, 55. Jonathan Edwards Jr., "No. 793 Jan. 19. 1783. Eph. 4.24," *Jonathan Edwards, Jr. Papers (Sermons)*, Hartford Seminary Library (Box 167, Folder 2742), 1–28.

[38]*LDES3*, 112. In the records of the White Haven Church is an account of the grounds of discipline taken by the church with Joseph Adams who was purported to have relations with a single woman who was niece and his housekeeper. The account gives recognition to the births of children through fornication. Perhaps after a period of time, they were accepted into the church again upon their public confession. This shows a considerable effort in pastoral relations if these are the same individuals brought back into communion. David Austin, "Communications and Actions of the White Haven Society Regarding the Discipline of Church Members: Joseph

that Edwards Jr.'s topic was "Benevolence" at a crowded college chapel on November 14, 1784.[39] The thoughts recorded in Ezra Stiles's diary should serve as a counter-balance to the negative storyline handed down as Stiles.

These examples highlight the potential for an alternative view of Edwards Jr.'s capacity as a preacher. Edwards Jr.'s parishioners' listening diet consisted of unpublished sermons preached Sunday after Sunday, rather than the occasional published sermons intended to create dialogue with other theologians in New England. Harry Stout points out that "the most accurate guide we have to what people actually heard are the handwritten sermon notes that ministers carried with them into the pulpit."[40] Although Stout's *The New England Soul* was published in 1985, he presents a convincing case for a careful examination of Edwards Jr.'s handwritten sermon notes.

A decade after Stout's work, Mark Valeri also perpetuates the spiritless preaching caricature even as Valeri compares a few of Edwards Jr.'s manuscripts with his mentor Joseph Bellamy. Valeri states that while Edwards was "never an engaging communicator, [he] marveled at Bellamy's ability to make doctrine accessible to common folk."[41] Yet there is evidence that Edwards Jr. could reach the common folk. After preaching in the rural outpost of Stockbridge, Massachusetts in April 1782 (Sermon No. 747 was preached two months earlier in New Haven), his father's successor, Stephen West (1735–1819), sent him a letter to not only console Edwards Jr. after

---

Adams, 1780," in *White Haven Church Records, Series 1*, New Haven Museum (MSS 9, Box 1, Folder U).

[39] *LDES3*, 141. Edwards Jr.'s text for that occasion was from Matthew 5:46. He had previously preached this sermon at the Association at Guilford, CT on May 28, 1783 as well as Sheffield, MA on July 27, 1783, then in the morning of November 14, 1784 in New Haven. Jonathan Edwards Jr., "No. ___ Novr. 14, 1784. Mat. 5. 46," *Andover Newton Miscellaneous Personal Papers Collection*, Yale Divinity Library (Box 168, Folder 5): 1–30.

[40] Harry S. Stout, *The New England Soul: Preaching and Religious Culture in Colonial New England* (New York: Oxford University Press, 1986), 5.

[41] Mark Valeri, *Law and Providence in Joseph Bellamy's New England* (New York: Oxford University Press, 1994), 173. In addition, see Richard D. Shiels for another rendition of the "abstract, metaphysical preaching" caricature in, "The Second Great Awakening in Connecticut: Critique of the Traditional Interpretation," *Church History* 49, no. 4 (December 1980): 403–406. To be fair to Valeri, his essay titled "Jonathan Edwards, the New Divinity, and Cosmopolitan Calvinism" in *After Jonathan Edwards* recognizes Edwards Jr.'s attempt to balance intellectual rigor with the evangelical tradition which "stressed personal conversion in terms of union with Christ" and "the conviction that God worked especially to convict many of the unregenerate at the same place and time—in other words, through revival." Oliver D. Crisp and Douglas A. Sweeney, eds., *After Jonathan Edwards: The Courses of the New England Theology* (New York: Oxford University Press, 2012), 19.

his wife's untimely death, but among other things, to thank him for his time with them.[42] West indicates that "the religious attention" produced a "visible" affect "among" them, "when you [Edwards Jr.] were here, [and religious attention] is greatly increased; and divine mercy is wonderfully magnified toward us."[43] Items like these, again, suggest that the spiritless caricature of the biographical articles is unbalanced.

To this day, other than Donald Weber's chapter in *Rhetoric and History in Revolutionary New England*,[44] not much has been done to disprove Nathan Strong's theory that all Edwards Jr. needed in order to have revival was to adjust his pulpit manner. Nathan Strong's advice to not prove propositions of gospel truth, if followed, may or may not have produced the desired responsiveness in New Haven. In other words, adapting one's style to accommodate an audience does not necessarily induce the Holy Spirit to do

---

[42] Sermon 747 indicates that the same message delivered in New Haven on February 3, 1782 was reused in Stockbridge in April 1782, and then again in October 1782 in Northampton. This full manuscript is based on Isaiah 45:19 "I said not unto the seed of Jacob, Seek ye me in vain." Jonathan Edwards Jr., *Andover-Newton Miscellaneous Personal Papers Collection,* Yale Divinity Library (RG 295 Box 168, Folder 5).

[43] Stephen West [of Stockbridge, MA], letter sent to Jonathan Edwards Jr. July 16, 1782, *Jonathan Edwards Papers, Series V. Edwards Family Correspondence, Edwards, Jonathan 1745–1801 Incoming Letters,* Beinecke Rare Book and Manuscript Library (Gen MSS 151, Box 1, Folder 5); His brother Timothy, also mentions that "great things are taking place here, in the minds of some. The number has been gradually increasing ever since you was [sic] with us, in a manner and among persons and characters, which results great glory to God—at least one person if not more was [sic] first made to attend by your preaching. May God have the glory." Timothy Edwards, letter sent to Jonathan Edwards Jr. July 23, 1782, *Jonathan Edwards Papers, Series V. Edwards Family Correspondence, Edwards, Jonathan 1745–1801 Incoming Letters,* Beinecke Rare Book and Manuscript Library (GEN MSS 151, Box 26, Folder 1440).

[44] Weber, "The Edwardsean Legacy: The Example of Jonathan Edwards Jr. of White Haven," *Rhetoric and History in Revolutionary New England* (New York: Oxford University Press, 1988), 47–43.

anything.⁴⁵ Indeed, Edwards Jr.'s unpublished manuscripts show that his style did not drastically change throughout his thirty-year ministry.

History does affirm that over twenty-six years at the White Haven church Edwards would see his congregants slip away to "competition" in town.⁴⁶ However, this slow bleed by itself does not necessarily affirm the spiritless preaching narrative per se. This slow bleed came from a variety of directions.⁴⁷ In spite of the loss of his congregation to other options in town, Edwards Jr. would live to see the Holy Spirit revive his listeners in the early days of the Second Great Awakening. Instead of changing styles, Edwards Jr. changed congregations. In his next ministry phase (December 1795–July 1799), and to his delight, this new flock in Colebrook, Connecticut responded sympathetically, if not enthusiastically, to some of the very same outlines

---

⁴⁵ Toward the end of the Great Awakening, there were occasions of extreme excess. Joseph Bellamy's Memoirist relates an incident by one of his students that "So great was this power, that Bellamy, when he first began itinerating, in the time of the 'great awakening,' was himself astonished at the effect he produced, and for a long time regarded it as the immediate and almost miraculous work of the Holy Spirit applying divine truth. Returning home, however, after repeated experience of this kind, he sat down and devoutly inquired, 'Am I right? Is it possible that the Holy Ghost so regard me, as in connection with my words and voice, to bring up a crowded congregation to their feet, or prostate them on the floor, with wailing or joy inexpressible? I have seemed able, at such moments of overwhelming excitement and agitation, to any thing I pleased with an audience. Can this be the work of the Holy Spirit? Can it be pleasing to Christ? Is it to salvation? No, I fear not. I feel that it must be mere animal excitement, and not the work of the Holy One. I will go out thus no more." Bellamy, *Works*, lxii–lxiii.

⁴⁶ According to Stiles, Edwards had preached away his congregation with his "incessant Preaching of his New Divinity and Rigidity in Church administrations." *LDES3*, 344. Weber, "The Edwardsean Legacy," 51.

⁴⁷ Mary Mitchell, historian of the United Church of New Haven (formerly the White Haven Church), in the bicentennial review notes that the formation of the Whitneyville Church contributed to a decrease in members as well. *History of the United Church of New Haven*, (New Haven, CT: The United Church, 1942), 29. C. C. Goen also describes the White Haven Church as always being a troubled work due to "patterns of dissidence" from its inception in 1742. New Haven was unique among the colonies, as most citizens of New Haven were permitted to choose the church to which they would belong, and a committee assigned persons who had no choice. "The voluntaristic plan marked the beginning of the end for the traditional parish pattern in Connecticut." Goen, *Revivalism and Separatism*, 86–89. After Edwards Jr. was installed in 1769, the pattern of discord would continue with the formation of the Fair Haven Church nine months later.

which had been preached in New Haven[48]—even producing appreciable revival and numerical growth.[49]

Unfortunately, most of what has been handed down about Edwards Jr. is deduced from the bias of a few individuals, declining church attendance, and midnineteenth novelists. There has not been original study on Edwards Jr. in nearly fifty years since Robert L. Ferm's biography, *A Colonial Pastor: Jonathan Edwards the Younger (1745–1801)* was published in 1976.[50] For example, when Ferm's biography was published he knew of the existence of Edwards Jr.'s spiritual diary, but neglected to consider it as evidence of a 'glowing mysticism' or 'natural piety' said to be absent by Haroutunian.[51] He also neglects Edwards Jr.'s involvement during the war, his missionary activity in New York State, and advocacy for justice. In locating manuscripts that were overlooked by Ferm, I have also fill important gaps in the last years of his White Haven ministry. These sources, which include reconciliation, bring balance to the standard interpretation that Edwards Jr. was simply a cold metaphysician who deliberately drove his church away. Therefore, a new examination of Jonathan Edwards Jr. is warranted. In the pages that follow is a renewed engagement with original sources to recover the life and piety of the younger, forgotten Edwards. This new work begins by returning to the sources to piece together Edwards Jr.'s biography. Since Edwards Jr. is described by nineteenth century testimonials as having challenges in personality, I will first provide a biographical sketch highlighting several aspects in his life that may have produced this account.

---

[48] Edwards Jr. recorded at the top of the title page of his sermon the volume number, place of composition, place preached with its date. Many of his earlier sermons preached in New Haven have been noted to have been preached at Colebrook as well. For example, his earliest "recycled" sermon later to be used in Colebrook was No. 478 May 17, 1776 from Isaiah 45:7 "I form the light and create darkness: I make peace and create evil: I the Lord do all these things." Preached for a Continental Fast in New Haven, he then again used it in Colebrook on April 6, 1798. Jonathan Edwards Jr., *Jonathan Edwards and Calvin Chapin Papers*, Beinecke Rare Book and Manuscript Library (Gen MSS 781, Box 1, Folder 2). This sermon was just five years into his ministry in New Haven when the congregation was still at least 480 strong. In 1772, Ezra Stiles estimates that his congregation was about 480. *LDES1*, 284.

[49] In 1798 Edwards admitted eleven members and by 1799 twenty-seven new members were added so that the membership had nearly tripled in size to over sixty members by the time of his departure. Ferm, *Edwards the Younger*, 151. Compare with Benjamin A. Dean, *History of the Colebrook Congregational Church 1795–1895: Centennial Address Delivered December 31, 1895* (Hartford, CT: Connecticut State Library, 1913), 23.

[50] Robert L. Ferm, *A Colonial Pastor: Jonathan Edwards the Younger, 1745–1801* (Grand Rapids: Eerdmans Publishing, 1976).

[51] See discussion of Joseph Haroutunian's caricature of Edwards Jr. above.

The second chapter will focus on forty-six sermons that are based on the Sermon on the Mount.[52] These sermons will show that he is not only a consistent Calvinist in the New Divinity movement but will also serve to begin the process to amend his negative caricature. The younger knew how necessary the Spirit was for true religion to flourish in his congregation and he sought for ways to encourage piety. In the third chapter, is a side-by-side comparison of Edwards Jr.'s thinking on the Spirit with that of his father. Theologically, Edwards Jr. is known best for his work on the moral government theory of the atonement, and so many are not aware that he also shared with his father a concern for the work of the Holy Spirit.

I have also included several new sermon transcripts in the appendix. Two sermon transcripts are relative to the execution of Moses Paul in 1772. A third sermon, preached in 1775, is also included to highlight the important role Edwards Jr. played in the struggle for liberty in the founding era. This sermon also displays his public theology derived out of the just war tradition. I also include a sermon from Revelation that features some of his thinking on the Holy Spirit. The other appendices provide material relevant to his life, ministry, and mentorship.

---

[52]All but three are unpublished handwritten full-manuscripts or note-form.

Chapter 2

A Biographical Sketch

IN A LETTER TO HIS GRANDMOTHER, Edwards Jr. revealed an awareness of his spiritual and theological heritage. As the third-generation ministerial student, young Jonathan had come to terms with his responsibility. He asked his grandmother Esther Stoddard Edwards to pray for his capacity to honor their legacy. This request for prayer occurred at time of deep spiritual reflection and sensitivity. Since the elder Edwards's namesake has been given a largely negative caricature, a focus on his 'natural piety' will be featured through his private diary and preparation for ministry.

The atmosphere in which Edwards Jr.'s early life developed included both spiritual nurture and difficulties for his parents. These key points of development will be considered as relevant to his piety and personality, in the overall flow of his life and ministry. This biography will also highlight a sensitivity to his father's thinking on the trinitarian expression of benevolence through the Holy Spirit. Specifically, Edwards Jr. applies this to public justice. By advocating abolition, Edwards Jr. seems to be keenly aware of his responsibility to carry forward the legacy of his father. In the overall trajectory of his life, one can observe a pastor who grew in his sensitivity through the trials he experienced. At the end of his life, he was eulogized by Robert Smith, who claimed he had observed "the tender charities of the heart."[1] And now we turn to a new examination of Edwards Jr.'s life.

---

[1] *JEW1*, 512.

Hardship and Spiritual Nurture

Jonathan Edwards's namesake was born on a "sabbath-day night, May 26, 1745, between 9 and 10 o'clock" as his father was drafting *Religious Affections* for publication.[2] Two months later, when just a babe in mid-July, his family was visited in Northampton for a week by George Whitefield (1714–1770) and his bride.[3] Whitefield had visited the Edwards five years earlier and was persuaded by the observation of Jonathan and Sarah's sweet marriage relations to cease bachelorship at the earliest opportunity.[4] Edwards Jr. grew up in a nurturing and spiritual home. In spite of the benefits which come from a pious and nurturing family,[5] difficulty on several fronts made parenting young Jonathan more difficult even if there were many helping hands. A large family was the unintended, but costly,[6] consequence of being spared of childhood mortality. Yet, the family was not altogether spared, and in some ways, grieved harder when Edwards Jr. was about three-years. The death of his older sister Jerusha (1730–1747) became a significant cloud[7]

---

[2] The younger's birth details are recorded in the Edward's family Bible in Edwards's "own handwriting" and a copy is preserved in print. Jonathan Edwards Sr., "Family and Descendants of President Edwards (1891)," *Jonathan Edwards Collection,* Beinecke Rare Book and Manuscript Library, Yale University (GEN MSS 151, Box 29, Folder 1586), 1.

[3] George M. Marsden, *Jonathan Edwards: A Life* (New Haven, CT: Yale University Press, 2003), 310.

[4] Whitefield's nineteenth century biographer relates from his journal that "a sweeter couple I have not yet seen. Their children were dressed, not in silks and satins, but plain, as becomes the children of those who in all things ought to be examples of Christian simplicity. She is a woman adorned with a meek and quiet spirit, talked feelingly and solidly of the things of God, and seemed to be such a helpmate for her husband, that she caused me to renew those prayers, which, for some months, I have put up to God, that he would be pleased to send me a daughter of Abraham to be my wife. I find, upon many accounts, it is my duty to marry." Joseph Belcher, *George Whitefield: A Biography, with Special Reference to His Labors in America* (New York: American Tract Society, 1857), 179–180.

[5] Samuel Hopkins described Jonathan Edwards Sr. as a caring husband who "kept a watchful eye over his children, that he might admonish them of the first wrong step, and direct them in the right way [...] instructing them in the principles of religion; in which he made use of the Assembly's Shorter Catechism" (emphasis original). Edwards Sr. religiously guarded the Sabbath, and monitored his children's friends, mandating a curfew of nine o'clock. All of these disciplines promoted a wholesome environment in which to grow up. Samuel Hopkins, *The Life of President Edwards* (1764; repr., in vol. 1, *The Works of President Edwards,* New York: S. Converse, 1829), 46–47.

[6] "Edwards' salary, while relatively generous, was not keeping up with the combination of rising prices and a growing family. Also, since money was scarce, payments were often slow." Marsden, *Jonathan Edwards,* 301–305.

[7] In a letter to his friend, John Erskine across the Atlantic, Edwards Sr. revealed a melancholy which was lingering after about twenty months since the loss of his daughter. He thought

in a growing storm, which would break when Edwards Jr. was only five years old. The other clouds had been gathering for several years. Pastoral relations in Northampton had been strained by a poorly timed reversal of his revered grandfather Solomon Stoddard's Half-way Covenant and permissive policy on participation in the Lord's Supper. Edwards Sr. further aggravated the peace of the church in a poorly executed church discipline case involving the bad behavior of several young men.[8] The storm finally broke on June 18, 1750. A vote for the dismissal of Edwards Sr. unsettled the family. The stress and joy of weddings would also weigh on the family, as Sally (Sarah Jr.) wed just eight days before that watershed vote. Mary would stay behind in Northampton with her new husband as well.[9] The disconcerting uncertainty would persist for exactly a year from their father's farewell sermon in July 1, 1750 until their relocation to Stockbridge.

Added to the difficulty of parenting during this time, young Jonathan had an eye malady which persisted for several years. As a toddler and lingering into boyhood, Edwards Jr. suffered from "an inflammatory weakness in his eyes."[10] According to a medical journal from the first half of the nineteenth century, his condition was probably a chronic conjunctivitis, which at that time was called "Serofulous Ophthalmy."[11] This inflammation is said to have resisted "applications"[12] until his parents shaved his head "repeated often,

---

that perhaps this was from the Lord "to teach me how to sympathize with the afflicted." John Erskine had recently lost his father. Jonathan Edwards Sr., letter to John Erskine, October 14, 1748, *Letters and Personal Writings*, in *Works of Jonathan Edwards*, vol. 16 (New Haven, CT: Yale University Press, 1970), 265.

[8] Marsden argues that the episode of Timothy and Simeon Root might be described better as 'the young folks' Bible' than 'the bad book case.' The kind of behavior which was being engaged in would be described today as sexual harassment. Additionally, Edwards also had to deal with three paternity disputes in the parish during the 1740s. Marsden, *Jonathan Edwards*, 296–301.

[9] Sally (Sarah Jr.) would marry Elihu Parsons and Mary would marry Timothy Dwight Jr. Marsden, *Jonathan Edwards*, 363.

[10] Nathan Williams, John Smalley, and Benjamin Trumbull, eds., *The Connecticut Evangelical Magazine*, vol. 2 (Hartford, CT: Hudson and Goodwin, 1801), 377.

[11] "Occurs most from the period of weaning to the age of nine or ten. There is a very watery state of the eye, and extreme intolerance of light; the redness is often slight, at first on the lids, and generally only partly on the eye; the enlarged vessels run in fasciculi towards the cornea, and terminate on it, or the slerotia, or more frequently on the boundary between them, in phylctenulae or pustules, containing a clear or yellowish fluid. The disease is worse during the day." John Fife and A. Taylor, eds., "On Diseases of the Eye (Continued)," in *Provincial Medical and Surgical Journal* (1844–1852) 10, no. 17 (1846): 193.

[12] Williams, *Evangelical Magazine*, 378. In a later issue of the *Provincial Medical and Surgical Journal*, this condition is said to be treated with "fomentations and poultices" and in milder cases may be corrected by "tonics and good diet." John Fife and A. Taylor, eds., "On Diseases

and for a long time." Coupled with his eye condition were the difficulties of relocation and absence of a school in the settlement. Thus, his learning to read was delayed "until a much later period than is common in New England."[13] While not having capacity to learn visually, his auditory aptitude was nevertheless evident as he became fluent in the Mahican tongue. Reflecting on his upbringing, Edwards Jr. wrote,

> The Indians being the nearest neighbors, I constantly associated with them; their boys were my daily schoolmates and playfellows. Out of my father's house, I seldom heard any language spoken besides Indian. By these means I acquired the knowledge of that language, and a great facility in speaking it. It became more familiar to me than my mother tongue. I knew the names of some things in Indian that I did not know in English. Even all my thoughts ran in Indian; and though the true pronunciation of the language is extremely difficult to all but themselves, they acknowledged that I had acquired it perfectly, which, as they said, never had been done by any Anglo-American.[14]

Later in his life, Edwards Jr. would have the honor of supplying a copy of his linguistic study of Mahican to President George Washington for him to pass on to a "Society of Literati" in Europe.[15]

Growing up with the Indians, most certainly would have influenced young Jonathan's disposition and demeanor. Edna Gerstner describes how Mahican children aged they would learn "not to show enthusiasm, or any expression" on their faces.[16] This distant poker-face became a defining characteristic of Edwards Jr.[17]

---

of the Eye (Continued)," in *Provincial Medical and Surgical Journal (1844–1852)* 10, no. 20 (1846): 228–29.

[13] Tryon Edwards, "Memoir," in *JEW1*, xiii.

[14] Jonathan Edwards Jr., "Observations on the Language of the Muhhekaneew Indians; in which the Extent of that Language in North America is Shown [...]," in JEW1, 469.

[15] George Washington, letter to Jonathan Edwards Jr. on August 28, 1788, in *Jonathan Edwards Jr. and Calvin Chapin Papers,* Beinecke Rare Book and Manuscript Library (MSS 151, Box 26, Folder 1461).

[16] Although a historical fiction, this book is based upon the Edwards family journals and likely paints an accurate picture of life in Stockbridge. Edna Gerstner, *Jonathan and Sarah: An Uncommon Union, A Novel Based on the Family of Jonathan and Sarah Edwards (The Stockbridge Years, 1750–1758)* (Morgan, PA: Soli Deo Gloria Publications, 1995), 5–6.

[17] Timothy Mather Cooley relates that "[i]n his personal appearance he was far from being prepossessing, as any one must be convinced from the portrait of him that has been published

A Traumatic Apprenticeship

When Edwards Jr. was about nine years old, a providential request for a ministry partner would further remove Edwards Jr. from his family and civilization. In a letter to Joseph Bellamy, Gideon Hawley—missionary to the Oneida Indians of Onohquaughe in the New York wilderness (Ouaquaga[18] on the Susquehanna River)— described the need for a companion who could master the language.[19] Bellamy was probably already aware of young Jonathan's talents, and through correspondence with Edwards Sr. upon another matter, may have presented the idea of young Jonathan as Gideon's companion.[20] In short order the pieces of Hawley's linguistic puzzle would come together. Did Edwards Sr. desire his son to be another David Brainerd to the Indians? Perhaps so. Hawley's missionary society in Boston provided a monetary gift to the Edwards family for the provision of their young son to be an apprentice-translator.[21]

Mr. and Mrs. Edwards decided to send their nine-year old boy over two hundred miles away to minister among the Six Nations with Gideon

---

with his works. He was rather short, of a dark complexion, a piercing eye, and a severe countenance, strongly marked with the lines of thought. In his manners he was somewhat distant, and I believe there were comparatively few who felt much freedom in conversing with him." *AAP1*, 659.

[18] In Kenneth Minkema's dissertation on the three ministers of the Edwards family, he identifies the location as Unadilla, NY in *The Edwardses: A Ministerial Famliy in Eighteenth-Century New England*, (PhD diss., The University of Connecticut, 1988), 398; however, according to a hand-drawn map with latitude markings specifying N42°12' and N42°10', Gideon Hawley identifies a bend of river with islands and tributaries which better match Ouaquaga, NY. Gideon Hawley, letter to Jonathan Walter Edwards on March 14, 1803 in *Jonathan Edwards Papers*, Beinecke Rare Book and Manuscript Library (Gen MSS 151, Box 27, Folder 1487).

[19] "My companion has intended to quit the affair next Spring because among other reasons there [is] no prospect of his ever obtaining the Indian Language and where I shall [f]ind another I don't know—I purpose to go to Boston in the Spring [a]nd perhaps I may make you a visit in April, tho' I don't look upon it likely that I shall have time." Gideon Hawley, letter to Joseph Bellamy on February 3, 1755, *Joseph Bellamy Letters*, Hartford Seminary Library (Box 190, Folder 2955).

[20] Although the letter and pamphlet are unavailable, in the aforementioned letter to Joseph Bellamy, Gideon Hawley requests a pamphlet about the doctrine of the Moravians to be forwarded to Mr. Edwards on his behalf.

[21] In a return letter from Gideon Hawley to Joseph Bellamy, composed on April 18, 1755 in Stockbridge, Hawley indicates that the missionary society in Boston had granted funds to provide for a new companion. After visiting with Mr. Edwards, he presented them "20 £ sil[ver] for the encouragement of his son Jonathan who is to set out with me next Monday [April 28] for the Indian Country." Gideon Hawley, letter to Joseph Bellamy on April 18, 1755, in *Jonathan Edwards Collection*, Beinecke Rare Book and Manuscript Library (Box 28, Folder 1535).

Hawley on April 28, 1755.[22] Even with a good start, they would not arrive until the fall, as they spent time at the Castle of Hendrick in Canajoharie where a renowned Mohawk chief resided.[23] Timothy Edwards who was enrolled that year at the college of New Jersey also accompanied them. For reasons unknown, Hawley left Timothy and Jonathan there while he returned to Stockbridge. Once returned to Canajoharie, Hawley descended into Onohquaughe with Jonathan and Tommy Spencer (1749–1777)[24] in October. Timothy Edwards, on the other hand, returned home.

A month after young Jonathan's departure, his father wrote a letter dated on the day following his tenth birthday. In this letter, he comforts Jonathan with God's omniscience, while informing him that a playmate of his had died a week prior. Since his friend had not been much older than Jonathan, this death was a providential opportunity to examine his heart. Was there evidence that young Jonathan was "converted and become a new creature"?[25] The gravity of frontier life, coupled with the pressing need of continual self-examination, intensified young Jonathan's inherited introverted tendencies.

After Edwards Jr.'s death in 1801, Gideon Hawley would recount the thrilling tale of escape from the French-sympathetic Delaware Indians in

---

[22] In a letter to Edwards Jr.'s son Jonathan Walter Edwards, Gideon in his older age (fifty years later), may have mistaken the date of the beginning of travel as being April 8 (leaving out the 2 which makes 28), Gideon Hawley, letter to Jonathan Walter Edwards on June 10, 1802 in *Jonathan Edwards Papers,* Beinecke Rare Book and Manuscript Library (Gen MSS 151, Box 27, Folder 1487). "Mr. Hawley, and his young charge, set out on their journey in April 1755." Tryon Edwards, "Memoir," in *JEW1,* xiv.

[23] Edwards, "Memoir," xiv.

[24] Thomas Spencer was an Oneida, the son of an Oneida woman and the Presbyterian missionary Elihu Spencer. He was born about 1749 at Onoquaga, the Tuscarora-Oneida-Mohawk settlement on the Susquehanna River where Gideon Hawley conducted his mission work with Edwards Jr. He learned to speak and write English, probably from Hawley and his father. Thomas Spencer lived as an adult in Cherry Valley and did "message running" for Sir William Johnson and later "spy running" in Canada. "Biographical Sketch of Thomas Spencer," Mary King Research Library, Madison County NY Historical Society (File X00884).

[25] Jonathan Edwards, letter to Jonathan Edwards Jr. on May 27, 1755, *Jonathan Edwards Collection,* Beinecke Rare Book and Manuscript Library (Gen MSS 151, Box 22, Folder 1284).

two letters to Jonathan Walter Edwards (1772–1831).[26] Traveling in the dead of winter, Hawley relates that they had

> encountered every danger and difficulty—once one of our horses broke through the ice and lay near an hour in a depth of water—Once we were benighted—twice we met with strange Indians, that I suppose were hostile—we lay on the ground all but one night; when we had a warm comfortable wigwam—we were well, but the burden of the hardship were heavy on me and my Jonathan could not mount his horse without assistance from me or Tommy.[27]

They managed to get out with their horses through Cherry Valley leaving Thomas Spencer there. Hawley and young Edwards pushed on to Stockbridge arriving on January 21, 1756 to the embrace of the Edwards family.[28]

Loss of Family and Awakening

Not much is known about this period; however, Edwards Jr.'s son-in-law claims that during the year of his reunion with the family, Edwards Jr. found in his father's library Locke's *Essay on Human Understanding*, and "read it over and over again [...] with increasing delight."[29] This detail was intended to show philosophical aptitude; however, it also shows parental encouragement. Edwards Sr. wrote to encourage him while in the western frontier about his personal piety and this concern continued when he returned. For example, in a later diary entry, Edwards Jr. reveals his father's counsel to "watch over" his "natural temper."[30] Time with his parents did not last very long as tragedy would strike the family. Yet, between his return

---

[26] The detailed map of the river with Indian longhouses, wigwams, and fields with latitudinal ordinates is found in the second letter. Gideon Hawley, "Letter to Jonathan Walter Edwards on June 10, 1802 and March 14, 1803" in *Jonathan Edwards Papers*, Beinecke Rare Book and Manuscript Library (Gen MSS 151, Box 27, Folder 1487). In AAP1 the Oneida's are said to have carried young Jonathan "on their shoulders many miles through the wilderness to a place which they supposed beyond the reach of danger," 654.

[27] Hawley, "Letter to Edwards, June 10, 1802."

[28] Hawley, "Letter to Edwards, June 10, 1802."

[29] *AAP1*, 658.

[30] Jonathan Edwards Jr., "Diary," *Jonathan Edwards Papers*, Beinecke Rare Book and Manuscript Library (Gen MSS 151, Box 24, Folder 1357), 16.

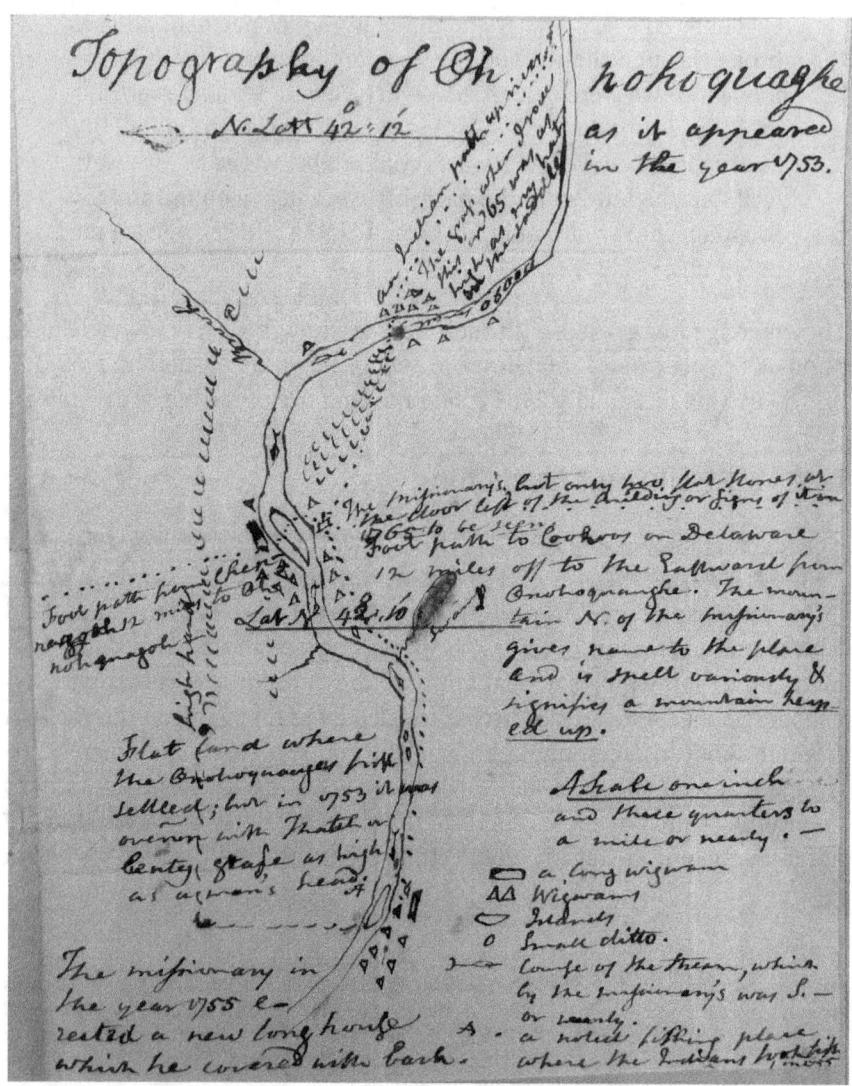

Figure A: Gideon Hawley's Hand-Drawn Map of Onohquaughe. Courtesy of the Beinecke Rare Book Library

home and his father's coming departure to Princeton, Robert L. Ferm characterizes as "exposure to the theological doctrines and to the spirit of his father's mind." In these couple years, his father was preparing manuscripts on *Original Sin, Nature of True Virtue,* and *Freedom of the Will* for publication. But he was also beginning to prepare young Jonathan for ministry.[31]

Late in 1757 Edwards Sr. received a request to fill the presidency at the College of New Jersey.[32] After consultation and deliberation, Edwards accepted the position on January 4, 1758, and at just thirteen years, young Jonathan would be unsettled again.[33] Unhappily for Edwards Jr. tragedy struck during this transitional year with the dramatic loss of his father, mother, *and* sister Esther Edwards Burr. These early childhood experiences would have had a sobering affect upon young Jonathan, contributing to his perceived distant disposition.

Upon the death of Edwards Jr.'s parents, his eldest brother Timothy took leadership of the home in Stockbridge.[34] Benefactors at Princeton would make sure that the younger Edwards was prepared for the College of New Jersey.[35] After a year of preparatory school, Edwards Jr. enrolled in the fall of 1761 while Samuel Finley was president and a frequent chapel preacher.[36] Samuel Finley, a graduate of William Tennent's "Log College," represented the New Side of Presbyterianism which emphasized the necessity of more than a mere subscription to doctrine and public worship. In the spirit of

---

[31] Ferm, *Jonathan Edwards the Younger,* 16–17.

[32] John Maclean, *History of the College of New Jersey, from Its Origin in 1746 to the Commencement of 1854* (Philadelphia: J. B. Lippincott, 1877), 170.

[33] Maclean, *History,* 173.

[34] Edna Gerstner suggests that with the sudden loss of both parents and ill-equipped, Timothy was "often out of temper and spoke harshly to them [his siblings]." Gerstner, *Jonathan and Sarah,* 235.

[35] From 1760–1763, at the annual synod of the Presbyterian Church, inquiry was made into the care of the education of poor and pious youths specifically back to the year 1758. After the synod made request year after year, it was finally learned that approximately five hundred pounds at six percent interest had been set aside by the College of New Jersey for this purpose. With interest to be dispersed annually (about 30 pounds) for the "education of poor and pious youth," this may have been the means to assist young Edwards prepare for college and to attend through his graduation in 1765. William Tennent was a trustee of the College during this time, and during the call of Edwards Sr., and the care of Edwards Jr. *Records of the Presbyterian Church in the United States of America: Embracing the Minutes of the General Presbytery and General Synod 1706–1788, Together with an Index and the Minutes of the General Convention for Religious Liberty, 1766–1775* (Philadelphia: Presbyterian Board of Publication, 1904), 299–323.

[36] Ferm, *Jonathan Edwards the Younger,* 19.

Whitefield, New Side preachers insisted upon a converted ministry in their revivalist preaching.[37]

Young Edwards had not yet been converted and without a mother or father to return to during school vacations, found himself with too much freedom and a propensity for mischief. During these mid-year holidays, he would often stay at "Staddle Hill," the residence of Judge Seth Wetmore in Middletown, Connecticut. Rather than observe the evening of the Sabbath, Timothy Dwight and Jonathan would steal down to the kitchen early and then go out to "visit some young ladies, living in the neighborhood." On one such evening, the plan went painfully wrong as both boys spilled scalding pudding on themselves in their haste.[38] Perhaps the Spirit was beginning to speak loudly through pain for when Edwards Jr. would return to school, he would be caught up in an awakening.

According to William E. Schneck, in the fall of Edwards Jr.'s second year of college (1762), "it pleased God again to pour out his Holy Spirit with an uncommon power" in the college and neighboring community "lasting for about a year." This revival produced conversions in the freshman class spreading upward to the older students to a total of about fifty percent of the student body.[39] George Whitefield came to Princeton on the heels of

---

[37] Ferm, *Jonathan Edwards the Younger*, 29.

[38] According to the tradition recorded in the Wetmore Family genealogy, one such escapade went humorously wrong. "The supper for Saturday night was invariably "hasty pudding" and milk, for host, guest and servant. The pudding was boiling in an enormous kettle, such as the old fashioned, capacious kitchen fireplaces of those days alone could hold. But the young men were impatient, stole into the kitchen (where the old negress "Membo" was the acknowledged mistress). Calling, in an undertone, "Membo, Membo, won't you give us our supper?" and then admitted her to their confidence. "De Lor bress you," says Membo, "de hasy puddin not done." "Never mind" (they replied), "we will eat it," and into the pantry they went, and brought out two large pewter plates, as bright as silver, and with the ladles which they had provided themselves with, they commenced dipping the pudding from the kettle. According to the custom of the time, they were dressed in short breeches, with long silk stockings and low-quartered shoes. Membo stood aside, quite grieved, that her authority was so unceremoniously interfered with, and particularly, to see her young favorites helping themselves. "Now massa Ed'ards. Now! massa Dwight, see what you gone and done." They had both dropped the boiling, tenacious pudding upon their silk hose, and were dancing around the floor with pain their impatience had caused them. Membo assisted them in removing the pudding, and applied a remedy to their burns, at the same time giving them a lecture upon being in a hurry, and the impropriety and sin of "gowin to see de girls on Saturday night, de beginnin ob de Lor's day." James Carnahan Wetmore, *Wetmore Family of America, It's Collateral Branches: Genealogical, Biographical, And Historical Notices* (Albany, NY: Munsell and Rowland, 1861), 283–285.

[39] The related account of Dr. Woodall, a freshman in 1762 while Edwards Jr. was a sophomore. Woodall reports that "every class became a praying society and the whole college met once a week for prayer" and that of the fifty students converted a large percentage "devoted themselves

this revival, preaching several times "with much approbation and success."[40] Edwards Jr. was deeply affected by these outpourings of the Spirit that summer and early fall (1763), so that he penned a declaration of faith "to draw near to the Lord's Table" for the first time.[41] In the coming year, Edwards Jr. would keep a private diary[42] in an effort to work out his salvation with fear and trembling demonstrating a great sensitivity to sin and the Spirit.

This diary was designed to prayerfully root out besetting sin and stoke the fire of the Spirit in his soul. His diary begins the day before his nineteenth birthday and is carried through the New Year (May 25, 1764–January 13, 1765).[43] Contemplating God's salvific mercy a year prior, he outlines his purpose this way:

> Although it is near a year since I hope God has showed me mercy, yet I find my life has been by no means answerable to my profession. But that I have been in general too careless and negligent about the concerns of my Soul and that I have sometimes been led into sin to the wounding of my soul especially that of machy anitauhauwongkon wonk anannahkaun [Mahican], which seem to be my thorn in the flesh to buffet me and the sin which does most easily beset me and therefore needs more particularly to

to gospel ministry." John Frelinghuysen Hageman, *History of Princeton and Its Institutions,* 2nd ed., vol. 2. (Philadelphia: J. B. Lippincott, 1879), 82–83.

[40] Hageman, *History of Princeton,* 83.

[41] This declaration of faith will is located in appendix 5. Jonathan Edwards Jr., "Confession of Faith September 17, 1763," *Jonathan Edwards Papers,* Beinecke Rare Book and Manuscript Library (Gen MSS 151, Box 24, Folder 1355).

[42] Tryon Edwards noted the existence of this diary; however, when Wesley Ewert curated the manuscripts at Hartford Seminary for his biographical dissertation in 1953, he claimed that "there was no trace of the diary." Tryon Edwards, "Memoir," in JEW1, xv.; Wesley Carl Ewert, *Jonathan Edwards The Younger: A Biographical Essay,* vol. 1 (PhD diss., Hartford Theological Seminary, 1953), 5.; Robert L. Ferm bypasses even a mention of this diary in 1976, but a decade later, Kenneth Minkema found it for his dissertation *The Edwardses: A Ministerial Family in Eighteenth-century New England* (1988). Donald Weber also interacted with the diary briefly in "The Edwardsean Legacy: The Example of Jonathan Edwards, Jr. of White Haven," in *Rhetoric and History in Revolutionary New England* (New York: Oxford University Press, 1988), 47–73, 49.

[43] Each diary entry keeps pace at about once per week as reflection typically after corporate worship. Various texts are described as preached by Dr. Finley, Mr. Murray, Mr. Hadley (was a tutor under Edwards Sr.'s brief tenure), Mr. Thomson, Mr. Brainard, William Tennent (younger), and "The Doctor." Jonathan Edwards Jr., "Diary," *Jonathan Edwards Papers,* Beinecke Rare Book and Manuscript Library (Gen MSS 151, Box 24, Folder 1357), 1–19.

> be guarded against. For this purpose; namely, to find out the deceitfulness of my heart so as the last appearance of evil and keep my heart right with God; I now begin a diary as some short account of the workings of it, and pray God he would assist me in searching into the deep recesses of it and enable me to be faithful to myself; that it may be a happy means to reform my life and conversation and make me live more circumspectly for the future.[44]

In other places, he will specifically talk about a difficulty with anger, unbelief, laziness in corporate worship, pride, carnality, worldliness, and busyness. According to Carl Masthay and Ives Goddard, linguists familiar with Mahican, this phrase (*machy anitauhauwongkon wonk anannahkaun*) means "evil thoughts and deed."[45] As Edwards Jr. lay bare his inner thoughts, he uses this phrase three times in the diary.[46] The use of Mahican words interchangeably with English, is a testament that "all my [Edwards Jr.'s] thoughts ran in Indian," was so.[47]

Further, this passage is evidence of his sensitivity to the Spirit's innermost workings. On June 17 he boldly declares his shame and regret over

> some difference which happened in the week past between M.[48] and myself has been a mean to set my heart at a greater distance from God. I find in my heart so much corruption and depravity that I am carried away by the least temptation to sin. Lord make to depend on thee alone for the future! [. . . June] 18) Lord God, when shall I gain ye conquest over every passion! Wilt thou O God suffer me to fill up the measure of my iniquity and heap up wrath against the day of wrath and the righteous judgement of God? Have I been all this while playing the hypocrite, deceiving

---

[44] Edwards Jr., "Diary," 1–2.

[45] According to Carl Masthay, a Native American linguist, "'Mahican' is the single language, and 'Mohican' is an ethnic group and cultural fusion, now consisting of several Algonquian ethnic groups genetically mixed." Email message on September 6, 2019 with Carl Masthay of St. Louis, Missouri. Carl and his associate Ives Goddard assisted me in the translation of this obscure Mahican phrase. In addition, Larry Madden of the Stockbridge-Munsee Band of Mohicans assisted me by creating a connection with Chris Harvey, a linguist from Toronto, Ontario, Canada.

[46] Also on August 19 and September 22, 1764. Edwards Jr., "Diary," 15, 17.

[47] Edwards Jr., "Observations on the Language of the Muhhekaneew Indians," 469.

[48] The name of the person is hidden by the initial M.

myself and lying to God? Lord thou knowest what is in man! Do thou search my heart and purge out from these all the seeds of iniquity, every evil thought and idle imagination and enable me to live the religion I profess![49]

The diary trails off after the New Year; however, later that May, on his twentieth birthday, Edwards Jr. would pen on a scrap of paper a prayer in Mahican, translated:

> Oh my Lord, these things that you do for me are what you never again have to protect me from, by taking away sin, whether *I am doing it or thinking about it*. Now help me, oh my Lord God, so that I will not ever be in darkness. Jonathan. Edwards [Jr.]. N. H. [New Haven] May 27, 1765.[50]

The italicized words correspond to the Mahican phrase in his diary, and therefore suggests that God had given him confidence through "the special influences of his holy Spirit" in the completed work of Christ.[51]

In spite of an objective faith in Christ's work, the susceptibility to slip into the darkness was ever present for Edwards Jr. In a letter to his brother just over a decade later, he described a particularly dark season in which he "experienced much weakness, and great affliction from an utmost lowness of spirits during the summer season, the effect of a great relaxation of the whole system of nature." Perhaps due to an illness, he fell into discouragement, and with gratitude he relates to Timothy that "as the cold weather came on, I began to obtain relief."[52] Edwards Jr.'s son-in-law Calvin Chapin relates that throughout his life, he was self-conscious of his irritability; however, "[h]e watched, and prayed, and struggled, against it, as the besetting infirmity of his nature; and those who had an opportunity of observing, knew that his earnest efforts were not in vain."[53] On September 2, 1764, he confessed to

---

[49] Edwards Jr., "Diary," 8–9.

[50] Emphasis added. Jonathan Edwards Jr., "Prayer in Mahican May 27, 1765," trans. Carl Masthay (see note 32 above), *Jonathan Edwards Papers*, Beinecke Rare Book and Manuscript Library (Gen MSS 151, Box 29, Folder 1596).

[51] Edwards Jr., "Diary," 7.

[52] This letter was written just two years after the passing of his namesake Jonathan. Jonathan Edwards Jr., letter to Timothy Edwards December 18, 1777, *Edwards Family Correspondence, Jonathan Edwards 1745–1801 Outgoing Letters*, Beinecke Rare Book and Manuscript Library (Gen MSS 151, Box 26, Folder 1424).

[53] *AAP1*, 658. From Calvin Chapin's viewpoint, Edwards suffered a "self-jealousy," or what some might call morbid self-introspection; however, this trait may stem from the combination of

his diary, "I have been made to see, that I have generally been too careless about my natural temper, have not watched over so diligently as I should have done, according to my father's last counsel to me."⁵⁴ Nevertheless, in a letter to his grandmother shortly before he finished his diary, Edwards Jr. expressed his earnest desire that God would be gracious to allow him to be "a guide and instructor to youth, and make me to follow the example my parents and grandparents."⁵⁵

At the end of his senior year (1765), Edwards "delivered 'with great Propriety and Spirit' a pre-commencement Latin oration 'On the Evils to which a People is Liable, when involved in debt.'"⁵⁶ After graduating that fall with a Bachelor of Arts, he was invited to spend the winter with Samuel Hopkins to review his father's manuscripts. Hopkins then sent him on to study under Joseph Bellamy in Bethlehem, Connecticut.⁵⁷

---

genuine spirituality combined with the brilliance of his inherited introversion. George Marsden describes Edwards Jr.'s grandfather Timothy Edwards as "an intensely disciplined perfectionist, a worrier about details, a firm authoritarian who was nonetheless capable of good humor and warm affection toward his family." In addition, there seems to have run a "psychosis" in the family through his great-grandmother, and mother of Timothy Edwards. Marsden relates that Jonathan Edwards Sr. "is sometimes criticized for having too dim a view of human nature, but it may be helpful to be reminded that his grandmother was an incorrigible profligate, his great-aunt committed infanticide, and his great-uncle was an ax-murderer." This biological background may have predisposed Edwards Jr. to have genius idiosyncrasy. Marsden, *Jonathan Edwards*, 22.

⁵⁴Edwards Jr., "Diary," 16.

⁵⁵Jonathan Edwards Jr., letter to Esther Stoddard Edwards, 1765 April 12. MS, one leaf. *Shepard Family Collection,* Beinecke Rare Book and Manuscript Library. Kenneth Minkema graciously shared his transcription of this document as the original was, at the time of my research, en route from the Yale Divinity Library to the Beinecke Rare Book Library.

⁵⁶James McLachlan, *Princetonians: A Biographical Dictionary 1748–1768* (Princeton, NJ: Princeton University Press, 1976), 494.

⁵⁷Bethlem later became Bethlehem. Samuel Hopkins sent the following introduction to Bellamy on July 7, 1766: "Sir Edwards will, I hope, get a great deal of good at your house. He will take it kindly if you converse with him particularly about his personal religion, and act the part of a father to him, in freely giving him your best counsel and advice. He is, I think, an honest, conscientious lad, and in consequence of my kind treatment of him, he trusts me as a father. He has a high taste for good speaking and will be of service to your pupils with respect to this, if you promote the matter" in William Patten, *Reminiscences of the Late Rev. Samuel Hopkins, D. D. of Newport, RI [...]* (Providence, RI: I. H. Cady, 1843), 45–47. However short his stay with Hopkins, as noted in the introduction above, the occasion proved to impress upon young Edwards's mind his father's theology.

Early Ministry and Marriage Tragedy

The New England finishing school for preachers occurred under the roof of experienced pastors. Bellamy was a tough teacher, who through the Socratic method prepared a variety of questions to assist young preachers be ready theologically. In addition to theological preparation, Bellamy also critiqued his apprentices on their pulpit presentation or the lack thereof.[58] In spite of the rigor of Bellamy's apprenticeship,[59] Edwards Jr. was successful and accordingly licensed to preach on October 22, 1766 by the Litchfield Association.[60] Since he was now following in his father's footsteps, Edwards Jr.'s brothers and sisters signed over custody of their father's manuscripts to him in 1767.[61]

---

[58] According to Joseph Bellamy's memoirist, "after reading select experimental and practical discourses, [his students were] to prepare sermon on similar subjects, which he revised and corrected. And that his students might be trained, not only to prepare, but properly to deliver their discourses, it was his rule that those who were licensed should preach, in turn, at appointed stations in the outskirts of the parish. On these occasions, he rode, with all his students, to attend the service; on returning from which, he usually criticized the performance, generally with reference to the peculiar character of the speaker, and always in way not likely to be forgotten." The memoirist follows up with several humorous examples of critique. *The Works of Joseph Bellamy*, vol. 1 (Boston: Doctrinal Tract and Book Society, 1850), lviii–lix.

[59] Edwards Jr.'s earliest sermon manuscript was completed under the watchful eye of Joseph Bellamy in August 1766. After his licensure, he would preach it at Samuel Hopkin's church in Great Barrington, Massachusetts. The sermon consists of an exposition of 2 Peter 2:22 in which a pig and a dog return to the mire and the vomit. Out of this text are the early formations of a New Divinity concern for "real religion and true piety." Jonathan Edwards Jr., "Sermon III. August 1766. 2 Pet. 2.22.," *Jonathan Edwards, Jr. Papers (Sermons)*, Hartford Seminary Library (Box 165, Folder 2725), 3.

[60] According to Robert L. Ferm Edwards Jr. was licensed to preach on Oct 21, 1766 (*Edwards the Younger*, 23); however, according to the records of the Litchfield Association which met with the Consociation at Southbury, the examination began on the twenty-first and continued the following morning at "6 o'clock [...] according to our stated rules with respect to his knowledge in the Liberal arts and Sciences, and Acquaintance with matters of religion, doctrinal and experimental: And this Association approve, license and recommend him as a meet person to preach the Gospel, wherever God in his Providence shall call him hereto." Comprising his examination committee were John Graham, Joseph Bellamy, Thomas Canfield, Jonathan Lee, Nathaniel Taylor, Hezekiah Gold, Abel Newell, Cotton M. Smith, Sylvanus Osborn, Noah Wadhams, Noah Benedict, and Ammi R. Robbins. Litchfield Association Records, 1752–1852, in the *General Association of Connecticut Collection* (Boston: Congregational Library and Archives), 119–120.

[61] "Agreement, arranging for deposit of Edwards manuscripts to Jonathan Edwards, signed by seven of his siblings, March 27, 1767," *Jonathan Edwards Collection, Series 10*, Beinecke Rare Book and Manuscript Library (Gen. MSS 151, Box 37, Folder 1666).

Returning to the College of New Jersey, he provided pulpit supply while tutoring.[62] According to a classmate of Edwards Jr., "Dr. Finley often submitted to be taught by him, especially in mathematics."[63] Edwards Jr. turned down his father's mission in Stockbridge in 1767, and later a professorship of Mathematics and Languages at Princeton in 1768.[64] Instead he pursued a pastorate in New Haven, Connecticut. This pastorate would further challenge and shape the temper of the younger Edwards.

The White Haven Church in New Haven (today the United Church on the Green) had been formed in protest to the leadership of the First Church during the days of the Great Awakening.[65] In the heady days of the awakening, Joseph Bellamy demonstrated support of the separates by preaching to them,[66] and consequently exercised an influence on their selection of a new minister. At the time of Edwards Jr.'s call, his uncle James Pierrepoint was still active along with about forty-three others who remembered the first split.[67] According to Samuel Dutton, trouble already was brewing in the church, as the church had readopted the Half-way Covenant in 1760, which they had eschewed back in 1742.[68] Then Samuel Bird resigned the pastorate

---

[62] Wesley Ewert provides a variety of towns in which Edwards Jr. provided supply in his dissertation. Ewert, *Jonathan Edwards the Younger,* vol. 1, 15–16.

[63] McLachlan, *Princetonians,* 494.

[64] Somewhere in the fall of 1767 Edwards Jr. visited Stockbridge, and according to Stephen West in a letter to Andrew Eliot, Edwards communicated that he might have a greater usefulness at the college, yet he would eventually turn that opportunity down as well. Minkema, *Edwardses,* 447, n49. During that school year a concerted effort was made to advance Samuel Hopkin's name for professorship, but it would be to no avail. By the following year John Witherspoon would become the president of the college. James Caldwell, letter to Joseph Bellamy March 16, 1767, *Joseph Bellamy Letters,* Hartford Seminary Library (Box 188, Folder 2935, Item 81332). According to Joseph A. Conforti, Witherspoon lost no time in purging New Divinity influence out of the school. Edwards Jr. resigned his tutorship, pursuing a pastorate in New Haven. Joseph A. Conforti, *Samuel Hopkins and The New Divinity Movement: Calvinism, the Congregational Ministry, and Reform in New England Between the Great Awakenings* (Grand Rapids: Christian University Press, 1981), 74.

[65] The story of the split is recorded by Samuel William Southmayd Dutton in an address honoring the hundredth anniversary of the church. *The History of the North Church in New Haven: From Its Formation in May 1742, During the Great Awakening, to the Completion of the Century in May 1842: in Three Sermons* (New Haven, CT: A. H. Maltby, 1842). The North Church was the amalgamation of the White Haven and Fair Haven Churches after Edwards Jr.'s pastorate.

[66] Mark Valeri, *Law and Providence in Joseph Bellamy's New England: The Origins of the New Divinity Revolutionary America* (New York: Oxford University Press, 1994), 19.

[67] Valeri, *Law and Providence,* 60.

[68] Valeri, *Law and Providence,* 58.

in January 1768 at only forty-four years because of 'bodily infirmities.'[69] Mr. Bird's departure signaled to some that unwelcomed changes were in the wind. After Edwards Jr. was introduced to the congregation through a lengthy pulpit supply, and finally given invitation to settle in September 1768, a dissatisfied minority[70] arose in opposition to the New Divinity principle of fully owning the covenant. Robert L. Ferm and Douglas Sweeney suggest that there is no evidence that Jonathan Edwards Jr. was involved in overturning the Halfway Covenant, but an anxious letter to Joseph Bellamy late in November suggests otherwise.[71] By December, the majority under Roger Sherman's leadership would overturn the Half-way Covenant, making way for Edwards Jr.'s ordination on January 4, 1769.[72]

---

[69] Struck from the report is this line: "[...] and that the church look out for some suitable person to supply his place and that he is willing to assist them therein." In the "Committee Report of the Resignation of Samuel Bird, December 30, 1767," *White Haven Church Records, Series 1*, New Haven Museum (MSS 9, Box 1, Folder Q).

[70] A month after an invitation to settle in September 1768, on October 17th a petition with twenty-five names was submitted to the leadership of the White Haven church that Mr. Fisk of Stonington be considered for the position. "Petition Requesting the Calling of Mr. Fisk," *White Haven Church Records, Series 1*, New Haven Museum (MSS 9, Box 1, Folder Q).

[71] Robert L. Ferm suggests that there is no evidence that the Half-way Covenant was to be rescinded at Edwards Jr.'s request in *Jonathan Edwards the Younger*, 73. Citing Ferm, Daniel W. Cooley and Douglas A. Sweeney suggest the same in "The Edwardseans and the Atonement," *A New Divinity: Transatlantic Reformed Evangelical Debates during the Long Eighteenth Century*, ed. Mark Jones and Michael A. G. Haykin, Reformed Historical Theology Series, 49 (Gottigen, Vandenhoeck and Ruprecht Verlage, 2018), 116; however, in a letter sent to Joseph Bellamy on November 31, 1768, Jonathan Edwards Jr. in coordination with Roger Sherman seems to be maneuvering in this direction. "I suppose Mr. Sherman has given you full information of what was done at our last society meeting. I had some thoughts of riding up to Bethlem this week: but have concluded to defer it till next week. President Daggett and Mr. Trumbull are of opinion that the opposition, which has hitherto appeared is sufficient discouragement. The Half-way Covenant is now under consideration. They say there will be no great difficulty in the church. The danger is hat the society will take it in dudgeon [a feeling of offense or deep resentment]—But time will well shew the event. They have not fixed any salary as yet; but have left it at large, only promising to support me; and Mr. Sherman seems to be of opinion that it is best it be left so. But it is contrary to the opinion of the above named gentlemen. I beg you will send me your opinion upon this head by Mr. Sherman, who I expect will return on Monday next, to be before the church's meeting. Or if you have an opportunity sooner please to embrace it. My mind is much agitated about the affair. And I am determined not to give any answer till I see you, if not some others of my friends at a distance—I hope you will be at home next week.—With kind regard to the family and the young gentlemen there, I am, Your most affectt. Humble Servant, Jonathan. Edwards." Jonathan Edwards Jr., letter to Joseph Bellamy, November 31, 1768, *Jonathan Edwards Papers, Series V Edwards Family Correspondence, Jonathan Edwards 1745–1801 Outgoing Letters*, Beinecke Rare Book and Manuscript Library (Box 26, folder 1414).

[72] An invitation to the ordination went to Bellamy and a delegate to attend the examination at Mr. John Pierpont's home the day before at noon. White Haven Church, letter to Joseph

Nevertheless, sixty-eight people subscribed to a petition opposing his installation, which was delivered during the evening of the council meeting of ministers.[73] While sixty-eight signed, only twenty-five were eligible to vote and a calculation of the ratable estate was about one fourth of the society's financial capacity. After hearing the concerns, the council determined that after "mature deliberation, and after taking a large view of the affair were of the opinion that there was no sufficient objection against their proceeding to the ordination of Mr. Edwards according to the desire of the church and the society."[74] Through the winter and spring, negotiations for a colleague pastor as a half-way solution came to naught. Finally, in July a church council was called two months prior to the split. In this council, three points of grievance were outlined:

> *First.* That the Reverend Mr. Edwards was ordained to the pastoral care of the society and church while so many timely manifested their opposition thereto. Second. That Mr. Edwards and the church under his care do not allow the admission of peoples to baptism upon their owning the covenant without coming to sacrament of the lord's supper. Third. That Mr. Edwards's preaching on some particular accounts, is not so much to their satisfaction and edification as they could desire.[75]

Momentum toward independent worship finally took over and services began on September 19, 1769, under the discipline of the Half-way Covenant at the state house. Not surprisingly, the new church would be led by their former pastor Mr. Bird.[76] The attendant consequences of a split coupled with the impressions of the disaffected would begin to create a narrative, which would stick to Edwards Jr. in years to come; however, church documents show how the dissatisfied had already begun to resist New Divinity leadership a year

Bellamy December 20, 1768, *Joseph Bellamy 1719–1790 Correspondence*, Beinecke Rare Book and Manuscript Library (MSS 151, Box 28, Folder 1531).

[73] "Narrative Recording the Formation of the Fair Haven Society, 1769–1772," *White Haven Church Records, Series 1*, New Haven Museum (MSS 9, Box 2, Folder B).

[74] "The Result of the Council at Ordination of Mr. Edwards January 3, 1769," *Connecticut Miscellaneous Manuscripts Collection*, Manuscripts and Archives, Yale University Library (MS 149, Series III, Box 20, Folder 215).

[75] "Miscellaneous Records of the Fair Haven Society," in *White Haven Church Records, Series 1*, New Haven Museum (MSS 9, Box 2, Folder A1).

[76] "Narrative Recording the Formation of the Fair Haven Society, 1769–1772," *White Haven Church Records, Series 1*, New Haven Museum (MSS 9, Box 2, Folder B).

before the split. In all likelihood, by the time of Mr. Bird's resignation, a full two years ahead of Edwards Jr.'s ordination, forces were already well in play. Even with this split, Ezra Stiles estimated that White Haven had four hundred and eighty, while the new church had two hundred.[77]

The ensuing years would bring joy and grief to Edwards Jr. At the late age of twenty-five, Samuel Hopkins officiated his wedding of Mary Porter in Hadley, Massachusetts on October 4, 1770. Together they would have three surviving children: Jonathan Walter, Jerusha, and Mary.[78] According to Robert L. Ferm "the Edwardses had four children but we know little about them; the name of one child who died in infancy is even lost."[79] Yet, this is not entirely true, as he would dedicate sermon 417 on April 2, 1775 for "the occasion of the death of my child *Jonathan*."[80] For Edwards Jr., as much as for his wife, he chose John 14:1 "Let not your heart be troubled" as his text. Jonathan Walter, like his sister Jerusha, would perpetuate his father's memory of a cherished sister, and now, a lost son.[81]

After twelve years of marriage, a remarkable tragedy occurred and would test Edwards Jr.'s ministry before his people. On Monday, June 24, 1782, while on her way to conduct personal business, Mary Porter Edwards left Edwards Jr. at their hay lot and travelled on alone in a horse drawn carriage. Stopping at a pond to water the horse, she allowed it to step into the water and misjudged the depth and grade.[82] The carriage descended quickly, and losing her balance, she struck her head. Unable to respond in her trauma,

---

[77] *LDES1*, 284.

[78] Birthdates are as follows: Mary, July 11, 1773; Jonathan Walter, February 26, 1775; Jerusha, February 4, 1776. Ferm, *Edwards the Younger*, 79 n7.

[79] Ferm, *Edwards the Younger*, 79 n7.

[80] Jonathan Edwards Jr., "417. April 2. 1775. John 14.1," *Jonathan Edwards Jr. Papers (Sermons)*, Hartford Seminary Library (Box 166, Folder 2735), 1–4. Given the lateness of Jonathan Walter's birth (Feb. 26, 1775) relative to the death of first Jonathan (March 1775), seems to indicate the loss of the eldest son at the age of two or three. Walter may have been his second son's birth name with Jonathan added a few months later. In other words, See note 76 for additional rationale. Also see appendix 1, figure D for a photo of this sermon title.

[81] There is no reason to think that the trend of naming children after deceased siblings was dramatically different in the rest of New England. For example, in a study of child-naming practices in Hingham, Massachusetts during the last half of the eighteenth century "necronymic succession occurred for nearly ninety percent of dying children with the same name as one of their parents and for over threefourths of dying children not named for a parent." Daniel Scott Smith, "Child-Naming Practice, Kinship Ties, and Change in Family Attitudes in Hingham, Massachusetts, 1641 to 1880," *Journal of Social History* 18, no. 4 (Summer 1985).

[82] Ezra Stiles describes the water depth as being fifteen feet and her body was believed to have been found about an hour later. *LDES3*, 28.

Mary drowned.[83] The next day, Ezra Stiles would preside over the funeral which was held with a full meetinghouse.[84]

Edwards Jr. did not speak on the following Sunday. He did return to the pulpit on the first Sunday of July, and preached twice from texts fitted to his loss.[85] This loss occurred at the highwater mark of Edwards Jr.'s ministry in New Haven when, according to Ezra Stile's calculations, White Haven had about eight hundred in its parish.[86]

Over the last thirteen years of his ministry in New Haven, Edwards Jr. would work through several pastoral challenges as he saw his congregation slip away; however, by his side he would have Mercy Sabin who became his

---

[83] Details of the event are preserved in a letter to his nephew Timothy Dwight and future president of Yale. Jonathan Edwards Jr., letter to Timothy Dwight, July 18, 1782, *Andover Newton Miscellaneous Personal Papers Collection,* Yale Divinity Library (Box 168, Folder 1).

[84] Stiles gives details of the funeral: his preaching text was from Philippians 1:21, Charles Whittelsey of the First Church made the first Prayer, Psalm 89 was sung, and Mr. Street prayed. Edwards Jr. was comforted by the presence of eleven other ministers of whom seven had lost their wives. In spite of his grief, Edwards Jr. spoke at the grave. *LDES3,* 28.

[85] In the morning sermon, Edwards Jr. focused his heart in the pattern of "true religion" from the great commandment to love God and neighbor found in Matt 22:37-38. Love for God is observed in "patience under trials. [Indeed,] trials will be trials. [God] designed [that they] should be. [It is] not duty— not. [Yet trials are] to feel [as a duty]. Yet [if we] may be patient [and] not murmur, and if [we] love [God], [then we will] see and believe right. [We will have] no wonder." Jonathan Edwards Jr., "No. 769 July 7. 1782. Mat. 22.37, 38.," *Jonathan Edwards Jr. Papers (Sermons),* Hartford Seminary Library (Box 167, Folder 2742), 4. In the second sermon that day, he spoke from Job 14:1 "Man that is born of a woman is of few days and full of trouble." His opening remarks place trials as an opportunity as "training for [our] better" and that we are "children at school" who do not always enjoy the experiences of life. Jonathan Edwards Jr., "No. 770 July 7. 1782. Job. 14.1," *Jonathan Edwards Jr. Papers (Sermons),* Hartford Seminary Library (Box 167, Folder 2742), 1.

Both sermon themes arise in his letter to Timothy Dwight. For example, "My trials are indeed great, but I hope I do not murmur against God or call into question his righteousness [...] I think I have some desire, that I may hereby be made a better man and a better minister and and I ask your prayers that that may be the case." Edwards Jr., letter to Dwight, July 18, 1782. Even after five years, in a letter to John Ryland Jr., Edwards Jr. reveals how affected he was by his beloved wife's death. He writes: "Your affliction in the loss of Mrs. Ryland is truly affecting! As you mention my "former affliction," I suppose you have heard, though I know not how, of my peculiar trial, in the loss of a most amiable comfort. She was accidently drowned. A most surprising and afflicting scene! So that you see, I can feel for you. "May all things work together for your good"! I have for near four years been agreeably resettled in married life but I have as yet no offspring by the second marriage. I hope you continue to pray for me. You may be sure, that I do not forget you." Jonathan Edwards Jr., letter to John Ryland Jr. October 2, 1787, *Edwards Family Correspondence, Jonathan Edwards 1745–1801 Outgoing Letters,* Beinecke Rare Book and Manuscript Library (GEN MSS 152 Box 1, Folder 3), 1–2.

[86] First Church numbered about nine hundred, White Haven numbered eight hundred, Fair Haven numbered nine hundred and fifty, and the Episcopal two hundred and fifty. *LDES3,* 14.

Figure B: Portrait of Jonathan Edwards Jr. by Reuben Moulthrop (ca. 1780)

loyal and loving wife and mother of his children. They would never have children of their own.[87]

Revolution and Benevolent Justice

The decade leading up to the sudden passing of Mary in 1782 was relatively stable for the White Haven Church in spite of the national upheaval created by the Intolerable Acts and subsequent war with Great Britain. According to Tryon Edwards, his grandfather participated in revolutionary rhetoric along with many other pastors in New England.[88] These tumultuous years were fruitful for the younger Edwards. To both the war effort and to the welfare of the oppressed by injustice he lent his voice. In both of these experiences, he demonstrated a consistency of thought with his father.

Advocating Justice

During the lead-up to war with England, Edwards Jr. provided spiritual counsel to Moses Paul, a Native American man facing execution for murder at a local tavern of a man from out of town. When Moses Paul was eventually hanged on September 2, 1772, an execution of a Native American had not occurred in New Haven since the turn of the eighteenth century. Even though residents of New Haven had witnessed the hanging of a "habitual criminal" just four years previous,[89] the uniqueness of the accused drew a large crowd of witnesses. While hangings were not common, guilt for murder was even more rare as the prosecution necessarily had to demonstrate premeditation. The lesser verdict of manslaughter was handed down more frequently. When

---

[87] On December 18, 1783, eighteen months after his loss, at thirty-eight Edwards Jr. remarried the daughter of Hezekiah Sabin, a New Haven merchant who had originally been a subscriber in opposition to Edwards Jr.'s installation. "Signers Against Mr. Edwards Ordination, Dec. 16th, 1768," *Connecticut Miscellaneous Manuscripts Collection,* Manuscripts and Archives, Yale University (MS 149, Series III, Box 20, Folder 215).; Mary Hewitt Mitchell, *History of the United Church of New Haven* (New Haven, CT: The United Church, 1942), 164. Mary was twenty-five; however, they would not have children, but she would accept his children as her own. LDES3, 102; Ferm, *Edwards the Younger,* 81.

[88] "Many of his sermons preached during the revolution, show the intelligent and warm interest which he, in common with the great body of the New England ministers, felt in the welfare of his country, and in her success in that eventful struggle." Edwards, "Memoir," in *JEW1,* xxxii.

[89] Isaac Frasier was hung in New Haven for being a "habitual criminal." See "Capital Punishment in Connecticut," *Connecticut State Library,* libguides.ctstatelibrary.org; https://libguides.ctstatelibrary.org/law/capitalpunishment/personsexecuted; accessed on August 22, 2020.

convicted of manslaughter, the criminal could be deprived of property or publicly whipped and would then be branded with the letter 'M' on the hand, which guaranteed the gallows should he or she offend a second time. Although the courts treated Indians as legal subjects of the Crown, the tendency to move toward a murder charge rather than manslaughter was more frequent for Native Americans than for whites who killed other whites.[90]

Prior to an execution, a condemned person would spend time with a minister to make themselves right with God. This ritual often led to a confession of guilt. In "True Confessions and Dying Warnings in Colonial New England," Lawrence Towner observed that preparation for eternity frequently caused confessions to occur during proceedings. These confessions might be provided to visiting ministers in the prison.[91] However, Moses Paul did not conform to this pattern even though he had been visited by several of the pastors in town. In fact, according to Louis P. Masur, Moses Paul was one of four capital crimes in the late eighteenth century who refused to confess to a crime they had been sentenced for either in court or on the scaffold. Significant to both Moses Paul and Jonathan Edwards Jr. is another man who claimed innocence.[92]

Masur's observation is significant because Joseph Mountain, a free black man convicted of rape and executed in 1790, had also been visited by Jonathan Edwards Jr.[93] Both Paul and Mountain had at least two ministers

---

[90] Ava Chamberlain, "The Execution of Moses Paul: A Story of Crime and Contact in Eighteenth-Century Connecticut," *The New England Quarterly Journal* 77, No. 3 (Sept. 2004): 414–450, 448–49.

[91] Lawrence W. Towner, "True Confessions and Dying Warnings in Colonial New England," in *Sibley's Heir: A Volume in Memory of Clifford Kenyon Shipton.*, 523–539 (Boston: Colonial Society of Massachusetts, 1982), 533.; For example, Patience Boston confessed to a minister that she had drowned an eight-year-old boy even against the advice of some because she had felt burdened to remove the blood-guilt from the land. Stuart Banner, *The Death Penalty: An American History* (Cambridge, MA: Harvard University Press, 2002), 15.

[92] Louis P. Masur, *Rites of Execution: Capital Punishment and the Transformation of American Culture, 1776–1865* (New York: Oxford University Press, 1989), 43.

[93] Joseph Mountain's memorial was published for the benefit of the female who he had attacked about a mile outside of New Haven. In this memorial he details his birth into a slave-owning home in Philadelphia, and then his life of lawlessness in Britain and France as a 'foot-pad' and then a highwayman. Upon his return to America, he acknowledges and confesses with regret his brutal attack; however, he denied following through on the act of rape. Joseph Mountain, *Sketches of the life of Joseph Mountain, a Negro, who was executed at New-Haven [...]*, ed. by David Daggett (New Haven, CT: T and S Green, 1790) in *Early English Books Online Text Creation Partnership*, 2011, https://quod.lib.umich.edu/e/evans/N17364.0001.001, accessed 5 September 2020.

involved in their departure sermons. Both men asked Edwards Jr. to provide sermons in these tradtional worship services for the condemned.[94] This fact is significant on its own. Yet, most remarkably, Edwards Jr. recycled the *very same sermon* manuscript for Joseph Mountain. The rarity of a persistant innocence plea, coupled with the very same manuscript, suggests an insight on the part of Edwards Jr.'s in spite of the different capital crimes committed.

Edwards Jr.'s sermon explicated various issues of theology from Psalm 55:23. Overall, it walks a fine line in its practical application of potentially misapplied justice. When compared with another sermon for Joseph Mountain provided by the other pastor in town, this conclusion becomes stronger. James Dana, of the First Church, preached and addresses the potential misjustice of justice. He proposed imprisonment for life might be a more just solution than execution. While recognizing Mountain's life of lawlessness, in the application section of his sermon, Dana says that he would not have agreed to participate in an execution sermon if he "did not think it at least possible, that there may yet be mercy in store for you."[95] This "passing comment" indicates that Dana agreed to preach while appeal was being made; however, it is also a subtle statement on Mountain's case: when in doubt, there is no harm done, should a judge commute the death penalty to a life sentence.

That Edwards Jr. used the same sermon manuscript for Joseph Mountain *and* Moses Paul is significant given the content of both minister's sermons. Couple this fact with the significant statistic of participation in two of the four "not guilty" pleas, and Edwards Jr.'s sense that a misapplication of justice in Moses Paul's case becomes more certain. An examination of this sermon will also bear this out below. Only a few years into his pastorate, Edwards Jr. began to prepare himself to advocate for the just treatment of all people under the law. In time he would become an ardent abolitionist.

Moses Paul initially selected Edwards Jr. to be a preacher of his first execution sermon on June 7, 1772. After Moses Paul's appeal was received and his execution postponed to September, Edwards Jr. would then preach a second sermon on August 30, 1772 and then Samson Occom would preach

---

[94] On the actual day of Joseph Mountain's execution, James Dana of the First Church in New Haven would preach his first such execution sermon at Mountain's request. James Dana, *The intent of capital punishment. A discourse delivered in the city of New-Haven, October 20, 1790. Being the day of the execution of Joseph Mountain, for a rape* (New Haven, CT: T. and S. Green, 1790) in *Early English Books Online Text Creation Partnership*, 2011, https://quod.lib.umich.edu/e/evans/N17366.0001.001, accessed 5 September 2020.

[95] Dana, *The intent of capital punishment*, 22.

the final sermon just a few days later at the courthouse on September 2.[96] Why did Moses Paul select Edwards Jr.? Ava Chamberlain indicates that Edwards Jr. may have had a common bond with Moses Paul due to a similar age and upbringing.[97] The similarity of age is true; however, the second is possibly coincidental. In 1772, Edwards Jr., on the one hand, had been pastor of the White Haven Church for three years, newly married, and just twenty-seven years old at the time of the execution. Moses Paul, on the other hand, was slightly older at thirty,[98] single, and a one-time soldier.[99] With regard to upbringing, Edwards Jr. had grown up on the edge of the frontier mixing with the Mohican tribes, even learning the nearly impossible language better than English. Moses Paul, however, was of Wampanoag descent, his parents having already integrated into an English way of life, even apprenticing young Moses to an English couple in Windham, Connecticut. Chamberlain suggests that Paul considered Edwards Jr. to be sympathetic on a cultural basis.[100] We may not fully know the reason for the interest in Edwards Jr.; yet, there is similar concern for justice found in Jonathan Edwards Sr. In this way, Edwards Jr. demonstrates that he did receive his father's spiritual sensitivity and concern for justice.

It is true that Edwards Sr. participated in keeping enslaved people, yet in spite of this fact, he seemed to have a concern for their well-being, even speaking out against the trade in the Hampshire brief for a neighboring congregational consociation.[101] While Edwards Sr. was not as vocal on a civil-political level, he was nevertheless an ardent defender of Native American interests in Stockbridge. During his brief pastorate in Stockbridge, Edwards Sr. wrote often to the mission commissioners in Boston to warn them of the corruption in the school. Roy M. Paul suggests that during

---

[96] A transcript of both Edwards Jr.'s sermons can be found in appendix 3; Samson Occom, *A Sermon at the Execution of Moses Paul, an Indian [...]*, ed. Jonathan Edwards Jr. (1788; repr. London: Buckland, 1789).

[97] Ava Chamberlain's excellent article details the story of supposed murder and the stages of the trial in *New England Quarterly*. Ava Chamberlain, "The Execution of Moses Paul: A Story of Crime and Contact in Eighteenth-Century Connecticut," *The New England Quarterly Journal* 77, No. 3 (Sept. 2004): 414–450, 432.

[98] Jonathan Edwards Jr., "Volume 225," *Jonathan Edwards Jr. Papers (Sermons)*, Hartford Seminary Library (Box 166, Folder 2732), 25.

[99] *Collections of the Connecticut Historical Society,* Vol. 10 (Hartford, CT: Connecticut Historical Society, 1905), 363–364.

[100] Chamberlain, "The Execution of Moses Paul," 418.

[101] Kenneth P. Minkema, "Jonathan Edwards's Defense of Slavery," *Massachusetts Historical Review,* vol. 4 (2002), 38.

Edwards Sr.'s time in Stockbridge his presence created a caution to would be oppressors seeking land for rum. Remarkably, only five land sales occurred during his seven-year term, while in the ten years after his tenure eighty-seven occurred.[102] These exchanges of land were often grossly inequitable. Having lived with the Indians, Edwards Jr. most likely inherited his father's benevolent concern for their well-being, and desired justice on their behalf.

As noted earlier, both Moses Paul and Joseph Mountain had pled innocent to the charges laid upon them by the justice system. This fact is important, but even more important evidentially and theologically is how Edwards Jr.'s used the same text and manuscript for both pending executions. Eighteen years later Edwards Jr. chose to reuse the same manuscript with the same arguments for a man who likewise plead not guilty to the specific crime. Instead of revision, Edwards Jr. simply put brackets around key terms relative to both men, while keeping the same arguments regarding benevolence and justice.

While we may not know for certain whether either man was guilty of the stated crime, we do have the opportunity to observe the Edwardsean principle of benevolence in practice. But there is also an honest dealing with retributive justice benevolently as Edwards Jr. will present a theological proposal to commute an execution penalty when there is reasonable doubt. Edwards Jr. proposed that "there is a difference between our state and the state of the church under the law."[103] Arguing from silence in the "Mosaic Dispensation" regarding eternal torments,[104] Edwards Jr. proposed that the emphasis in the gospel dispensation is such that a greater warning exists. Since in the old dispensation temporal punishments were used to encourage a responsiveness to the sacrificial system, this justly implies that the weight of eternal punishment ought to compel people in a greater way. On the basis of this reasoning, Edwards Jr. says that temporal punishments of the old era "do not necessarily follow."[105] While not proposing the discontinuance of capital punishment per se, Edwards Jr. recognized that there are times when God's infinite wisdom allows for a delay in justice now. Yet, this delay is

---

[102] Roy M. Paul, *Jonathan Edwards and the Stockbridge Mohican Indians* (Peterborough, Canada: H&E Publishing, 2020), 93.

[103] Jonathan Edwards Jr., "Volume 225," Jonathan Edwards Jr. Papers (Sermons), Hartford Seminary Library (Box 166, Folder 2732), 9.

[104] In using the term dispensation to distinguish between the mosaic and gospel periods within the covenant of grace, Edwards Jr. demonstrated that he had been editing his father's sermons for publication as *The History of the Work of Redemption* (1774).

[105] Edwards Jr., "Volume 225," 9–10.

for reasons he may not disclose. In other words, Edward Jr. is encouraging his listeners to practice a benevolent application of the law, while trusting in God's ultimate justice, should the evidence in this temporal world be inconclusive.

Before moving on quickly to the application of the sermon, I should say that this line of reasoning was not original with Edwards Jr. That he was intent on extending or bolstering his father's legacy is evident by the inclusion of this argument derived from *A History of the Work of Redemption*. At the time of this execution sermon, Edwards Jr. was preparing to send a transcript of his father's redemption sermons to Scotland for printing in 1774. In the fourth sermon in this thirty-part redemption series, Edwards Jr. leans upon his father's observation that "the revelations that God gave of himself in those days [under the Mosaic dispensation] used to be accompanied with much more terror than in these days of the gospel." In other words, the argument for mercy in this lifetime had a rational basis "since a future state and the eternal misery of hell is more clearly revealed, and since the awful justice of God against the sins of men has been so wonderfully displayed in the sufferings of Christ." Not only does this demonstrate the patriarchy of ideas, but also demonstrates a clear biblical argument to commute a punishment should the evidence be too thin in this lifetime. In other words, God will sort out the details in time, if man is unable to arrive upon just retribution.

Before he made personal application to Moses Paul, Edwards Jr. provided a careful argument for God's just application of eternal torment. Using a kind of apophatic reasoning, Edwards Jr. asks his listeners if it is just for God to cast off those who have already cast him off? In other words,

> sin against God is to rise in rebellion against him; it is to say by our conduct that God is not worthy to [be] feared and obeyed, and therefore to treat him with contempt. [...] If the sinner rises up against and cast off God, [then] is God unjust to cast the sinner off? If [he] refuses to continue in his allegiance to God [then] is it not just that God should refuse to admit him to the enjoyment of the benefit of his faithful subjects? If he despises the happiness of heaven, as every impenitent sinner under the gospel does, where is the injustice in suffering him to remain without it? And [where is the injustice should he] never to taste of the rich supper which he has provided and serves up in the heavenly state. If they despise the blessings of the gospel [and] walk—to death, as all impenitent sinners under the

gospel do, certainly it is no more than just that they should be suffered to have their own choice, and enjoy the death which they choose.[106]

In this execution sermon, Edwards Jr. does a couple things. First, he addresses the contemporary question regarding the necessity of capital punishment and God's retributive justice. Second, he addresses the contradiction of a penitent prisoner who was willing to admit up to a point and the appearance of a "final" retributive justice in this lifetime. What if he was not actually guilty of premeditated murder? Would this really be a just retribution?

Moses Paul was willing to admit to intoxication but not to premeditated murder. Ava Chamberlain, in her otherwise strong article, seems to misunderstand Edwards Jr.'s rhetoric. She proposes that Edwards Jr.'s sermon contains "a subtle polemic *against* Paul's claim that he had been unjustly sentenced."[107] This conclusion, however, does not adequately consider Edwards Jr.'s claim that the state is not obligated to apply retributive justice in a gospel dispensation as it did in the Mosaic dispensation. From God's benevolent application of justice, Edwards Jr. is showing that God may allow error in the application of justice for purposes of his own choosing. The rhetorical value of this point would draw the listener to conclude a better way might be delay of "apparent" justice now, when no one will be able to escape "actual" justice in the future life. Nevertheless, this inability to secure "true" justice now, ought to cause us to pursue God as "the foundation of hope of escape ... from eternal wrath" should human government misapply justice in the present.[108]

In the personal application, Edwards Jr. again leaves open the door the possible misapplication of justice on Moses Paul's account. He leaves room for reasonable doubt by saying, "How far in reality the character of a [bloody] man belongs to you God and your own conscience best know. But this we all know that you have [been] legally convicted of this character; and therefore it is to be presumed that this is your true character."[109] By

---

[106] Edwards Jr., "Volume 225," 19–20. The argument for benevolent application of the law and trust in God's ultimate justice was derived from Jonathan Edwards Sr., "A History of the Work of Redemption," in *The Works of Jonathan Edwards Vol. 9*, trans and ed. by John F. Wilson (New Haven, CT: Yale University Press, 1989), 168–69.

[107] Chamberlain, "The Execution of Moses Paul," 433.

[108] Edwards Jr., "Volume 225," 21.

[109] Edwards Jr., "Volume 225," 25.

addressing the conscience and using the word "presumed" Edwards Jr. is not ascribing an absolute verdict; rather, he is stating the necessity of public reliance upon a system of justice to be just.[110] In the same paragraph, knowing full-well that an appeal had been made that would either postpone or reverse the execution, Edwards Jr. modified his manuscript by describing his impending death as "ere long," striking out the word "shortly."[111] Even thought he had made a formal appeal, unfortunately for Moses Paul, he did not receive another hearing. The higher court affirmed the lower court ruling without any consideration of new arguments. This being the case, with a new execution date, Moses Paul invited Samson Occom to preside over the second service.[112] Edwards Jr. also preached a second sermon the Sunday prior to the execution at Moses Paul's request.

While Moses Paul's actual guilt was legally inconclusive, the Edwardsean principle of benevolence is present in Edwards Jr.'s second sermon as well. While attempting to encourage the application of true benevolence in the second sermon, he also dealt with the apparent injustice done by man in the first sermon (see appendix 3 for a transcript of both sermons). Benevolence which is based on mutual love for self and others is the central argument for abolition.

Advocating Benevolence

Kyle Strobel, in his dissertation (2014), shows that Edwards Sr. understood that the pure acts of benevolence by people can be an outflow of the Holy Spirit's love. A pure act of love by image bearers replicates the mutual beatific delight of the Trinity for one another.[113] The Holy Spirit, as gift of God to sinners, is a benevolent principle producing a love for God and others. As we consider benevolence as it relates to justice, a careful distinction should be made with regard to the Hopkinsian *disinterested* benevolence. Neither

---

[110] In Samuel Johnson's *Dictionary of the English Language* (1766), the word presume carries a connotation of assertion without conclusive evidence. In other words, the public must rely on others to rightly apply the law, but can only presume upon what is received through the reception of others. Samuel Johnson, "Presume," in *Dictionary of the English Language [...]* (London: A. Millar, 1766).

[111] Edwards Jr., "Volume 225," 26.

[112] Chamberlain, "The Execution of Moses Paul," 442, n.69.

[113] See Kyle C. Strobel's helpful restructure of Edwards theology as a prioritization of the Trinitarian outworking of the "mutual beatific delight" for one another in redemption history. Kyle C. Strobel, *The Theology of Jonathan Edwards: A Reinterpretation*, ed by John Webster, Ian A. McFarland, and Ivor Davidson (New York: Bloomsbury T & T Clark), 2014.

Edwards Sr. nor his son believed Samuel Hopkins's extreme expression of benevolence, summed up in the phrase "willing to be damned for God's glory," was helpful.[114] Rather, the Edwardsean principle of benevolence is found to be consistent with a desire for God's own happiness.[115]

The younger Edwards sought to be faithful to his father's theological vision of benevolence while harmonizing it with retributive justice. In the second execution sermon (based on John 3:16), Edwards Jr. highlights God's benevolence as the outflow of God's love in this world.[116] Edwards Jr. argued that few people love with the view toward the general honor of God. In God's government of the universe, love is seen through justice propounding the glory of God if not by salvation, but also by damnation.[117] This love is freely bestowed on those who have "nothing to pay" but out of "compassion [for people who have] nothing worthy of delight. [This lack of worth is] exciting [to] the divine compassion. [And] thus appears the motive—God's pure love—compassion—pure compassion."[118] This pure love, which manifests as compassion, is the essence of the divine benevolence which orders the divine government of the universe. While Moses Paul might not have caught the subtle expression of the overflow of the mutual beatific desire of the Trinity into this world for unworthy sinners, nevertheless, herein is found a conceptual understanding of his father's thoughts on the Holy Spirit.

---

[114] Jonathan Edwards, "A Faithful Narrative," in *The Great Awakening, Works of Jonathan Edwards Online Vol. 4*, ed. C. C. Goen (New Haven, CT: Yale University Press, 1957–2008), 170.; In a letter to Samuel Hopkins on October 29, 1793, Jonathan Edwards Jr. advised Hopkins against the inclusion of this particular view in the second edition of his *System of Doctrines, Contained in Divine Revelation, Explained and Defended [...]*. Jonathan Edwards Jr., "Letter to Samuel Hopkins, October 29, 1793," *Park Family Papers Collection*. Sterling Memorial Library, Yale University (MS 384 Box 10, Folder 120 (Vol. 4).; Stephen Post, "Disinterested Benevolence: An American Debate Over the Nature of Christian Love," *Journal of Religious Ethics* 14, no. 2 (Fall 1986): 356–368.

[115] Jonathan Edwards Jr., "Remarks on the Improvements Made in Theology by His Father, President Edwards," in *The Works of Jonathan Edwards, D.D., Late President of Union College. With a Memoir [...]*, ed. Tyron Edwards, vol. 1, 481–492 (New York: Dayton and Newman, 1842), 481.

[116] Jonathan Edwards Jr., "Volume 242," *Jonathan Edwards Jr. Papers (Sermons)*, Hartford Seminary Library (Box 166, Folder 2732). The transcript of this sermon is in appendix 3.

[117] Edwards Jr., "Volume 242," 2.

[118] Edwards Jr., "Volume 242," 3–4.

Advocating Abolition

A year after Moses Paul's execution, Edwards Jr. would, with Ebenezer Baldwin, coauthor a series of articles that would appear in the *Connecticut Journal* and the *New Haven Post Boy*. Twice in October 1773 and December 1773 these articles shed unsettling light upon the slave trade and slavery in general. The primary argument in these articles is based upon the Edwardsean principle of benevolence inherent in the golden rule (Matthew 7:12). In the leading argument, he suggests that the American colonies were jealously motivated to secure their "own liberties," but have been negligent, and even "inattentive to our own conduct in enslaving the Negroes, or at least in joining in the trade, whereby they are enslaved."[119] The golden rule is the quintessential maxim which summaries the Edwardsean principle of Spirit imparted benevolence. Why? For pure love, which exists within the Trinity, to occur between men there must be a reception of the Spirit. In *Original Sin,* Edwards Sr. demonstrates how a prior principle of love must be provided by the Spirit prior as it was in the beginning with Adam and Eve in order that acts of benevolence may occur.[120]

Edwards Jr.'s participation in these execution sermons highlights a way in which he extended his father's legacy. This benevolent principle was inherited from his father's writings. Concern for the just application of God's benevolence is the essence of true religion. In spite of this effort to raise awareness about the horrors of slavery and the slave trade in general, his work toward the end of slavery in Connecticut was interrupted by the oppressive acts by Great Britain over her colonies. Even as Edwards Jr. was working through the publication of his father's sermons, which became known as *A History of the Work of Redemption* (1774), Parliament began to issue the Intolerable Acts. This geo-political shift caused Edwards Jr. to shift his focus from the slave trade to public theology in general in the revolutionary era. Yet, the interest in benevolence for the enslaved did not disappear.

Edwards Jr. remained active theologically and politically in those years between the execution of Moses Paul and Joseph Mountain (1772–1791). In these execution sermons are themes of justice and benevolence, which

---

[119] Ebenezer Baldwin and Jonathan Edwards Jr., "Some Observations upon the Slavery of Negroes," *Connecticut Journal, and the New-Haven Post-Boy* (October-December 1773), in *Am I Not a Man and a Brother: The Antislavery Crusade of Revolutionary America 1688–1788*, ed. Roger Burns (New York: Chelsea House, 1977), 293.

[120] Jonathan Edwards Sr., *Original Sin*, in *Works of Jonathan Edwards*, Vol. 3, ed. Clyde A. Holbrook (New Haven, CT: Yale University Press, 1970), 225–229.

would be significant topics in his more famous governmental theory of atonement. But in these sermons are also those foundational arguments which contribute to abolition that appear in his widely published abolition sermon in 1791.[121] In the broader storyline of Edwards Jr.'s life, his direct interest in the oppressed is evidence of his a genuine spirituality.

Patriotism and Revolution

The spirit of revolution was not limited to that contentious era separation at occured at the White Haven Church. Revolution was in the air as Britain began to pressure the colonies with legislation that prompted pastors to consider whether resistance to authority was biblical. Yet, even prior to the shots fired at Concord and Lexington, Massachusetts, Edwards Jr. began to identify with the concerns of the merchant and legal class in his wealthy congregation.

In a sermon delivered on the eve of the departure of the faction opposed to his installation, he preached a sermon which was intended to instruct on the proper method of dealing with those with whom you disagree. Yet in the applications made, he hints at an increasingly unsettled relationship with England. Preaching from Exodus 3:7–8, he taught that "It is the duty of a people under affliction and public calamities to cry to God for deliverance."[122] The proper approach in seeking deliverance from "civil tyranny" is to "petition king and chief magistrates of any nation for deliverance from oppression."[123] This application and illustration was within recent memory. The British Crown had the passed the Stamp Act (1765) just four years earlier that caused the colonies to resist and request a reversal of policy.

On the eve of the first Continental Congress, a Fast was proclaimed throughout the colonies. Jonathan Edwards Jr. led his congregation to consider the adversity which they were experiencing from Britain's heavy hand. In this August 31, 1774, sermon from Ecclesiastes 7:17, and after a lengthy exposition of his text, he summarized the concerns of his congregation in this way:

---

[121] Jonathan Edwards Jr., "The Injustice and Impolicy of the Slave Trade, and of Slavery," in *The Works of Jonathan Edwards, D.D., Late President of Union College. With a Memoir [...]*, ed. Tyron Edwards, vol. 2, 75–97 (New York: Dayton and Newman, 1842).

[122] Jonathan Edwards Jr., "Sermon 74, August 31, 1769," *Jonathan Edwards Jr. Papers (Sermons)*, Hartford Seminary Library (Box 165, Folder 2727).

[123] Edwards Jr., "Sermon 74."

But here it may be proper for us to inquire in what are the calamities which we suffer and have reason to fear. The sum of all these calamities is that the parliament of Great Britain claims a right to make laws for us here in America, to tax us and to dispose of our lives, liberty and property according to their own pleasure, without any consent of ours given, or even asked. And upon this right they have not any claimed, but have acted upon it; and if we sit down quickly, that they will still act upon it, to the utter ruin of us and our children. – Upon this claim of the British parliament they not long since passed the odious stamp act, whereby vast sums of money were to be raised upon us, entirely without our consent; and the burden of this act fell with peculiar weight upon the poor, the widow and the fatherless. By the vigorous and unified opposition of America, and by certain other motives, they were induced indeed to repeal this act, but not to renounce the claim upon which it was founded. But soon after, being determined to prosecute their claim, they passed another act, imposing duties upon *paper, glass, painter's colours* and *tea,* for the sole and express purpose of raising a revenue, or extorting money from us to be paid here in America; at the same time utterly prohibiting us from furnishing ourselves with these articles from any other quarter, but from Great Britain.[124]

By same manner, Edwards Jr. lays out the case that oppression still existed as the taxation of tea remained in force in spite of a repeal of unjust taxation in the other areas. Edwards Jr. chronicled the Intolerable Acts which included the suspension of the New York legislature, the forced quartering of soldiers, military tribunals in Rhode Island, blockades in Boston harbor, recension of the Massachusetts Bay Colony's charter, and potential extradition to England. All these incidents are summed up by Edwards Jr. as indicative of the "great whore of Babylon" who does not allow any to buy or sell without the mark or by the name of the beast.[125]

In this first major sermon on the escalating concerns with England, Edwards Jr. warned that Britain had recently decreed direct rule in Quebec.

---

[124] Jonathan Edwards Jr., "390. Preached on a fast appointed by authority on occasion of the late acts of the British Legislature relating to Boston, the Massachusets [sic], Quebec, and America in general. Aug. 31. 1774," *Jonathan Edwards Jr. Papers (Sermons),* Hartford Seminary Library (Box 166, Folder 2735), 32–34.

[125] Edwards Jr., "390," 36.

By all appearances the crown was intent on the massive resettlement of papists from Ireland and would not hesitate to encroach upon America's religious freedoms.[126] Rhetorically, he focused on the distressing irony of Britain's actions. As if bewildered, he asks, and then answers his own question: "[Is] the king of Great Britain supreme head of papists in Canada? A king of the House of Hanover, which was brought to the throne chiefly to keep out Popery from Great Britain—a king who has solemnly sworn to maintain the Protestant Reformed Religion, now establishing it by law in a part of his dominions."[127] The remainder of the sermon picks up the familiar themes of taxation, deprivation of property, and self-rule.

Yet, from this collection of worries, he appeals to the patriotic "boast of Englishmen" in their constitution that "provides for the life, liberty and property of the subject," which will soon be lost so that they would in effect become "no longer Englishmen [...] freemen, [...but] arrant slaves."[128] Theologically, Edwards Jr. appeals to the doctrine of benevolence when he identifies unity and steadfastness as essential "in this important case, big with the greatest and most lasting consequences." Their success depended upon cooperation of colonies as well as each family and merchant. He encouraged the merchant and the farmer to not complain if their bottom line was not as strong as it had once been. Instead, each should consider how to "divest ourselves of all selfishness, and views to our own present interest."[129] Gerald McDermott recognized that in Edwards Sr.'s *Nature of True Virtue* almost every case the "private-publick distinction" is compared, he always put the private tendency in a negative connotation. In other words, a concern for the public good above one's own private interest consists in a benevolence that is consistent with true religion.[130] This concern for the public good is an important precondition to ensure liberty for all.

During these years Edwards Jr. prepared his congregation for war with England, even preaching to several companies of troops that were organizing

---

[126] Jonathan Edwards Jr., "390. Preached on a fast appointed by authority on occasion of the late acts of the British Legislature relating to Boston, the Massachusetts, Quebec, and America in general. Ecc. 7.14. August 31. 1774.," *Jonathan Edwards Jr. Papers (Sermons)*, Hartford Theological Seminary (Box 166, Folder 2735), four-page unnumbered insert between page 40–41.

[127] Edwards Jr., "390," 36.

[128] Edwards Jr., "390. Preached on a fast," 54–56.

[129] Edwards Jr., "390. Preached on a fast," 67–68.

[130] Gerald R. McDermott, *One Holy and Happy Society: The Public Theology of Jonathan Edwards* (University Park, PA: Pennsylvania State University Press, 1992), 103–104.

in New Haven.[131] To General David Wooster's troops, who were keeping Sabbath in New Haven, Edwards Jr. encouraged uncertain troops that their cause was glorious. Even at the end of May 1775, many were still wondering whether their cause was righteous or not, so Edwards preached the benevolence of their cause to restore the relationship of the king and his subjects.[132] He drew his doctrine from the biblical admonition to seek the benefit of others instead of one's own interest (1 Cor. 10:24). Man's tendency, he said, was to seek what they chiefly love but how much better when men seek "the good of the public." Therefore, "the nature of true religion [is] in a disinterested spirit."[133] In seeking the good of the nation, these soldiers could be confident that their service had a greater purpose than their own private interest. In other words, their military movements directed toward their king, was part of the re-establishment of God's moral government.

In support of a 'civil war' with Britain, Edwards Jr. claimed that in the controversy with Great Britain, America had not been looking for war; rather, in "taking up arms against your king; and what not [...] is the way most effectually to establish the king upon his throne."[134] In other words, the troops should not be disheartened; rather, they are participating in a kind of restoration of monarchy, which also occurred in England during the deposition of Stuarts and restoration by the House of Hanover. These noble purposes "have abundant reason to encourage you and to make you *be strong and of good courage* and to excite you to quit yourselves like men in such a glorious cause."[135] Even as late as January 1776 the armed conflict with Britain was still being described as a civil war rather than a war for independence.[136]

---

[131] Jonathan Edwards Jr., "454. Decr. 22. 1775. Delivered at the desire of the officers of several companies belonging to the town, to them and their companies," *Jonathan Edwards Jr. Papers (Sermons)*, Hartford Seminary Library (Box 166, Folder 2736), 1–32.

[132] Jonathan Edwards Jr., "424. 1 Cor. 10.24. Delivered by the desire of General Wooster to several companies of his Regiment who then kept Sabbath in town. May 28. 1775.," *Jonathan Edwards Jr. Papers (Sermons)*, Hartford Theological Seminary (Box 166, Folder 2735).

[133] Edwards Jr., "424," 2–3.

[134] Edwards Jr., "424.," 9–10.

[135] Edwards Jr., "424.," 9–10.

[136] Jonathan Edwards Jr., "460. 1 Ki. 20.11. On a Public Fast on Account of the Civil War. Janry. 17. 1776.," *Jonathan Edwards Jr. Papers (Sermons)*, Hartford Theological Seminary (Box 166, Folder 2736).

These uniformed men were the "guardians" of the people, interposing themselves against tyranny, to "fight for religion," and our "happiness and liberty so long favored."[137] In their fight and exposure to danger, the militia is to "imbibe that noble principle of benevolence."[138] Even a year into the war, Edwards Jr. advocated that benevolence was the answer for victory in war saying, "That [if] the strength of our love to the public is small, [then] this is [the] case of public calamity; [however,] if strong public benevolence, [then we will] not [be] easily overcome."[139]

After the Declaration of Independence was published, he became active as an evangelist hopeful that God's Spirit would stir up new conversions. At the beginning of 1777, he even planned a four-part series of revival sermons "to awaken sinners."[140] That year appeared bleak for the Colonies, until the unexpected surrender of General Burgoyne's army. Appropriate to the occasion, Edwards Jr. preached his November 1777, Thanksgiving sermon from Psalm 118:23 "This is the Lord's doing, it is marvelous in our eyes."[141]

These war years brought great pressure upon Connecticut. They were the second largest suppliers of men and raw materials for the conflict, and his own town would be asked to pay a price for liberty more directly. Three years after the first Declaration of Independence, forty-eight British men-of-war left New York Sound to pillage and burn the Connecticut coast. Their first stop on evening of July 4, 1779, was an anchorage just at the mouth of New Haven. With two divisions of Regulars and Hessians—a combined force of nearly three thousand troops—Major General Tyron and Brigadier General Garth landed on either side of the harbor the next morning.[142]

---

[137] In a very dramatic appeal to the men in arms, he whips up the Protestant antipathy for the papacy. He warns: "the pope in Canada—so here soon—not speak against the 'man of sin'—whore of Babylon, drunk with the blood of Saints—makes kings drink cup of fornication. Not fight valiantly for this? Our fathers did—suffered, burnt at the stake—so we if—your country—entirely ruined in a political respect if not make a stand." Edwards Jr., "1 Cor. 10.24." 10–12.

[138] Edwards Jr., "1 Cor. 10.24." 12.

[139] Jonathan Edwards Jr., "No. 526. Prov. 24.10, April 27, 1777." *Jonathan Edwards Jr. Papers (Sermons)*, Hartford Theological Seminary (Box 166, Folder 2737), 5.

[140] Sermons 512, 516, 517, 518. *Jonathan Edwards Jr. Papers (Sermons)*, Hartford Seminary Library (Box 166, Folder 2737).

[141] Jonathan Edwards Jr., "No. 537. Novr. 20.1777. On a Thanksgiving soon after the defeat capture of Genl. Burgoyne and his whole army," *Jonathan Edwards Jr. Papers (Sermons)*, Hartford Seminary Library (Box 167, Folder 2738), 1–8.

[142] George Hare Ford, "The Defense of New Haven and Resistance Made Against Invading Troops Along the West Shore, July 1779," in *Revolutionary Characters of New Haven [...]* (New Haven, CT: Sons of the American Revolution, 1911), 31–32.

With orders to converge upon New Haven Green from either direction, the next hours brought chaos in the town as a residential militia of just one hundred and fifty endeavored to hold back the enemy. Acting President of Yale Naphtali Daggett rode out upon his horse to meet the enemy with his fowling gun followed by enthusiastic Yale students.[143] With the general population outnumbered by the invaders, much of the town evacuated until adequate militia could be aroused to meet the enemy. As rumors of a gathering military response was received, the English generals decided to re-embark after the second day of occupation and sailed up the coast to do the same to Fairfield and Norwalk.

New Haven was providentially spared burning,[144] but in all, this British excursion up the coastline, was estimated to have incurred a loss of about one hundred thousand pounds sterling.[145] Several from Edwards Jr.'s congregation had been either killed, wounded, or captured. While not in his congregation, his future brother-in-law, Hezekiah Sabin Jr. from the Fairhaven Church, was also captured by the British.[146] After the town began to put themselves back together again, stories would be told of atrocities by the British, and of the heroism by the townspeople. According to Ezra Stiles, when he returned to town the day after the British left, he surveyed the "desolations, dead Corpses, and conflagrations," and declared:

> It was a scene of mixed joy and sorrow—plunder, rapes, murder, bayoneting, indelicacies towards the sex, insolence and abuse and insult towards the inhabitants in general. Dwellinghouses and stores just setting on fire at East Haven in full view, etc. Joy and rejoicing that the buildings had escaped the flames in the compact part of the town; yet mixed with fears of relanding and future conflagration of which they had left rigorous threatings.[147]

---

[143] According to a report, a British detail was sent to capture Daggett when he did not fall back with the rest, and was asked, "What are you doing, you old fool, firing on his majesty's troops?" "Exercising the rights of war, sir," was his reply, and off went his fowling piece again." Ford, "The Defense of New Haven," 35.

[144] According to Charles Townshend, Edmund Fanning, a graduate of Yale College and son-inlaw of General Tyron interceded on the town's behalf so as not to be put to fire. His reason not to burn the town, according to General Garth from the view of the State House, was that "Tis too pretty a place to burn." Charles Hervey Townshend, *The British Invasion of New Haven, Connecticut [...]*, (New Haven, CT: Tuttle, Morehouse and Taylor, 1879), 7, 17.

[145] *LDES2*, 359.

[146] Ford, "The Defense of New Haven," 35.

[147] *LDES2*, 357.

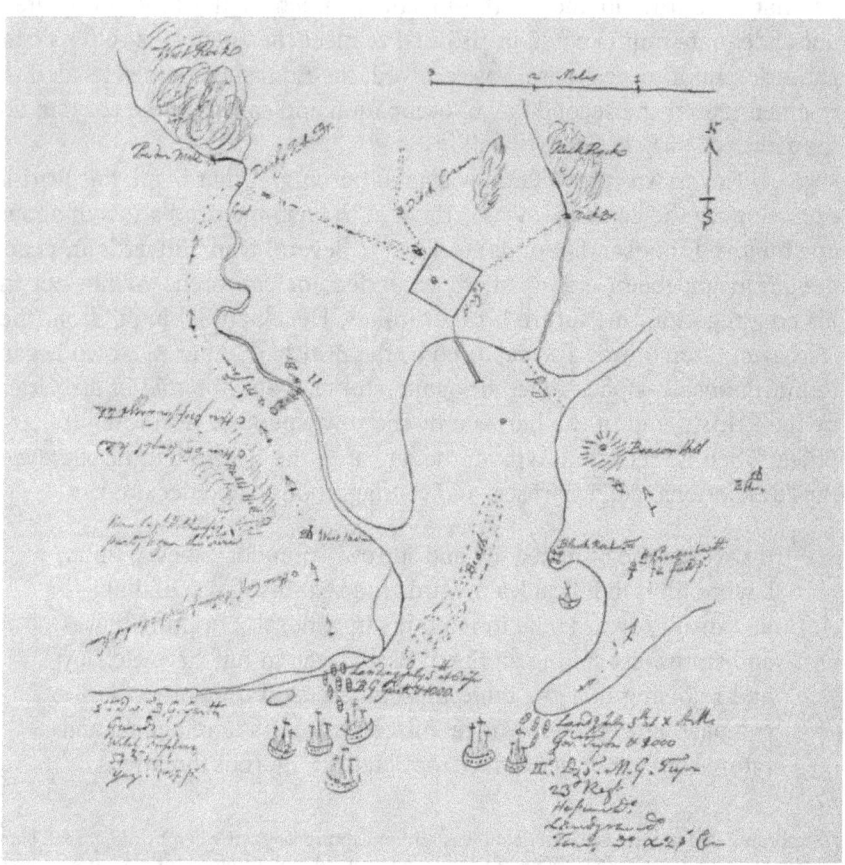

Figure C: Sketch, by Dr. Ezra Stiles, of the Invasion of New Haven. The Literary Diary of Ezra Stiles: March 14, 1776–December 31, 1781. Vol. 2. Edited by Franklin Bowditch Dexter. New York: Charles Scribner's Sons, 1901

Edwards Jr. provided spiritual comfort for his people on August 12 at a specially called fast by local leaders. While the British spared the town, they nevertheless destroyed eight dwelling houses, three barns, six warehouses at the docks, and seven merchant vessels.[148] These last two casualty of war alarmed the community and drew them to consider now their livelihood was severely damaged.[149]

In this sermon, he encouraged his people to consider what God might be saying through the providential reproof of invasion: "We [have] been more particularly reproved. We not only suffered the common calamities. [Ours was] some special [loss of shipping]. [Indeed,] we depended on trade."[150] Erza Stiles attended this sermon "at Mr. Edwards's meeting in the forenoon" and conveyed that "the presence of God seemed to be with us all day. Blessed be God that he has put it into the hearts of his people to seek him in the hour of distress, especially now that we are threatened with the return of the enemy to lay New Haven in ashes."[151] The task of repairing his congregation, in light of the ongoing difficult trial of the war, was made even more challenging after the invasion.

Defense of the Gospel and Displacement

Edwards Jr.'s final period of ministry (1782–1795) in New Haven is often the source for the negative caricature; however, the oft-referenced difficult pastoral relations typically miss several factors. First, ministerial challenges came from several directions. Not least of which was the effect of the war upon New England and migration toward New York, Pennsylvania, Ohio, and Vermont.[152] Second, at about the time of the loss of his wife in 1782 and with the stress of a young family, the nation also experienced a severe inflationary run. During this time, with expenses rising and need to manage

---

[148]*LDES2*, 364.

[149]*LDES2*, 362.

[150]Jonathan Edwards Jr., "No. 624. Aug. 12.1779. On a fast kept by the town on account of the late invasion and present danger," *Jonathan Edwards Jr. Papers (Sermons)*, Hartford Seminary Library (Box 167, Folder 2739), 3.

[151]*LDES2*, 362.

[152]"But the greatest emigration of all those directly following the Revolution took its way into New York, the more conservative element staying nearer the eastern boundary, the venturesome ones going out into the wilderness. A strong current set out in 1783–1784 from the New England States, and speedily the western shore of Lake Champlain and the older towns on the Hudson felt the influence of the newcomers." Lois (Kimball) Mathews Rosenberry, *The Expansion of New England* (Boston: Houghton Mifflin company, 1909), 153.

his household, he asked his church to consider renegotiating his original contract. Later, in 1786 as difficulties began to present themselves, he felt compelled to give explanation as to how he had requested compensation four years earlier.

Referring to his request in 1782, he reminded them that he had been hired in 1769 as a single man on one hundred pounds, and that since then his circumstances had changed remarkably to provide for a family of seven. He goes on to say that "I presume that the society did not think my salary was too large before the war; or to be fair, that it would have been too large had my family consisted then of the same number of persons, of what it now consists. Yes we all know, that the expenses of supporting a family now, are much greater than they were then."[153] Inflationary pressure and mass migration created a significant pressure upon congregational churches throughout the state.

A greater pressure than migration and economics was, thirdly, the theological pressures upon New Divinity pastors who were striving to be faithful to the Edwardsean tradition. As the inheritor of his father's manuscripts and name, Edwards Jr. felt compelled to answer the Universalist and Arminian. *The Salvation of All Men Strictly Examined* was published in 1790 and *Dissertation Concerning Liberty and Necessity* in 1797 and responsed to each error respectively. The former manuscript was prepared while at New Haven and the later in Colebrook. His literary efforts served to provide an accusation for some who were becoming disgruntled.

According to David Austin, a deacon at the White Haven Church, Edwards Jr. spent too much time answering theologians and not enough time "studying how he may win his people to the practice of virtue and religion."[154] In particular, chairing a committee to discover the absence of several parishioners, Austin had uncovered some malcontent leveled against Edwards Jr. by Ebenezer Beardselee. In a letter to Roger Sherman, Austin said that Beardselee had been prohibited from attending the Lord's Table for being a Universalist. In addition, Beardselee complained that Edwards Jr. accused him publicly instead of approaching him privately. Furthermore, he charged that Edwards Jr.'s sermons were unedifying for his family as they tended toward "idle distinctions of school Divinity, metaphysical, abstruse,

---

[153] Jonathan Edwards Jr., Letter Sent to the Society of White Haven January 31, 1786, *Connecticut Miscellaneous Manuscripts Collection*. Manuscripts and Archives, Yale University Library (MS 149 Series III. Box 20. Folder 215), 2–3.

[154] David Austin, letter to Roger Sherman February 20, 1790 in Ferm, *Edwards the Younger*, 141.

unintelligible, and dangerous speculations, with perverse disputing."[155] Roger Sherman, on the other hand, defended Edwards Jr. as among the best preachers of his day, and furthermore, Beardselee was widely known to embrace Universalism.[156]

In 1782 John Cornwell, a former member of White Haven, wrote a reconciling letter stating that in time past he had been too rash in desiring to leave the church. In his rashness, he had asked permission to join the Separates[157] because Edwards Jr. "did not preach the necessity of the Spirit."[158] In his letter, he acknowledges that

> I then thought Mr. Edwards preaching wrong in that he did not insist an entry more, and more frequently on the views and exercises of the sinner under awakenings and convictions which take place before regeneration; and this is what I chiefly meant by remarking as I did in the church meeting, that Mr. Edwards did not enough preach the Spirit. But I now see that the Scriptures insist much more on the exercise of true grace after regeneration, than on those affections which take place before it. And in general, I approve of that system of sentiments which are held and preached in this church, so far as I know them. This satisfaction I have obtained by a careful perusal the Scriptures, of the writings of the late President Edwards, and by free conversation with the pastor of this church and by those sermons of his, which I have lately had opportunity of attending

---

[155] "Committee Report on Enquiry of Several Brethren, August 20, 1789," *White Haven Church Records, Series 1,* New Haven Museum (MSS 9, Box 1, Folder U1).

[156] "You observe that I have been much absent and so have not had an opportunity to attend and be acquainted with his preaching in general of late years. I know that this has been the case but I have frequently attended his ministry had conversation with him on religious subjects to my great satisfaction. When I have been absent I have heard many good preachers which I esteem orthodox and pious, but I have found none that in all respects suits me better than Dr. Edwards." Roger Sherman, letter to David Austin March 1, 1790 in Ferm, *Edwards the Younger,* 143.

[157] C. C. Goen describes at length the characteristics of the Separates' preaching and worship including the peculiarities of the "holy whine," impressions, enthusiasm, and "improvement of spiritual gifts." Goen, *Revivalism and Separatism in New England,* 174–184. At about the mid-point of Edwards's preaching career in New Haven (1781), the Separates officially became a denomination. Goen, *Revivalism and Separatism,* 172.

[158] According to church records on December 23, 1777. Ewert, *Jonathan Edwards the Younger,* vol. 1, 31.

to. And I cannot but recommend it to any who happen to view things, as I formerly did, to seek satisfaction in the same way.[159]

Cornwell recognized Edwards Jr.'s preaching as consistent in doctrinal manner with his father (President Edwards). However consistent with his father he may have been, the slanderous actions of Cornwell and Beardselee would have created an atmosphere of doubt in the congregation's mind toward their pastor.[160]

As difficulties mounted the unraveling relationship between pastor and congregation began to accelerate during this last half of his ministry in New Haven. When affected by vacant pews, the temptation to preach church attendance often works against itself, and at different seasons Edwards Jr. yielded to this temptation. For example, in a sermon delivered in 1781 during the war, he makes leaving his church easy with "[p]erhaps you don't like the preacher—if he does not deal in the truth, he should deal in it. If he does preach the truth, you ought to like it, and if you don't, you can go elsewhere."[161] Wesley Ewert chronicles the seasons of bad and better feeling between Edwards and his people through this last decade.[162]

By December 31, 1791, Ezra Stiles had begun to take notice, and he noted in his diary that "Dr. Edwards's people are exceedingly alienated from him."[163] Yet the relationship had not been altogether irreparable. Attempt had been made. Due to Edwards Jr.'s loyalty to his father's position on the Half-way Covenant, he took a conservative view and avoided fellowship with mixed churches like First Church who were not zealous for true religion. In a letter to Edwards Jr., about thirteen men privately expressed their desire that the White Haven Church participate with the two other churches in town. Yet, in their appeal, they decided that in the bonds of brotherly love to "quietly content ourselves with the ministrations of our Pastor: sincerely burying all animosities . . . [and] if at the present or at any future time, our Pastor

---

[159] John Cornwell, letter to White Haven Church and Jonathan Edwards [Jr.], May 27, 1782, *White Haven Church Records, Series 1,* New Haven Museum (MSS 9, Box 1, Folder U1).

[160] Ezra Stiles noted in his diary that Edwards Jr.'s congregation had grown disgusted with how he carried out the Beardeslee affair, but that the issues ran deeper into doctrinal discontent. "This is a pretext. In truth his incessant preaching of New Divinity and rigidity in church administration has disgusted them." *LDES3,* 343.

[161] Jonathan Edwards Jr., "No. 710 June 3. 1781 Psal. 73.28.," *Jonathan Edwards Jr. Papers (Sermons),* Hartford Seminary Library (Box 167, Folder 2741), appendix.

[162] Ewert, *Jonathan Edwards the Younger,* vol. 1, 32–36.

[163] *LDES3,* 438.

should find himself at liberty to join with us in opinion, that maintaining Christian communion with the other two congregational churches in this place, would be productive [...] that he would please to signify it to us."[164]

In response, Edwards Jr. effusively expressed his love and gratitude toward his "brethren and friends" for their show of mature response to "bury all animosities, to forgive all injuries, real or supposed, and to forget all grievances. It also affords, a peculiar satisfaction to find you, my Christian brethren and friends, joining in strengthening my hands in the labours of the ministry."[165] He assured them that if he felt liberty that he would propose joining the other church in the furtherance of true religion. Nevertheless, over the next four years, the White Haven Society came to the conclusion that they could no longer pay Edwards Jr. adequately[166] as they had dwindled so, and that dismission to another church was the only alternative.

Loss of congregants might suggest that Ebenezer Beardselee's metaphysical characterization, or a more spirited style as John Cornwell desired was the root of the problem; however, Leonard Bacon, historian of the First Church, notes that in James Dana's congregation, and others, retention was not much better:

> [T]he period immediately following the revolutionary war, when the disastrous and demoralizing influences of that long conflict were felt most powerfully in all the Churches [...] was just [at] the deepest—the period in which the ministry of so gifted and evangelical a divine as the younger Edwards, came to an end in this very town for want of success—the period just before the commencement of those great, successive, spreading reli-

---

[164] "Conciliatory Propositions in White Haven Between Dr. Edwards and Others, April 3, 1790," *Connecticut Miscellaneous Manuscripts Collection*, Manuscripts and Archives, Yale University Library (MS 149, Series III, Box 20, Folder 215).

[165] Jonathan Edwards Jr., Letter Sent to David Austin April 3, 1790, *Connecticut Miscellaneous Manuscripts Collection*, Manuscripts and Archives, Yale University Library (MS 149, Series III, Box 20, Folder 215), 1.

[166] Benjamin A. Dean's records in his history of the Colebrook church the local speculation on how such an affluent church could not collect a hundred pounds for his salary when they could muster ninety plus wood. The conclusion was inferred that the Half-way Covenant controversy had reared itself up again. *History of the Colebrook Congregational Church 1795–1895: Centennial Address Delivered December 31, 1895* (Hartford: Connecticut State Library, 1913), 12–14; also see *AAP1*, 655. According to Kenneth Minkema, David Austin and Jeremiah Atwater had growing resentment to Edwards Jr.'s intolerance toward churches practicing the Half-way Covenant. In general, the mood of the town was changing toward rigid doctrinal standards. Minkema, *The Edwardses*, 549.

gious awakenings, which characterized the last forty years of our ecclesiastical history.[167]

As a testament to Bacon's depiction of the spirit of the age, in 1788 a committee was formed by the General Association to draft an exhortation on the subject of the increasing neglect of "public Worship of God [...] to be publicly read, in the various Congregations, through the State."[168] Bacon's generous observation is likely true in the main and certainly not symptomatic of Edwards Jr.'s ministry particularly; however, given the peculiarities of Jonathan Edwards Jr.'s on-going challenge of personality and predilection toward analytical theology would likely create a less pleasing narrative in the community.[169] No doubt, his older brother's wise words struck a chord with his younger brother, when Timothy wrote:

> In this day of adversity it becomes you to consider. Enquire wherein you have failed of the wisdom of the serpent and harmlessness of the dove. If you are what you profess to be your heavenly Father sees that you want chastisement and inflicts it in infinite goodness to you. [...] Dwell not on the ingratitude of your people but on your own heart and life.[170]

In spite of being relieved from ministry in New Haven on May 19, 1795,[171] Edwards Jr. would be the commencement speaker at Yale that Septem-

---

[167] Leonard Bacon, *Thirteen Historical Discourses, on the Completion of Two Hundred Years: From the Beginning of the First Church in New Haven, with an Appendix* (New Haven, NY: Durrie and Peck, 1839), 277–278.

[168] Lavalette Perrin, William DeL. Love Jr., and Charles H. Clark, eds., *The Records of the General Association of Ye Colony of Connecticut: June 20, 1738–June 19, 1799* (Hartford, CT: The Case, Lockwood and Brainard Co., 1888), 127.

[169] Timothy wrote in 1795 to warn and encourage his brother saying, "This is a great event and will effect your character in several ways. However fully you exonerate yourself or may be so by a counsel—It is therefore a frown of Providence a heavy chastisement." Timothy Edwards, "Letter to Jonathan Edwards Jr. May 18, 1795," *Series V. Edwards Family Correspondence*, Beinecke Rare Book and Manuscript Library (GEN MSS 151, Box 26, Folder 1440).

[170] Timothy Edwards, "Letter to Jonathan Edwards Jr."

[171] Benjamin Trumbull was the chosen moderator, represented in the clergy by John Marsh, Thomas Bray, Samuel Eells, William Robinson, Wilaim Lockwood, Benoni Upson, David Beebee. Delegats consisted of Solomon Tuttle, Josiah Hart, Joel Rose, Jonathan Russel, Timothy Clark, Daniel Buckingham, Amos Gridley, and Phinehas Peck. "Broadside, New Haven, May 19, 1795," *Jonathan Edwards, 1745–1801, in Edwards Family Collection,* Princeton University Library (AM 13472, Box 1, Folder 24).

ber.[172] Taking leave of ministry in New Haven, Edwards Jr. began a new pastorate in Colebrook, CT until his call to the presidency of Union College in Schenectady, New York in 1799.

Before taking leave to Union College, Edwards Jr.'s participation in the Second Great Awakening, recognition must be paid to a nearly forgotten aspect of his biography. Although Edwards Jr. had turned down opportunity to pastor his father's missionary outpost in Stockbridge, he nevertheless put energy into the westward effort of Congregationalist expansion. While the constitution of the Connecticut Missionary Society formed in 1798 indicates that his tenure was short due to his coming relocation to Union, Edwards Jr. was named to the board of trustees on the basis of his prior involvement in the General Association.[173]

Edwards Jr. was active in the promotion of missionary church development as early as the mid-1780s through his participation in the General Association. In a summer meeting of 1788 in the home of Nathan Perkins, Edwards Jr. participated in a committee to consider best practices for the advancement of churches in the new settlements of Vermont and New York.[174] At the June 21, 1791, meeting as the secretary, Jonathan Edwards Jr. recorded the resolution to study "the most proper and feasible mode of sending missionaries to new settlements, and communicate them to the next General Association."[175] And study, he did.

---

[172] Edwards Jr. had rapport with the faculty. At one point, he had been considered for a professorship of divinity; however, political pressures would cause the appointment not to materialize. In Ezra Stiles' diary, he notes on May 16, 1788, the passing thoughts of someone who asked, "why not choose Dr. Edwards? Dr. W. replied [in jest] why not at once choose Dr. Bellamy—President, Mr. Hopkins—Prof. of Divinity.and" *LDES3*, 317. Edwards Jr. would on occasion serve as an examiner. At these semi-annual examinations, Edwards Jr. would often interpose haud rect (not correct). Samuel Dutton relates: "The students on one occasion, not liking as the college phrase goes, 'to be screwed,' expressed their dissatisfaction with the Dr.'s mode of examination, by 'scraping.' 'Very well,' says he, 'young gentlemen, you may take your course, I shall pursue mine;' and screwed them tighter and tighter, till they concluded that their wisest course was, to be still. They gave him, however, the name of 'Old *haud recte*,' by which he afterwards went among the students." Dutton, *History of the North Church*, 72, note.

[173] Nathan Perkins, ed., *The Constitution of the Missionary Society of Connecticut: with an Address from the Board of Trustees, to the Peoples of the State, and a Narrative on the Subject of Missions* [...] (Hartford, CT: Hudson and Goodwin, 1800), 4.

[174] Ewert, *Jonathan Edwards the Younger*, vol. 1, 54–56. Perrin, *The Records of the General Association*, 126.

[175] Ewert, *Jonathan Edwards*, 137–138. In a joint letter, responding to a disgruntled Vermonter who was offended that missionaries would come to his state, Edwards Jr. along with Ezra Stiles and Benjamin Trumbull assert that "there are very few new settlements in the northern and western parts of the United States, which on account of their infancy and other circumstances are unable to support the preaching of the gospel for themselves, is a matter of public notoriety:

Within two months, Edwards Jr. traveled west to Oneida County, NY to survey and assist three fledgling congregations organize as congregational churches (New Hartford, Paris Hill, and Clinton). According to local records on "August 29, 1791, Dr. Edwards came up the narrow trail through the forest, from another little settlement—now the village of Clinton." There he assisted the residents of Paris Hill to become "The Second Church of Christ in Whitestown."[176]

The 'First Church' was formed in New Hartford (Whitestown) just a few days before on August 27 in the barn of Col. Jedediah Sanger.[177] On that day, he met with thirteen signers, and baptized eight children.[178] From New Hartford to Paris Hill, and from Paris Hill to Clinton proceeded Edwards on a course of about a week. To each of these churches he provided a similar confession of faith, covenant, and rules of admission. Of the three churches, only the Clinton and New Hartford church retain a copy of the original documents.[179]

Upon his return to New Haven, Edwards Jr. with his committee developed a strategy to provide pastors for these new settlements. At the meeting the following year (1792), at the General Association meeting, Edwards Jr. and Mr. Williams provided a report. This report was prepared for publication and over the next year (1793) the raising of money would commence.[180] Edwards Jr. would preside over Dan Bradley's ordination and recommend

---

and the inhabitants of those settlements, in letters to us, abundantly attest this fact." Ezra Stiles, Benjamin Trumbell, and Jonathan Edwards Jr., "Letter to the Editor," in *The Connecticut Courant*, vol. 24, no. 1512 (Hartford, CT: Hudson and Goodwin, January 13, 1794).

[176] Mary Head Wicks, *Historical Sketches of the Paris Congregational Church: 1791–1941* (Utica, NY: Paris Congregational, 1941), 2. See also, Henry J. Cookinham, *History of Oneida County New York: From 1700 to the Present Time*, vol. 1 (Chicago: S. J. Clarke Publishing Co., 1912), 298–299.

[177] A Book Containing an Account of the Formation and Proceedings of the First Church in Whitestown, trans. Harry Young (New Hartford, NY: New Hartford Presbyterian Church, n.d.), 1.

[178] According to this baptism record, these children were baptized earlier in the week on August 23, 1791. Kathy Last, "New Hartford Presbyterian Church Baptisms," transcribed by Daughters of the American Revolution, n.d., accessed July 5, 2020, http://oneida.nygenweb.net/towns/newhartford/NHbaptisms.htm.

[179] A faithful transcript of the statement of faith, covenant, and rules of admission are provided in appendix 7.

[180] Perrin, *The Records of the General Association*, 140–148.

him to the New Hartford church. To the Clinton church he recommend Asahel S. Norton.[181]

Deacon David Austin's letter to Roger Sherman in early 1790 suggesting that Edwards Jr. might be too preoccupied elsewhere may be true to the extent that the White Haven Church may not have had as an expansive vision as their pastor.[182] During these later years, Edwards Jr. not only labored for Congregationalism's westward advancement, but upon his return from the Oneida County settlements, he preached an impactful sermon on "The Injustice and Impolicy of the Slave Trade, and of Slavery" on September 15, 1791 in New Haven.[183] This sermon, in some ways, was the culmination of his efforts at previous General Association meetings dating back to 1788 when he had been appointed to a committee "to draw up an address and petition to the General Assembly, that some effectual Laws may be made for the total abolition of the Slave Trade, to be laid before this body."[184]

Second Great Awakening and Union

Edwards Jr. was a natural choice for the Colebrook congregation, for a number had been baptized and received into the church of his grandfather Timothy in Windsor, Connecticut. Windsor Township had laid out the new town of Colebrook, and the memory of the Edwards Family, at that time, was still being carried by the second generation.[185] Nineteen ministers and fifteen delegates came together to install Edwards Jr. on December 31, 1795, including Edward Dorr Griffin[186] whose ordination he had preached earlier that summer.[187] According to a history of the town, Mr. Robbins who had known Edwards Jr. for over thirty years began the examination by saying,

---

[181] Jonathan Edwards Jr., "All Divine Truth Profitable," in *JEW2*, 98, n.1.; *AAP2*, 332.

[182] Ferm, *Edwards the Younger*, 141.

[183] Jonathan Edwards Jr., "The Injustice and Impolicy of the Slave Trade, and of Slavery," in *JEW2*, 75, n.1.

[184] Perrin, *The Records of the General Association*, 126–127.

[185] Dean, *History of Colebrook Congregational*, 11. "Sarah Pierrepoint's sister was also the aunt of one of the lady members of the church [by marriage to] Nathaniel Russell; whose father and grandfather were long pastors at Rocky Hill and doubtless were known to Dr. Edwards' father and grandfather." Dean, *History of Colebrook Congregational*, 12.

[186] Dean, *History of Colebrook Congregational*, 14.5.

[187] At New Hartford, Connecticut on June 4, 1795. *JEW2*, 210–223.

"Well, brethren, the sea is before you, now dive, dive!"[188] Although a short pastorate, due to a call to serve as the second president of Union College in Schenectady, New York (May 2, 1799), Edwards Jr. observed that in his time the "effusions of his Holy Spirit" had brought some in the church "to the saving knowledge of the truth, and to awaken and convince others."[189] This was a modest appraisal of his time with them, for in 1798 Colebrook Congregational Church admitted eleven members. By 1799 twenty-seven new members were added so that the membership had nearly tripled in size to over sixty members by the time of his departure.[190] These converts were the first fruits of the Second Great Awakening.

Mr. Andrew Yates, member of Union's board of directors, delivered the invitation to accept the call to Union's Presidency. Hoping to convey the offer in person, nevertheless, Yates was unable to because Edwards Jr. was out of town at the time. Edwards Jr., like his father, deferred to a council of an association of ministers. The council then advised him to accept the position after due process.[191] After departing his dear flock, he found the transition to be smooth. In his coming to Schenectady, contrary to the rumors, Edwards Jr. surprised all to be "mild and affectionate."[192]

Even while he increased the rigor and discipline of student life,[193] Edwards Jr. promised to be a very winsome leader for his young students. Thomas Palmer a graduate of 1803 recalled Edwards Jr. needing to dismiss his class because he "laughed so immoderately in his philosophy classroom."[194] In spite of an unfortunately short tenure, Edwards Jr. did much

---

[188] Dean, *History of Colebrook Congregational*, 14.5.

[189] *JEW2*, 229.

[190] Ferm, *Edwards the Younger*, 151. Compare with Dean, *History of the Colebrook Congregational*, 23.

[191] Ferm, *Edwards the Younger*, 155.

[192] B. B. Edwards, ed., *The American Quarterly Register*, vol. 3 (Boston: American Education Society, 1836), 295.

[193] Edwards Jr. extended the required attendance at morning and evening prayers to a full seven days, adding Saturday morning instruction. English was added to the curricula to assist in writing and public speaking. Additional rules regarding billiards, gambling, and prohibition on keeping wine and liquors in rooms. Spring examination period was extended to four days from three. Wayne Somers, *Encyclopedia of Union College History* (Schenectady, NY: Union College Press, 2003), 251.

[194] Somers, *Encyclopedia of Union*, 251.

for the school's morale in settling student unrest,[195] securing state funds, and assisting interdenominational cooperation.

Edwards Jr.'s greatest contribution at the College came in the broader Presbyterian movement in which partnership with Congregationalists occurred in the Plan of Union (1801). This plan facilitated a mission partnership as the nation expanded westward. Sadly, in spite of his warm reception in the Albany area, six weeks after the passage of the Plan of Union, Edwards Jr. caught an "intermittent fever" and died on August 1, 1801.[196] The fever's progression was just eight days. Both he and his father died shortly after accepting a college presidency. His last known words were "It becomes us cheerfully to submit to the will of God. He is wise and gracious. He orders everything for the best. The blood of Christ is my only ground of hope."[197] On August 3, 1801 in the Reformed Dutch Church at Schenectady, Robert Smith preached his funeral oration. Smith, had been the pastor of the First Presbyterian Church of Schenectady up to a month prior to Edwards Jr.'s death,[198] and had observed that people often mistook his "composed eye" for a coldness of spirit, when "in fact, far from being a stranger to the tender charities of the heart [...] he has sometimes been known to have been melted into tears even by a plaintive tune sung by a worshipping assembly."[199]

The inherited caricature of Edwards Jr. as a spiritless preacher is certainly related to his reserved personality, upbringing, and pastoral sorrows. Nevertheless, in spite of Edwards Jr.'s idiosyncrasies, the congregational churches of the new nation experienced great pressure to respond to enlightenment thought while providing spiritual counsel to their respective flocks. As hard as New Divinity pastors may have tried, not all succeeded in balancing both of these concerns. Even then, both father and son found themselves at war with congregations over the infamous Half-way Covenant. Yet, in spite of these conflicts, Edwards Jr. seemed to have a vital piety that resonated with his father's theological focuses. In the next chapter, a survey of Edwards Jr.'s manuscripts from the Sermon on the Mount will show that he was a faithful

---

[195] Edwards arrived in town as several student protests with regard to perceived partiality of teachers and incompetence. Somers, *Encyclopedia of Union*, 251.

[196] Ferm, *Edwards the Younger*, 169–170.

[197] Dutton, *History of The North Church*, 69–70; also, in *JEW1*, 514.

[198] George R. Howell and John H. Munsell, *History of the County of Schenectady, N.Y., from 1662–1886* (Schenectady: Munsell and Company, 1886), 101–102.

[199] *JEW1*, 512.

inheritor of his father's concern for a regenerate church membership whose affection for God is nurtured by Holy Spirit.

Chapter 3

A Shared Relish for True Religion

As a unique school of thought, New England Theology might have been cut short by Edwards Sr.'s untimely death. But instead of fading away, the new theological brand was sustained and nourished by his primary pupils—Joseph Bellamy (1719–1790) and Samuel Hopkins (1721–1803)—who made a pact to preserve its integrity.[1] With Jonathan Edwards Jr. (1745–1801) who had recently graduated Princeton in 1765, the three created an impressive intellectual triumvirate. However strong they may have been in their day,[2] pressure from diverse sources mounted during the pre-Civil War era to extricate Edwards from his successors. Conservatives at Princeton University began to question the origin of this received New England Theology,[3] largely as a response to Charles G. Finney (1792–1875), who also claimed a theological lineage back to Edwards.[4] In 1852 Edwards

---

[1] An earlier version of this material appeared in *Evangelical Quarterly* and is here republished with permission of the editor. John S. Banks, "Jonathan Edwards Jr.'s Relish for True Religion: The Advance of the New England Theology in the Sermon on the Mount.," *Evangelical Quarterly*, 91.1 (Jan 2020): 66–92.

[2] According to Edwards Amasa Park (1808–1900), on the eve of the American Civil War over a hundred New England pulpits favored this variation on covenant theology, which he attributed to Jonathan Edwards himself. However, not all agreed with Park's genealogy. Edwards Amasa Park, "The New England Theology," *Biliotheca Sacra*, 9 (1852): 175.

[3] Park, "The New England Theology," 175–76.

[4] Charles G. Finney, *Lectures on Systematic Theology, Embracing Lectures on Moral Government, The Atonement, Moral and Physical Depravity, Natural, Moral, and Gracious Ability, Repentance, Faith, Justification, Sanctification, andc.* (Oberlin, OH: James M. Fitch, 1846), 492. Also see Doug Sweeney and Allen Guelzo, *New England Theology: From Jonathan Edwards to Edwards Amasa Park* (Grand Rapids: Baker Academic, 2006), 227–228.

Amasa Park responded to Princeton[5] emphatically declaring: "Idle, idle is the late attempt to draw a line of demarcation between the elder Edwards, Bellamy, on the one side, and the younger Edwards, Emmons, West, on the other, with regard to these three principles."[6]

While the conservatives were at war over the mantle of Edwards Sr.,[7] emerging liberals like Harriet Beecher Stowe (1811–1896) began to depict Edwards Sr.'s successors as terrifying New England with unnecessary metaphysical abstractions in her novel *The Minister's Wooing*.[8] In particular, she drew her sights upon Edwards Jr. and Hopkins for tilling up mysteries which should not be unearthed.[9] *The Minister's Wooing* (1859), published seven

---

[5] Charles Hodge, "The New Divinity Tried," in *Princeton V. The New Divinity: The Meaning of Sin, Grace, Salvation, and Revival* (Cambridge, UK: The Banner of Truth Trust, 2001), 141–70. Edwards Amasa Park described the "incursion of Dr. Hodge" of Princeton as an ill-informed and unskilled military maneuver into theological territory on par with Napoleon's failed invasion of Russia. See Park, "The New England Theology," 170.

[6] The "three radical principles" related to (1) sin consisting in choice, (2) natural power equals, and (3) also limits duty. Park, "The New England Theology," 175.

[7] "The Princetonians, and those who succeeded them through Westminster Theological and Reformed Theological seminaries, could not avoid bowing in respect to the figure of Edwards, but it was an Edwards carefully sculpted to resemble Princeton Calvinism and an Edwards with no heirs." Sweeney, *New England Theology,* 19.

[8] Mary, the heroine of Stowe's novel, desires to marry a bolder and more dashing suitor but has resigned herself to marry Samuel Hopkins, a stodgy minister in Newport, RI. In chapter 23 ("Views of Divine Government"), Stowe personifies in the Mrs. Marvyn the theological trauma inflicted by the logical conclusions of the New England Theology of ministers upon their congregations. Mrs. Marvyn, Mary's potential mother-in-law, goes through a nervous breakdown when she contemplates her own spiritual destiny in light of the extremes of Hopkin's theology. However, the solution is not logic, but the simple love of the cross. This love is offered as a balm by her uneducated black slave Candace. After the love of the gospel is applied, Mrs. Marvyn is finally able to rest quietly. Harriet Beecher Stowe, *The Minister's Wooing* (New York: Derby and Jackson, 1859), 332–350.

[9] "The task they proposed to themselves was that of reconciling the most tremendous facts of sin and evil, present and eternal, with those conceptions of Infinite Power and Benevolence which their own strong and generous natures enabled them so vividly to realize. In the intervals of planting and harvesting, they were busy with the toils of adjusting the laws of a universe. Solemnly simple, they made long journeys in their old one-horse chaises, to settle with each other some nice point of celestial jurisprudence, and to compare their maps of the Infinite. Their letters to each other form a literature altogether unique. Hopkins sends to Edwards the younger his scheme of the universe, in which he starts with the proposition, that God is infinitely above all obligations of any kind to his creatures. Edwards replies with the brusque comment,–"This is wrong; God has no more right to injure a creature than a creature has to injure God;" and each probably about that time preached a sermon on his own view, which was discussed by every farmer, in intervals of plough and hoe, by every woman and girl at loom, spinningwheel, or wash-tub. New England was one vast sea, surging from depths to heights with thought and discussion of the most insoluble of mysteries." Stowe, *The Minister's Wooing*, 334–35.

years after her wildly popular *Uncle Tom's Cabin* (1852),[10] likely did much to sink both men beneath the waters of a spiritless preaching caricature.[11] Picking up cues from Stowe, and others unsympathetic[12] to the heirs of Edwards, "a line of demarcation between the elder Edwards" and the younger has prevailed.[13] In spite of the inherited caricature from Stowe, and to a lesser extent by Princeton, recent scholarship has "begun to show that the older 'decline and fall' narrative often associated with the [New Divinity] movement is [...] mistaken."[14] Crisp and Sweeney's *After Edwards* advances

---

[10] James McPherson retells how President Abraham Lincoln greeted Harriet Beecher Stowe in 1862 with these words: "So you're the little woman who wrote the book that made this great war." James McPherson, *Battle Cry of Freedom: The Civil War Era* (New York: Oxford University Press, 1988), 90.

[11] Another example of mid-nineteenth century characterization of New Divinity preachers is found in Doctor Johns (1866). This novel, like *The Minister's Wooing*, depicted the country parsons of New England in those days as being "heavy-minded, right-meaning man; utterly inaccessible to any of the graces of life; no bird ever sang in his ear; no flower ever bloomed for his eye; a man to whom life was only a serious spiritual toil, and all human joys a vanity to be spurned; preaching tediously long sermons, and counting the fatigue of the listeners a fitting oblation to spiritual truth; staggering through life with a great burden of theologies on his back, which it was his constant struggle to pack into smaller and smaller compass,—not so much, we fear, for the relief of others as of himself." Donald Grant Mitchell, *Doctor Johns: Being a Narrative of Certain Events in the Life of an Orthodox Minister of Connecticut*, Edgewood, vol. 8, *The Works of Donald G. Mitchell* (New York: Charles Scribner's Sons, 1907), 176.

[12] Two years before Stowe's influential novel, Edward Jr.'s entry in the three-volume *Annals of the American Pulpit* (1857) depicted him as an arid, metaphysical preacher through the subjective experience of Rev. Timothy M. Cooley. "His manner was the opposite of attractive. In his voice there was a nasal twang which diminished the effect of his utterance. He had little or no gesture, looked about but little upon his audience, and seemed like a man who was conscious that he was dealing in abstractions. Nevertheless, he was uttering great and profound thoughts; and those who were capable of estimating them, went away admiring the power of his genius, and edified by the striking and original views which had been presented to them." *AAP1*, 659–60.

[13] These sentiments are carried into the nineteenth century by George Nye Boardman, *A History of New England Theology* (New York: A. D. F. Radolph, 1899); into the twentieth century by Frank Hugh Foster, *A Genetic History of the New England Theology* (Chicago: University of Chicago Press, 1907); also see Joseph Haroutunian, *Piety Versus Moralism: The Passing of New England Theology from Edwards to Taylor* (1932; repr., Eugene, OR: Wipf and Stock, 2006).

[14] Crisp, *After Jonathan Edwards*, 5. See also Joseph A. Conforti, *Jonathan Edwards, Religious Tradition, and American Culture* (Chapel Hill, NC: University of North Carolina Press, 1995), 118–120. "Recent scholarship has begun to revise our understanding of Edwards's New Divinity disciples. For too long scholars uncritically accepted Joseph Haroutunian's magisterial neo-orthodox interpretation of the movement. In *Piety versus Moralism: The Passing of the New England Theology* (1932), Haroutunian all but dethroned the New Divinity men as legitimate theological heirs of Edwards. Hopkins, Bellamy, and the arid scholastics who followed in their train and reproduced themselves, drone-like, in their students, corrupted Edwards's theology and moralized his high Calvinism." Haroutunian, *Piety versus Moralism*, 118–119. See also, William Breitenbach, "Piety and Moralism: Edwards and the New Divinity," in *Jonathan Edwards*

a corrective view in general;[15] however, Edwards Jr. is generally neglected in most recent scholarship.[16]

This chapter will begin to amend the nineteenth century narrative showing that between the younger and elder Edwards there can be no line of demarcation either. This narrative of disconnect and decline, enlarged by Joseph Haroutunian in the early twentieth century, has been hard to break. Haroutunian theorized that the successors of Edwards Sr. were intent upon making Calvinism relevant to their age. He says that "in renouncing 'mysticism' the Calvinists repudiated the only chance they had of giving meaning to their theology." Because they attempted to make a science out of theology, they created a "metaphysical and unimaginative rationalism [that] was in no position to vindicate the theology of a socially dead religion. . . . Metaphysics breeds upon the remains of dead religion."[17]

In Haroutunian's day, due to the influence of German theological liberalism in the previous century, many centers of theological training in America were shifting in the early twentieth century. During his era, the teachings of Jesus in the Sermon on the Mount (hereafter SM) were thought to be the pure kernel of Christian doctrine.[18] Since the SM has been the traditional territory of twentieth century liberalism, this research will focus on Edwards Jr.'s forty-six manuscripts from the SM. Aside from three published

and the American Experience, ed. Nathan O. Hatch and Harry S. Stout (New York: Oxford University Press, 1988), 177–204.

[15] Crisp, *After Edwards,* 5. Joseph A. Conforti also signals that New Divinity pastors were often characterized as "arid scholastics who overintellectualized the vital piety of the colonial awakening" in the mid-nineteenth century and that this assessment may not properly account for their role in the Second Great Awakening in *Jonathan Edwards, Religious Tradition, and American Culture* (Chapel Hill, NC: University of North Carolina Press, 1995), 14.

[16] Aside from Robert L. Ferm and an unpublished biographical dissertation by Wesley Ewert, not much has been done to raise the awareness of Jonathan Edwards the younger. In recent scholarship Donald Weber's short essay in a collection of featured revolutionary pulpits is the only star in what is otherwise a dark sky. His alone begins to challenge the spiritless caricature as he shows Edwards Jr.'s rhetorical zeal for the glorious cause. Weber relates: "Edwards's language, both in the sermon fragments (which constitute the bulk of his extant performances) and a few fully penned discourses, emerges as plain and familiar." Donald Weber, "The Edwardsean Legacy: The Example of Jonathan Edwards, Jr. of White Haven," in *Rhetoric and History in Revolutionary New England* (New York: Oxford University Press, 1988), 47–73.; Robert L. Ferm, *Jonathan Edwards the Younger: 1745–1801* (Grand Rapids: Eerdmans Publishing, 1976); Wesley Carl Ewert, *Jonathan Edwards The Younger: A Biographical Essay,* vol. 1 (PhD diss., Hartford Theological Seminary, 1953).

[17] Joseph Haroutunian, *Piety Versus Moralism: The Passing of the New England Theology,* 1932; reprint (New York: Harper and Rowe, 1970), xxvii–xxviii.

[18] Adolf von Harnack, *What Is Christianity? Lectures Delivered in the University of Berlin during the Winter-Term, 1899–1900,* 2nd rev. ed. (New York: G. P. Putnam's Sons, 1901), 76–80.

manuscripts, these forty-six are the only surviving texts from Matthew 5–7 spanning his thirty-year preaching ministry.[19] As typical of his unique style, Edwards Jr.'s sermon notes from the SM are non-sequential, occasionally recycled, yet demonstrate a received New England Theology from his father *through* his mentors.[20] In particular, the younger will be seen to share his father's *relish* that *true religion* would flourish in his congregation.[21] Through six major divisions in the SM, I will show Edwards Jr.'s consistency with his father's thinking on the Spirit's role in piety. The manuscripts will be considered canonically *not* chronologically or thematically.[22] This approach may be counterintuitive; however, is designed to follow an exegetical approach. An exegetical approach will reveal how he interpreted Scripture with a view to the influence of his father's thinking on the Spirit in conversation with Bellamy and Hopkins.

The Beatitudes (Matt 5:2–12)

Edwards Jr. began the SM with Matthew 5:3 (1788)[23] emphasizing marks of spiritual poverty; whereas, eight years later in 1794, he reworked this outline to accent the gospel substance contained in the same text.[24] In the

---

[19] There are over twelve hundred unpublished manuscripts. Hartford Theological Seminary houses the vast majority of manuscripts, followed by the Beinecke Rare Book Library, Yale University, then Yale Divinity Library, and lastly, Princeton University Library. For a complete list of locations see Robert L. Ferm, *Jonathan Edwards the Younger 1745–1801: A Colonial Pastor* (Grand Rapids: Eerdmans, 1976), 184–190. In Ferm's appendix, he refers to manuscripts at Andover-Newton; however, the collection was transferred to Yale Divinity Library in 2017.

[20] In appendix 1 is a brief discussion of his preaching and manuscripts with visual examples.

[21] The term 'relish' was typical of those New Divinity pastors who fell into the "taste" scheme rather than the "exercise" scheme. "Tasters held that a spiritual substance, 'taste,' 'relish,' or 'disposition,' lay behind the will and governed choice; such a depraved taste, which was sinful itself, also led sinners certainly to choose sin. Exercisers denied knowledge of a spiritual substance in back of the will; choice was the immediate exercise of the heart or will without an antecedent passive principle or taste." Joseph A. Conforti, *Edwards, Religious Tradition*, 127. See also Joseph Bellamy: "thro their [humanity's] exceeding great Depravity, intirely [sic] void of a right *Taste* and *Relish* for *true Beauty*, they could not but be even ravished with the divine Being," in *True Religion Delineated; or, Experimental Religion, [...]* (Boston: S. Kneeland, 1750), 43.

[22] See appendix 8 for a list of Jonathan Edwards Jr.'s complete list of MSS derived from the Sermon on the Mount in *chronological* order of delivery.

[23] Jonathan Edwards Jr., "No. 1032. April 6. 1788. Mat. V.3," *Jonathan Edwards and Calvin Chapin Papers*, Beinecke Rare Book and Manuscript Library (Box 1, Folder 3), 1–4.

[24] This sermon was prepared in 1794 for an undesignated purpose, but then preached in Colebrook on May 1, 1796. Jonathan Edwards Jr., "[Unnumbered] Augt. 24. 1794 Mat. V.3,"

first edition of this sermon, Edwards Jr. warned his listeners of the tendency to misread blessedness in materialistic ways. Rather a blessed person will be conscious of being "destitute of holiness,"[25] and "groan under [this lack]."[26] In particular, a person will sense his *spiritual* poverty and

> feel themselves blind
> [as] depravity brings
> on blindness—
> [they are] blind [to] the true beauty
> of holiness—the divine
> character.[27]

The awareness of a "native blindness thence forth becomes light in the Lord" bringing a sense of desperation.[28] Bellamy is in the background as the sense of blindness is part of the awakening work of the Holy Spirit. According to Bellamy, all that is necessary to overcome our native blindness is for the Holy Spirit to impart a "spiritual taste [... so that] we may be awakened to a realizing Sight and Sense of *what* God *is*."[29]

Taste for spiritual beauty is an idea running back to Edwards Sr.'s *Religious Affections*. In the third test of a religious affection, Edwards Sr. introduces taste and relish as an analogy for spiritual apprehension. A taste for the "beauty of holiness" is something entirely outside of natural human experience.[30] Obbie T. Todd describes Bellamy as being dependent upon

---

Jonathan Edwards and Calvin Chapin Papers, Beinecke Rare Book and Manuscript Library (Box 1, Folder 4), 1–4.

[25] Edwards Jr., "No. 1032," 1.

[26] Edwards Jr., "No. 1032," 2.

[27] Edwards Jr., "No. 1032," 3.

[28] Edwards Jr., "No. 1032," 3.

[29] Bellamy, *True Religion Delineated*, 45.

[30] "[T]hose that are regenerated, a new supernatural sense, that is as it were a certain divine spiritual taste, which is in its whole nature diverse from any former kinds of sensation of the mind, as tasting is diverse from any of the other five senses, and that something is perceived by a true saint in the exercise of this new sense of mind, in spiritual and divine things, as entirely different from anything that is perceived in them by natural men, as the sweet taste of honey is diverse from the ideas men get of honey by looking on it or feeling of it; now this that I have been speaking, viz. the beauty of holiness, is that thing in spiritual and divine things, which is perceived by this spiritual sense, that is so diverse from all that natural men perceive in them: this kind of beauty is the quality that is the immediate object of this spiritual sense: this is the sweetness that is the proper object of this spiritual taste." Jonathan Edwards Sr., *Religious Affections*, in *Works of Jonathan Edwards*, vol. 2, ed. Paul Ramsey (New Haven, CT: Yale University Press, 1957–2008), 259–260.

Religious Affections however changing the focus from love to law, yet in this instance neither Bellamy nor Edwards Jr. seem to deviate from Edwards Sr.³¹ Todd, writing within the present decade, demonstrates a reliance upon the decline theory of Haroutunian.

Edwards Jr.'s later manuscript carries a definite revivalist tone, stressing the necessity of a poverty of spirit before conversion might occur. Poverty of spirit is a "deep humility." Humility is vital "for the Spirit to awaken, to convert, to sanctify [is necessary] for pardon [and] for salvation."³² This emphasis bears significant resemblance to the contrasted legal and evangelical humility his father described in *Religious Affections*.³³ A profound evangelical humility sustains itself with the awareness that mercy is "infinitely more than deserved."³⁴ An ability to respond to the gospel hinges upon a poverty of spirit. In other words, without a deep (evangelical) humility, it will be impossible to "exercise repentance" toward Christ by faith.³⁵ A sinner will not repent (exercise) without first a *taste* provided by the Holy Spirit. Positively, a poverty of spirit causes one to *relish* or "enjoy [the prospect of] heaven."³⁶ This enjoyment of heaven's prospect is inversely related to the dispelling of pride in an ever-increasing capacity.³⁷ In Edwards Jr.'s biography, we

---

³¹Obbie T. Todd, "The Grammar of Revival: The Legacy of Jonathan Edwards's Teleological Language in Religious Affections (1746)," *Calvin Theological Journal* 54, no. 1 (2019): 35–56.

³²Edwards Jr., "Augt. 24. 1794," 2.

³³"Men may be legally humbled and have no humility; as the wicked at the Day of Judgment will be thoroughly convinced that they have no righteousness, but are altogether sinful, and exceeding guilty, and justly exposed to eternal damnation, and be fully sensible of their own helplessness, without the least mortification of the pride of their hearts: but the essence of evangelical humiliation consists in such humility, as becomes a creature, in itself exceeding sinful, under a dispensation of grace; consisting in a mean esteem of himself, as in himself nothing, and altogether contemptible and odious; attended with a mortification of a disposition to exalt himself, and a free renunciation of his own glory." Edwards Sr., *Religious Affections*, 312.

³⁴Edwards Jr., "Augt. 24. 1794," 2.

³⁵Edwards Jr., "Augt. 24. 1794," 3.

³⁶Edwards Jr., "Augt. 24. 1794," 3. Bellamy writes that when the very temper of a person's heart is touched by the Spirit, they "naturally feel as they do in Heaven, and naturally speak their Language, *Holy, holy, holy, is the Lord of Hosts; the whole Earth is full of his Glory!*" Emphasis original. Bellamy, *True Religion Delineated*, 43.

³⁷In the *Miscellanies* Edwards Sr. notes that heaven's happiness, joy and holiness consist in a continual increase. Jonathan Edwards, "Miscellanies," No. 435, in *The Works of Jonathan Edwards*, vol. 13., ed. Harry S. Stout (New Haven, CT: Yale University Press, 1970), 483. Also, in a sermon titled "The Value of Salvation" (1722), Jonathan Edwards Sr. writes of heaven's necessary increasing joy in this way: "If the saints in heaven were sure they should enjoy heaven some thousands of years, and after that it should be at an end, it would cast a great

had seen that Edwards Jr. was accused by his parishioner John Cornwell of not preaching the Spirit, but this sermon is a vindication of Edwards Jr.'s teaching on the need for the Spirit in the awakening process.

Edwards Jr.'s next text (Matt 5:4) was preached a month after the White Haven Church in New Haven had issued a call to him as pastor on September 16, 1768. In some ways, this sermon is a call to a corporate self-examination. Are they a true, visible church—one in which a successor of Edwards Sr. could pastor? Beginning with a theological examination of mankind's natural thirst after happiness from Psalm 4:6 "Who will shew us any good," Edwards Jr. queries if there might be a tinge of blame in this question. If the celestial host has a "great an appetite for good, and relish the happiness of that blessed world, as much yea as much more, than mankind relishes any good in this world,"[38] then any doubt is without excuse. This conclusion is parallel to Bellamy in recognizing human blindness as rebellion which is justly punishable by the Law.[39] Edwards Jr. continues:

> That blindness, whereby men are doubtful concerning the true good is certainly criminal, and God might justly leave them in their blindness to suffer the just demerit of it. But, God so loved the world that he gave his only begotten Son, that whosoever believeth on him, shall not perish but have everlasting life. He gave him to die that through him the way might be opened for the enjoyment of true happiness.[40]

This sermon begins on a dour note, giving the appearance that happiness is inaccessible; nevertheless, Edwards Jr. points his audience to the gospel as a means to find and enjoy true happiness in this pivotal passage. An evangelical impulse drives this sermon to the conclusion that *true happiness comes via meekness because all* the beatitudes connect to meekness. The

---

damp upon their joys and delights," in "The Value of Salvation," in *The Works of Jonathan Edwards, Sermons and Discourses 1720-23*, vol. 10., ed. Wilson H. Kimnach (New Haven, CT: Yale University Press, 1970), 324.

[38] Jonathan Edwards Jr., "Sermon 24. Oct. 23. 1768. Matthew 5.5," *Jonathan Edwards and Calvin Chapin Papers*, Beinecke Rare Book and Manuscript Library (Box 1, Folder 1), 3.

[39] "We have Eyes to see, and Ears to hear, and his Glory shines all around us [...] and there is nothing hinders our seeing and hearing, but that we are rebellious Creatures. Our Contrariety to God makes us blind and spiritually dead. [...] And hence it is most evident, that the supreme Governour of the World has not the least Ground or Reason to abate his law, or to reverse the Threatening." Bellamy, *True Religion Delineated*, 108.

[40] Edwards Jr., "Sermon 24.," 3–4.

poor in spirit cannot be other than meek and meekness necessarily goes before a merciful or peaceable outlook. The blessings are "annexed to each of these characters, which are not made to any but the godly, or true Christians." Therefore, "the spirit of meekness is a distinguishing characteristic of true Christians."[41]

While logical in his approach, Edwards Jr. is not inaccessible to his listeners as he illustrates by metaphor the meek character which is woven into many biblical texts. Christians are described as lambs, sheep,[42] doves,[43] little children,[44] but most fittingly *"all true Christians resemble Christ their Lord and master."*[45] Remarkably, these metaphors are borrowed directly out of his father's eighth sign of a religious affection.[46] Improving upon his father is probably overstated; however, Edwards Jr. places meekness as the head or the tendency of every other Christian grace. All Christian virtue is to be found in or "immediately consequent upon" meekness.[47]

Throughout this sermon the word true is a frequently repeated descriptor of good, happiness, Christian, church, saints, grace, zeal, meekness, and most importantly, religion. This emphasis is likely calculated to highlight the need for regenerate church membership. Between the issue of a call on September 16, and his acceptance on December 15, 1768[48] the church would

---

[41] Edwards Jr., "Sermon 24.," 5.

[42] Edwards Jr., "Sermon 24.," 7.

[43] "Now what can be more harmless, meek and gentle than a dove? What can be a more proper emblem of love and peace? Yet because the true church has such a meek, gentle, as I may say, dove like temper and disposition, (it is said Cant. 1.15, Behold, thou are fair, my love; behold thou art fair; *thou hast dove's eyes*. And again, *thou hast dove's eyes within thy locks*. Again, speaking of the church it is said, *O my dove,* that art in the clefts of the Rock. Open to me my love, *my dove, My dove,* my undefiled is but one)." Edwards Jr., "Sermon 24.," 8.

[44] Edwards Jr., "Sermon 24.," 8–11.

[45] Emphasis original. Edwards Jr., "Sermon 24.," 11.

[46] "The same appears by the name by which Christ is so often called in Scripture, viz. THE LAMB. And as these things are especially the character of Christ, so they are also especially the character of Christians. Christians are *Christlike* [...] Christ the great Shepherd, is himself a lamb, and believers are also *lambs:* all the flocks are lambs; John 21:15, "Feed my lambs." Luke 10:3, "I send you forth as lambs, in the midst of wolves." [...] Christian affections, and a Christian behavior, is but the flowing out of the savor of Christ's sweet ointments. Because the church has a *dovelike* temper and disposition, therefore it is said of her that she has doves' eyes [...] 'Tis doubtless very much on this account, that Christ represents all his disciples, all the heirs of heaven, *as little children* [...]." Emphasis Added. Edwards, *Religious Affections,* 346–349.

[47] Edwards Jr., "Sermon 24.," 19.

[48] Ferm, *Jonathan Edwards the Younger,* 72–75.

need to reconsider its eight-year experiment with the Half-way Covenant. This sermon, with on-going negotiations,[49] likely encouraged leadership to return to the practice regenerate church membership on December 6.

The third text coming from the Beatitudes is Matthew 5:6 and occurs in five different manuscripts from 1774–1789. These manuscripts advance a general thesis that God will bless those whose are endowed with a spiritual disposition for personal holiness. Holiness is an alternative gloss for righteousness. This being the case, in the last dated sermon ("1113 No."), Edwards Jr. interprets the object of hunger as personal holiness rather than for imputed holiness.[50] Contrary to an antinomian interpretation, Edwards Jr. contends that a person may hunger for pardon but still not be filled with any grace. Rather "[t]he sincere desires of the Christian increase in grace. [This produces] greater conformity to God [and] more of the Spirit of God."[51] God does not give satisfaction to a person who merely has a carnal desire to escape damnation; rather, he gives eternal blessing to those who desire real holiness.[52]

Manuscript "No. 1113" was delivered during a lengthy discussion to renew relations with the First Church in town.[53] The First Church made reconciliation more unlikely with the untimely installation of James Dana, an Old Light graduate of Harvard. Old Lights allowed a mixed membership and participation at the sacred table; whereas New Lights required evidence of conversion to participate. This timely sermon may have buried any possibility of a shared communion with the First Church, as Edwards Jr. emphasized that "the converted only" hungers after this personal righteousness.[54] Earlier renditions are nearly identical with some slight variations.[55]

---

[49] Robert L. Ferm suggests there is no evidence that Edwards Jr. was involved in the attempt to influence a reversal of the Half-way Covenant. See previous chapter, footnote 72 on page 31 for an example of the negotiations regarding the Half-way Covenant.

[50] Jonathan Edwards Jr., "1113. No. Novr. 8. 1789 Mat. V.6.," *Jonathan Edwards and Calvin Chapin Papers,* Beinecke Rare Book and Manuscript Library (Box 1, Folder 4) 1–4.

[51] Edwards Jr., "1113. No. Novr. 8. 1789 Mat. V.6.," 2.

[52] Edwards Jr., "1113.," 3–4.

[53] Robert L. Ferm describes the question of renewing periodic communion worship in meetings which occurred in February, April, June, August, September and finally in November 1789 (the month of this sermon). Ferm, *Jonathan Edwards the Younger,* 135.

[54] Edwards Jr., "No. 1113," 4.

[55] No. 803 adds two pages to further develop the object of the hunger and thirst. Here again, righteousness is defined as spiritual righteousness or holiness—and this righteousness is seen specifically as love to God, love to Christ, love for brethren, and repentance from all else.

Throughout these manuscripts Edwards Jr. draws frequently from *Religious Affections*. For example, a desire to be holy "for its own sake" creating a strong aversion to sin[56] draws upon the doctrinal thread of disinterested love.[57] Additionally, Edwards Jr. uses his father's familiar analogy of honey which is used in *Religious Affections* to describe the difference between knowing about spiritual things and having a taste for them[58] (even if holiness requires a bitter pill).[59] Further, this desire for holiness increases the prospect of heaven in the imagination as one "spurns those things which tend to prevent his increase in holiness."[60] The logic of this inverse relation-

---

Jonathan Edwards Jr., "No. 803. March 9. 1783. Mat. 5.6.," *Jonathan Edwards and Calvin Chapin Papers*, Beinecke Rare Book and Manuscript Library (Box 1, Folder 3), 1–3. In sermons No. 352 and No. 803, Edwards Jr. explores what is *implied* by hungering and thirsting for righteousness, and what is *implied* by having one's appetite satisfied. Jonathan Edwards Jr., "No. 352. Feb. 27. 1774. Mat. 5.6," *Jonathan Edwards and Calvin Chapin Papers*, Beinecke Rare Book and Manuscript Library (Box 1, Folder 2), 1–4. Sermon No. 511 increases to seven points; whereas, No. 352 had only five points; and the later No. 803 drops back to four. Jonathan Edwards Jr., "No. 511 Jan. 19. 1777. Mat 5.6," *Jonathan Edwards and Calvin Chapin Papers*, Beinecke Rare Book and Manuscript Library (Box 1, Folder 2), 1–4.

[56] Edwards Jr., "No. 511," 2–3.

[57] Edwards, *Religious Affections*, 240–253.

[58] Edwards Jr., "No. 511," 2. "[T]hen it follows that the mind has an entirely new kind of perception or sensation; and here is, as it were, a new *spiritual sense* that the mind has, or a principle of new kind of perception or spiritual sensation, which is in its whole nature different from any former kinds of sensation of the mind, as tasting is diverse from any of the other senses; and something is perceived by a true saint, in the exercise of this new sense of mind, in spiritual and divine things, as entirely diverse from anything that is perceived in them, by natural men, as the sweet taste of honey is diverse from the ideas men get of honey by only looking at it, and feeling of it." Edwards, *Religious Affections*, 205–206.

[59] Remarkably, Edwards Jr. uses the very same metaphor of a bitter pill [medicine] which his father had used in a sermon preached at Portsmouth in January 1737 from Matthew 5:6. Jonathan Edwards Sr., "418. Matt. 5:6," *Sermons, Series II, 1737*, in *Works of Jonathan Edwards*, vol. 52, ed. Jonathan Edwards Center (New Haven, CT: Yale University Press, 2008).

> in men desire many things
> that they have no proper appetite to. they
> may desire a lance to Lay open a wound
> or a bitter medicine to save their lives
> but it cant be said that they have any appe
> tite to ~~these lance and bitter medicine~~
> because the desire of these things is not at
> all for the things themse.
> but for the sake of som~~ething else~~ other
> good thing they hope to obtain.

[60] Edwards Jr., "No. 511," 3.

ship was also noted by Bellamy in *True Religion Delineated* when he wrote that

> it is evident from the Nature of Things, that such a love as this will effectually influence us to do so. As Self-love naturally causes us to set up Self and seek Self-Interest: So this Love to God will naturally influence us to set up God and seek his Interest. As delight in the World naturally makes us seek after the Enjoyment of the world, so this delight in God will naturally influence us to seek after the Enjoyment of God. [...] So Saints in Heaven love God perfectly, and so the good Man on Earth begins in a weak and feeble Manner to love God.[61]

The pursuit of all heavenly things increases over time, and in some ways, this hunger and thirst intensifies with the anticipation of heaven.

The last Beatitude sermon, in which the blessed are pure in heart, is exposited by two manuscripts. The first of these texts prioritize the indwelling work of the Holy Spirit at a difficult time early in Edwards Jr.'s ministry. Nine months into Edwards Jr.'s first year of ministry in September 1769, a sizeable minority who had opposed his settlement finally decided to leave. Two months prior to the exodus, Edwards Jr. taught his congregation that no natural man can be pure in heart unless the Holy Spirit takes residence in their heart.[62] Consequently, a pure heart is tender, full of affection, ravished with the beauty of God, filled with delight in the majesty of God so that the "whole soul wrapped up in delight and joy. [...] all things else [are] tasteless."[63] Borrowing his mentor Joseph Bellamy's analogy of a person not full of benevolence, Edwards Jr. describes these people as being caught in "the narrow circle of self."[64] Bellamy used this phrase in *True Religion Delineated* (1750) demonstrating mentoring conversations with Edwards Sr. as the very phrase appears in *A Dissertation Concerning the Nature of True Virtue* (1765).[65] As Edwards Jr. pled with his congregation, he asked them

---

[61] Bellamy, *True Religion Delineated*, 15.

[62] Jonathan Edwards Jr., "Volume 66. July 16. 1769. Mat. 5.8.," *Jonathan Edwards Jr. Papers (Sermons)*, Hartford Seminary Library (Box 165, Folder 2727), 6.

[63] Edwards Jr., "Volume 66. July 16. 1769 Mat. 5.8," 3–4.

[64] Edwards Jr., "Volume 66.," 9. Compare with "But Hypocrites are confined within the narrow Circle Self." Bellamy, *True Religion Delineated*, 89.

[65] On the other hand, perhaps after reading Bellamy's published work in 1750, Edwards added the footnote to include Bellamy's analogy. "It may be here noted that when hereafter I use a

to consider "what an amiable thing is true Christianity! This purity is the very essence of true religion."[66] Since a portion of Edwards Jr.'s congregation apparently did not have "an ear to hear [...] what the Spirit saith unto the churches,"[67] the split would occur in spite of his attempt to woo his congregation. Edwards Jr. would not return to this text for another nineteen years.[68]

The Beatitudes in the hands of Edwards Sr. and his followers are seen to be evidential marks of true religion. To them, Jesus's teaching demonstrates a progressive movement that begins with awareness of one's spiritual poverty. Spiritual poverty is a result of blindness. The Spirit must increase this awareness while at the same time provide an aesthetic taste for holiness. This taste works to create an 'evangelical humility,' rather than a legal one, leading to deeper and deeper sensation of heaven's happiness. This spiritual outworking is evident in Edwards Jr.'s preaching, and is consistent with his father's emphasis in *Religious Affections*.

Introduction (Matthew 5:13–20)

Traditionally, Matthew 5:13–20 is the thematic introduction of the main themes of the sermon, and The Beatitudes are a kind of spiritual prerequisite to understanding the SM in general. In this part of the SM, Edwards Jr. developed the evidential light of the Holy Spirit. The Spirit will radiate through the acts of believers in distinction from the world. Thus, the salt metaphor in Matthew 5:13 is critical, and is exegeted in two separate

---

phrase as "private system of beings," or others similar, I thereby intend any system or society of beings that contains but a small part of the great system comprehending the universality of existence. I think that may well be called a "private system" which is but an infinitely small part of this great whole we stand related to. I therefore also call that affection "private affection" which is limited to so narrow a circle; and that "general affection" or "benevolence" which has Being in general for its object." Jonathan Edwards, *Dissertation Concerning the Nature of True Religion*, in *Ethical Writings Ethical Writings*, vol. 8, ed. Paul Ramsey (New Haven, CT: Yale University Press, 1957–2008), 554, n1.

[66] Edwards Jr., "Volume 66.," 11.

[67] Edwards Jr., "Volume 66.," 12.

[68] With some time and reflection, in Sermon "No. 1006," he described the pure in heart as partakers of the divine nature allowing them to see God's glory and enjoy him. Jonathan Edwards Jr., "No. 1006. Sepr. 30. 1787 Mat. V. 8.," *Jonathan Edwards Jr. Papers (Sermons)*, Hartford Seminary Library (Box 168, Folder 2746), 1–2. Edwards Jr. also describes purity of heart as creating peace of mind as "turbulence is subdued by grace." This inner grace produces a peace with God and man in the form of patience, contentment, hope, and courage. Edwards Jr., "No. 1006.," 3–4.

manuscripts. In the earliest sermon,[69] Edwards Jr. compared the character of salt with a spirited Christianity. His first point highlights the peculiar flavor which encompasses a Christian's apprehensions, temper, motives, conduct, relations, and privileges. Edwards Jr. is thorough in describing the latent effect of the Spirit upon the Christian's disposition setting him in contrast with the world. For example, the world may see the character of God as great, omniscient, just, holy, but "not the glory [however] the disciple does."[70] The very temper of a Christian is quite different from the world because it has a "spirit of benevolence, a spirit of holiness, a spirit of kindness, even a most amiable spirit."[71] These dispositions "give an agreeable relish to meats, [so how much] the more the disciples. So divine grace renders agreeable the characters of those to whom [grace is] communicated."[72] These themes are carried into the second manuscript on the same text. He preached the same text at his second pulpit in Colebrook on March 31, 1797 with an even greater focus on the theme of true religion. Specifically, the "true disciples" of Christ give "relish to the earth" by "spreading around true religion in the earth."[73]

In "Grace Evidenced by Its Fruits" a published exposition of Matthew 5:15, Edwards Jr. observed that when divine grace takes residence in the heart it will produce a visible display (light) through holy practice.[74] Preached for the first time in 1769, this sermon bears a striking similarity to his first Beatitude sermon from Matthew 5:5 in 1768. Both sermons use biblical metaphors to illustrate abstract spiritual qualities. Just as divine nature is compared to a seed, a fire, a precious ointment, a spring of living

---

[69] The earliest sermon was delivered on December 21, 1783 just after he had been remarried on Thursday of that week to Miss Mercy Sabin of New Haven. Edwards Jr.'s first wife, Mary Porter Edwards, died the previous June by drowning, a result of a tragic horse and carriage accident. Surprisingly, or not, his nuptial earlier in the week is not directly visible in this sermon. A detailed account of the accident was shared with his nephew Timothy Dwight in a letter. Jonathan Edwards Jr., letter to Timothy Dwight, July 18, 1782, *Andover Newton Miscellaneous Personal Papers Collection,* Yale Divinity Library (Box 168, Folder 1). Tryon Edwards, "Memoir," in JEW1, xxv.

[70] Jonathan Edwards Jr., "No. 839. Dec. 21. 1783 Mat. 5.13 Ye are the salt of the earth and," *Jonathan Edwards Jr. Papers (Sermons),* Hartford Seminary Library (Box 167, Folder 2743), 1–3.

[71] Edwards Jr., "No. 839.," 3–4.

[72] Edwards Jr., "No. 839." 4.

[73] Jonathan Edwards Jr., "[Unnumbered] June 29. 1794 At Colebrook March 31. 1797 Mat. V.13," *Jonathan Edwards Jr. Papers (Sermons),* Hartford Seminary Library (Box 169, Folder 2753), 1–2.

[74] Jonathan Edwards Jr, "Grace Evidenced by Its Fruits [circa 1769]," in *JEW2,* 387–400.

water, spirit (John 3:6), and the power of godliness (2 Tim 3:5).[75] Like other metaphors borrowed from his father, these are also found peppered throughout *Religious Affections*.[76]

Edwards Jr. concludes that divine grace is the same in nature (temper) and tendency (act). His father is very much behind these thoughts when he states that "through the saving influences of the Spirit of God, there is a new inward perception or sensation of their minds [...] then the exercises of it are also entirely a new kind of perception or sensation."[77] In other words, the Divine Nature will produce visible fruits including a "cordial belief" in the truth, a reliance upon God, true love to God, repentance, humility, love to men, gratitude, and hope.[78] On the other hand an absence of visible fruit is an indication of gracelessness. While the exact date of this sermon is uncertain (circa 1769), Edwards Jr. may in this sermon be issuing a warning to those ready to leave the White Haven Church, when he says,

> Men who have no cordial consent to the truth, but whose hearts wholly oppose it, are continually raising objections against it. And by this means they frequently persuade themselves into disbelief of it; at least they render it less practical to themselves, and are much less influenced by it in their conduct. But a saving belief of the truth sweeps away all these objections, and receives the truth in all its practical power and efficacy.[79]

In similar fashion, Bellamy argues that a "sense of his infinite glory immediately imparted to the Soul by the Spirit of God, whereby the Heart is thus divinely established in the Belief of the truth, is therefore that *Unction from the holy One*, which all the Saints meekness in The Beatitudes was described with vibrant metaphor, spiritual vitality of the have, whereby they are effectually secured from being finally led away by false Teachers."[80] The 'tendency' of the Holy Spirit, says Edwards Jr., is to produce righteous acts in a dark world.

---

[75] Edwards, "Grace Evidenced by Its Fruits," 389–392.

[76] The Spirit of God is identified as being called "the power of godliness" and "fire." Edwards Sr., *Religious Affections*, 100. In a later passage, Edwards Sr. compares the Spirit of God to living water, a precious anointing ointment, and a seed. Edwards Sr., *Religious Affections*, 200–201.

[77] Edwards Sr., *Religious Affections*, 205.

[78] Edwards, "Grace Evidenced by Its Fruits," 392–398.

[79] Edwards, "Grace Evidenced by Its Fruits," 394–95.

[80] Bellamy, *True Religion Delineated*, 80.

In the three manuscripts highlighting Christ's fulfillment of law (Matt 5:17–18), Edwards Jr. does not minimize the free grace of the gospel by the Spirit. In these three sermons, Edwards Jr. deals with soteriological objections. In particular, he addresses the legality of imputed righteousness which justification without penalty creates. To answer this problem, he turned to the moral government theory of the atonement[81] in which Christ satisfied the justice in "support [to] the honor of the law equally supported as if literally executed."[82] Therefore the Law is seen to be in "full force" with the only "condition of justification" having been realized in Christ.[83] In lockstep with Bellamy, Edwards Jr. balances God's justice while holding mankind responsible to obey the law of God.[84] Since Edwards Sr. had written such a glowing endorsement of Bellamy's *True Religion Delineated* in the "Preface," this backing, according to Obbie Todd, suggests that Edwards Sr. may have sown the seeds of the governmental theory of the atonement in his successors.[85]

While at least half the sermon argues humanity's danger "under the [abiding] sentence of the law," he nevertheless implores his listeners to

---

[81] Historically, the substitutionary theory embodied "The Anselm Need" for satisfaction. This satisfaction came through the payment of the elect sinner's debt. The need for satisfaction tended to create a God in man's debt. Instead of indebting man to God, the New Divinity described sin as the offence against God's moral government. This put man in God's due, creating moral accountability. The atonement was necessary so that God could offer redemption to sinners in general while still having an efficacy for the elect. New Divinity thinking moved from a strict penal substitutionary toward a moral governmental theory by viewing the atonement as the restoration of the Godhead's honor by securing justice ("so that [God] might be just and the justifier"). As a primary spokesman for the governmental theory, Edwards Jr. modified the analogy of penal substitution to the restoration of the happiness and glory of God primarily (moral government) by the punishment of sin in Christ. William Breitenbach, *New Divinity Theology and the Idea of Moral Accountability*, Dissertation Series (New Haven, CT: Yale University Press, 1978), 137– 46. Jonathan Edwards Jr., "Thoughts on the Atonement," *JEW1*, 493–507. Also, Edwards Jr.'s three sermons on the atonement in *JEW2*, 11–52.

[82] Jonathan Edwards Jr., "No.753 March 3. 1782. Mat. 5, 17, 18." *Jonathan Edwards and Calvin Chapin Papers*, Beinecke Rare Book and Manuscript Library (Box 1, Folder 3), 3.

[83] Accordingly, "the gospel does/not allow of pardon/but conditional/[upon] repentance [through] faith," Edwards Jr., "No.753 March 3. 1782 Mat. 5.17, 18," 1–2.

[84] Bellamy, *True Religion Delineated*, 70–80. This explanation comes from Bellamy's argument that man has natural capacity to carry out the duty of the Law, although the heart does not desire to until "A Sense of the infinite Glory of God, begets a Disposition in the Heart to conform to this Law and do this Duty." Bellamy, *True Religion Delineated*, 80.

[85] Obbie Tyler Todd, "Purchasing the Spirit: A Trinitarian Hermeneutic for Jonathan Edwards's Doctrine of the Atonement," *Puritan Reformed Journal* 10, no. 2 (July 2018): 165–67. Also see, Jonathan Edwards Jr., "Remarks on the Improvements Made in Theology by His Father, President Edwards," in *JEW1*, 486.

abandon all other "fallacious hope" by turning to Christ's free grace.[86] In a subsequent sermon (1793), the force of the Law's duty continues into the current day; however, the "free grace of the gospel consists in this, [anyone] may be saved [yet some] live how they will; [however, we are empowered to obey the law and] this [is] the liberty of the children of God."[87] Of the three sermons, the middle sermon (1786) is the most metaphysical.[88]

These sermons involving the moral government theory were intended to address the controversy of John Murray's preaching in New Haven Green. Murray, who was a Universalist, found in Edwards Jr.'s congregation some sympathetic adherents. In the previous chapter, Edwards Jr.'s apologetic preaching on this topic became a sore spot for Hezekiah Beardselee (a professing Universalist), sparking the characterization that Edwards Jr. was an arid, metaphysical preacher. Yet, these sermons on the atonement do not characterize the large majority of Edwards Jr.'s preaching surveyed in this chapter as overly metaphysical, nor spiritless.

If repetition of a sermon text is any indication of preference, then Matthew 5:20 could be seen as one of Edwards Jr.'s favorite texts as it was used in nine different locations. All three manuscripts bear the mark of the New Divinity revivalist rhetoric. His earliest manuscript (1771) highlights, like his father, how righteousness must exceed morality through the "inward temper."[89] In a sermon *on the same text,* Edwards Sr. recognizes the absolute necessity of a regenerate heart:

> If we would enter into the kingdom of heaven we must exceed the Pharisees in this that we must not only give God our outside but we must give him our heart.[90]

---

[86] Edwards Jr., "No.753," 4.

[87] Jonathan Edwards Jr., "[Unnumbered] Aug. 4. 1793. Mat. V. 17.," *Jonathan Edwards and Calvin Chapin Papers,* Beinecke Rare Book and Manuscript Library (Box 1, Folder 4), 3.

[88] Edwards Jr. recognizes that Christ's divinity, and thus equality with the Father, provides the necessary weight so that the atonement might be sufficient and just within the divine government. Further, this equality guarantees that the satisfaction and the greatest proof of the "displeasure of God against sin as the damnation of all men," Jonathan Edwards Jr., "No. 939. March 12. 1786. Mat. 5. 17, 18.," *Jonathan Edwards and Calvin Chapin Papers,* Beinecke Rare Book and Manuscript Library (Box 1, Folder 3), 2–4. Also see, "Thoughts on the Atonement," in which a robust understanding of the Trinity is vital in holding an orthodox doctrine of the atonement. Edwards Jr., "Thoughts on the Atonement," 505–507.

[89] Jonathan Edwards Jr., "Volume 124. Feb. 16. 1771. Mat. 5.20.," *Jonathan Edwards and Calvin Chapin Papers,* Beinecke Rare Book and Manuscript Library (Box 1, Folder 1), 2.

[90] Jonathan Edwards Sr., "418. Matt. 5:6," *Sermons, Series II, July–December 1740,* in *Works of Jonathan Edwards,* vol. 56 (New Haven, CT: Jonathan Edwards Center at Yale University, 2008).

The other two manuscripts are of similar concern. Like the original they were designed to awaken false professors to "rest not till your righteousness exceeds [the Scribes and Pharisees]," but be like the "young man in the gospel" and "flee to the mountain" like Lot.[91]

These 'Introductory' sermons keep in step with his Father's view of the Spirit. The overall emphasis on the law is based on the work of the Holy Spirit. If Obbie Todd is correct that the seeds of the atonement theory are derived from his father, then even what his detractors have suggested is no deviation at all. Joseph Haroutunian said of Edwards Jr. that he "had none of his father's glowing mysticism and natural piety. He was the arch-moralist among the Calvinists. In him that legalism which has previously been observed as creeping into Calvinism finds its supreme expression."[92] Clearly, Haroutunian did not survey Edwards Jr.'s sermons.

The Law of Christ (Matt 5:21–48)

From Matthew 5:21–22 Edwards Jr. observed that the Jews were generally outward professors of the Law because they had not internalized the law ("thus lost the spirit").[93] Therefore his listeners needed to ensure they were true professors by practicing the spirit of the law. Edwards Jr. included adultery and false swearing as examples of how the Jews interpreted the Law legally and not spiritually. This tendency, he says, produced a flat or superficial reading. Given this inclination, Edwards Jr. shows that Jesus's

---

Also consider how *The Life of David Brainerd* puts into visual effect a person who has true religion, that is, those genuine marks of *Religious Affection*. In the closing remarks, Edwards Sr. shows how professing believers need an honest evaluation of their inward temper so as not to be hypocritical: "So, I doubt not, but there are many deluded people, if they should read the preceding account of Mr. Brainerd's life, who, reading without much understanding or careful observation, would say without hesitation that some things which they have met with are of the very same kind with what he expresses: when the agreement is only in some general circumstances, or some particular things that are superficial, and belonging as it were to the profession and outside of religion; but the inward temper of mind and the fruits in practice are as opposite and distant as East and West." Jonathan Edwards Sr., *The Life of David Brainerd*, in *Works of Jonathan Edwards*, vol. 7, ed. Norman Pettit (New Haven, CT: Yale University Press, 1957–2008), 518.

[91] Edwards Jr., "Volume 124," 16.

[92] Joseph Haroutunian, *Piety Versus Moralism: The Passing of the New England Theology*, 1932; reprint (New York: Harper and Rowe, 1970), 150.

[93] Jonathan Edwards Jr., "Volume 379. July 17. 1774. Mat. 5. 21, 22.," *Jonathan Edwards and Calvin Chapin Papers,* Beinecke Rare Book and Manuscript Library (Box 1, Folder 2), 1.

teaching on degrees of punishment goes beyond the surface of this life.[94] Four years earlier, Edwards Jr. had already concluded that reconciliation with one's accuser in Matthew 5:25–26 had higher implications.[95] Edwards Jr. posits God as man's primary adversary and a dispute between men as secondary.[96] Inescapable consequences come to those who do not repent and therefore reconciliation with God is of utmost importance.[97] With great tenderness he encouraged his last congregation in Colebrook to heed God's mercy. "What a favourable opportunity is this [that] while in the way with our adversary! What a mercy that are [ours] yet [we may be reconciled] in the way with him!"[98] Rather than preaching the other legal aspects of Matthew 5:21–48, Edwards Jr. discusses them generally as typical of how "the Jews had imbibed false ideas [and] taught false maxims."[99] Edwards Jr. shows how the Pharisees had corrupted the public judicial principle of "an eye for an eye." As a way of conducting, one's private life, this principle tended to create more enemies than friends. For the Christian, "It is a law of the gospel, that we love our enemies" and is implied "in that general love of being [is] required of all men. If [we are to be] benevolent to all men of course [then we must be benevolent] to enemies."[100]

---

[94] "No; this the letter [has to it] besides a Spiritual meaning—Illustrate the degrees of punishment in hell." Edwards Jr., "Volume 379.," 3. Later on the same page, Edwards Jr. summarizes the following doctrine which he will develop in detail: "In hell there will be an exact proportion observed between the demerit of the sins which shall be punished and the degree of punishment which shall be inflicted." Edwards Jr., "Volume 379.," 3. Edwards Jr.'s interpretation is unique; however, not outside of church history, as Hilary of Poitiers also saw the potential that God would be man's ultimate adversary, if he refuse to be reconciled to his brother (Matt 5:23–24). David G. Hunter, ed., *St. Hilary of Poitiers Commentary on Matthew*, trans. D. H. Williams (Washington, DC: The Catholic University of America Press, 2012), 67–68.

[95] Jonathan Edwards Jr., "Volume 130 Oct. 1770 Mat. 5. 25, 26.," *Jonathan Edwards and Calvin Chapin Papers*, Beinecke Rare Book and Manuscript Library (Box 1, Folder 1), 1–8.

[96] "And as in this case [it is] best to be reconciled lest [you] be delivered to the judge, andetc. So [then reconciled] to God lest [he] do far worse. 1. All mankind have an adversary. 2. Have an opportunity to be reconciled. 3. Wise for them to [agree] with him." Edwards Jr., "Volume 130," 1.

[97] Edwards Jr., "Volume 130," 8. This greater reconciliation premise is refined and delivered twenty-four years later in a manuscript in New Haven. Jonathan Edwards Jr., "[Unnumbered] Augt 24, 1794 Mat. V. 25.," *Andover Newton Miscellaneous Personal Papers Collection*, Yale Divinity Library (Box 168, Folder 11), 1–4.

[98] Edwards Jr., "Augt 24. 1794.," 4.

[99] Jonathan Edwards Jr., "[Unnumbered] July 18. 1790 Mat. V. 43, 44," *Jonathan Edwards and Calvin Chapin Papers*, Beinecke Rare Book and Manuscript Library (Box 1, Folder 4), 1.

[100] Edwards Jr., "[Unnumbered] July 18.," 4.

On November 14, 1784, Ezra Stiles recorded in his journal that Mr. Edwards had been to chapel and "preached on Benevolence."[101] More accurately, however, the sermon develops the theme of *Disinterested* Benevolence, a significant New Divinity doctrine, which excludes all motive of self-love.[102] Some have suggested that the concept of disinterested benevolence is not part of Edward Sr.'s theology;[103] however, in *Original Sin* (1758) he very clearly states:

> Our esteem of God is fundamentally defective, if it be not primarily for the excellency of his nature, which is the foundation of all that is valuable in him in any respect. If we love not God because he is what he is, but only because he is profitable to us, in truth we love him not at all. If we seem to love him, our love is not to him, but to something else.[104]

---

[101] *LDES1*, 143. Jonathan Edwards Jr., "No. ____ Novr. 14, 1784. Mat. 5. 46," *Andover Newton Miscellaneous Personal Papers Collection*, Jonathan Edwards, Jr., Yale Divinity Library (Box 168, Folder 5), 1–30. The following manuscripts are drafts of the November 1784 manuscript and may give insight into Edwards Jr.'s composition process. Jonathan Edwards Jr., "No. 805. March 23, 1783 Mat. 5.46," *Jonathan Edwards and Calvin Chapin Papers*, Beinecke Rare Book and Manuscript Library (Box 1, Folder 3), 1–4.; Jonathan Edwards Jr., "[Unnumbered and Undated] Mat. V. 46 [fragments]," *Jonathan Edwards and Calvin Chapin Papers*, Beinecke Rare Book and Manuscript Library (Box 1, Folder 3), 1–4 and loose page.

[102] "There is such an affection very common among men, as interested love or benevolence. This is when we love a man, merely because he is instrumental of promoting our good or happiness. . . . Now on the same principle we may love God himself; because he hath done us good in temporal or spiritual respects or because we expect or hope that he will do us good. This kind of love to God hath been and is now common in the world, and is the essence of the religion of many. Yet there is no real religion, no holiness, no true virtue in it, any more than there is in loving ourselves and in seeking our own private interest." Edwards Jr., "[Unnumbered and Undated] Mat. V. 46 [fragments]," 3–4. Joseph Bellamy writes in a similar way: "From this divine Benevolence, arises a free and genuine Disposition to dedicate, consecrate, devote and give up our selves entirely to the Lord forever; to walk in all his Ways, and keep all his Commands, seeking his Glory. [. . .] And if SELF be highest in Esteem, then Self-Interest will be the principal Motive and last End." Bellamy, *True Religion Delineated*, 12–13.

[103] Paul Ramsey is probably correct to say that in some senses Samuel Hopkin's expression of disinterested benevolence is outside of his mentor's thoughts. In other words, Edwards Sr. would not articulate a benevolence as that which creates the motive to be damned for the glory of God if He so wills. That being said, nonetheless, in this area there is a greater continuity of thought from the elder to the younger Edwards through Bellamy rather than Hopkins. "Appendix One: Joseph Bellamy's Copy of the Charity Sermons," *Ethical Writings*, in *Works of Jonathan Edwards*, vol. 8, ed. Paul Ramsey (New Haven, CT: Yale University Press, 1970), 648. n6.

[104] Jonathan Edwards Sr., *Original Sin*, in *Works of Jonathan Edwards*, vol. 3, ed. Clyde A. Holbrook (New Haven, CT: Yale University Press, 1970), 144.

In the same sermon, Edwards Jr. also addressed the tendency of deists like Thomas Paine to reject divine revelation in favor of "the light of nature."[105] Edwards Jr. objects that on the basis of an interested benevolence ("the light of nature"), the priest and Levite "were perfectly right in neglecting their half dead, perishing country-man."[106] As the sermon progresses, Edwards Jr. concludes that "in loving ourselves only, we make ourselves our ultimate and supreme good."[107] This reversal of goods creates a deleterious effect upon society because "self-love is so far from being the source of virtue, that in the inordinate indulgence of it, it becomes the source of all vice."[108] Vice breeds vice.

Edwards Jr. deduces, based on the mathematical law of proportions, that an infinite injustice occurs against God's universal system through even one individual sin. A divine necessity is created, and out of the "light of nature," requires a disinterested benevolence toward God and neighbor from the Law as a reflection of the character of God. Accordingly, the infinite evil of sin requires an eternity of hellfire. Edwards Jr. recognizes that the age of reason is devoid of any gospel hope.[109] Thus an infidel lacks any advantage in the life to come, or in the present life[110]—so, it would be wise to embrace the Christian system.[111]

What then is the duty of man? In a sermon on the final verse in the Law of Christ section (Matt 5:21–48),[112] Edwards Jr. considers the Christian calling to perfection (v. 48). In the last year of his ministry in New Haven (August 3, 1794), he defines divine perfection as a positive attribute which is by definition out of reach; however, because of man's limited nature,

---

[105]"The word of God is the creation we behold: And it is in this word, which no human invention can counterfeit or alter, that God speaketh universally to man." Paine Thomas, "The Age of Reason," in *The Writings of Thomas Paine*, vol. 4 (New York: G. P. Putnam's Sons, 1896), 45. Edwards Jr.'s introduction proposes the problem of looking to "the light of nature" for all necessary revelation regarding man's necessary benevolence but writers like Paine are placing "the whole of religion radically in self-love" and "they attempt to show that it is sufficiently plain by the light of nature." Edwards Jr., "No.___," 1.

[106]Edwards Jr., "No.___," 8.

[107]Edwards Jr., "No.___," 16.

[108]Edwards Jr., "No.___," 19.

[109]Edwards Jr., "No.___," 28–29.

[110]Thomas, "Age of Reason," 22.

[111]Edwards Jr., "No.___," 30.

[112]Jonathan Edwards Jr., "[Unnumbered] Augt. 3. 1794 Mat. V. 48.," *Jonathan Edwards and Calvin Chapin Papers*, Beinecke Rare Book and Manuscript Library (Box 1, Folder 4), 1–4.

freedom from sin (apophatic approach to perfection) is not just the goal, rather, is man's duty.[113] While others might be tempted to slacken the requirement of the Law, Edwards Jr. does not; although he is a realist ("I speak of Christian perfection— [...] not that we shall ever do it—"),[114] he recognizes that the Law instills humility.[115]

In the longest section of the Sermon on the Mount, and dealing with the law, Edwards Jr. demonstrates a revivalist spirit in step with his father. But even theologically, when speaking about benevolence, he shows a dependence upon his father's understanding of mathematical proportionality. Proportionally to an infinite deity is the necessity of punishments in proportion to his infinite holiness. Proportion, says McClymond and McDermott, is a "distinctive concept" found in Edwards Sr.'s trinitarian thinking.[116] In the sermon on benevolence we see Edwards Jr. applying these concepts regarding eternal punishment and eternal happiness.

The Lord's Prayer (Matt 6:10–13)

In the batch of sermons developed on the Lord's prayer, Edwards Jr. provided practical ways for his hearers to evaluate the quality and depth of their faith. In the prayer's six petitions, Edwards Jr. showed how they provide timeless instruction for the church. Edwards Jr., like his father, desired that the visible church would be consistent with the true church. In other words, as he preached, he called his church to strive for a purity of membership so that God's will (or kingdom) would be on earth as it is in heaven. Edwards Sr.'s scientific effort in *Religious Affections* to distinguish the true church within the visible church,[117] is affirmed in *True Religion Delineated* and honed by the younger Edwards.

---

[113] Edwards Jr., "Augt. 3. 1794," 2.

[114] Edwards Jr., "Augt. 3. 1794," 4.

[115] Edwards Jr., "Augt. 3. 1794," 4.

[116] Michael J. McClymond and Gerald R. McDermott, *The Theology of Jonathan Edwards* (New York: Oxford University Press, 2012), 96–101.

[117] In the "Author's Preface" to *Religious Affections,* Edwards Sr. describes the seemingly indistinguishable mixture which exists in the visible church just "as it is with fruit trees in the spring; there are a multitude of blossoms [...] but many of them are but of short continuance, they soon fall off, and never come to maturity." Edwards Sr., *Religious Affections,* 85–86.

In Matthew 6:10, the first three petitions are distilled into aspects of God's kingdom.[118] Specifically, the kingdom consists of the "whole society of true subjects of God" in this world. The "visible church" ought to consist only of those who have "the kingdom of grace in the heart." Specifically, these professors of God's kingdom have renounced Satan's kingdom and have taken "God's [kingdom]—[through] Christ—[by the] Holy Spirit."[119] Edwards Jr. goes on to lay out the "usual method" of entrance into the kingdom of God that consists of awakening, amazement over the wrath of God without a sense of resolution, leading to the saving knowledge of the truth and a new heart.[120] Twenty years later, in a more concise way, Edwards says that praying for the kingdom will cause believers to desire the visible church to increase in genuine membership.[121] However genuine membership may require a "renewal of profession" on the part of his hearers.[122] To be actively engaged in the promotion of the kingdom (church) is further evidence of being in the kingdom. Edwards Jr. implores his hearers to come to God's kingdom (that is, the true church) for it is

> the happy state
> of true Christians
> You belong to
> this kingdom—
> to the family of God
> of all holy beings
> God your father
> Christ redeemer—
> Holy Spirit sanctifier.[123]

The following year, Edwards Jr. picked up the bread petition to encourage prayer for rain during a drought. Far from the sermon being metaphysical,

---

[118] By collapsing these three petitions together, the sermon directed his congregation "to pray much for the coming of God's kingdom." Jonathan Edwards Jr., "Vol. 211 March 1. 1772 Mat. 6.10," *Jonathan Edwards and Calvin Chapin Papers,* Beinecke Rare Book and Manuscript Library (Box 1, Folder 2), 1.

[119] Edwards Jr., "Vol. 211," 2.

[120] Edwards Jr., "Vol. 211," 3–5.

[121] Jonathan Edwards Jr., "July 1. 1792 Mat. VI.10.," *Jonathan Edwards and Calvin Chapin Papers,* Beinecke Rare Book and Manuscript Library (Box 1, Folder 4), 3–4.

[122] Edwards Jr., "July 1. 1792.," 1.

[123] Edwards Jr., "Vol. 211," 7.

Edwards Jr. shows how dependent on God his parish was for "rain and shine."[124] With extended famine on the horizon, he reminds his congregation of the legitimacy of prayer in distress, but not to overlook dependence when all is well. While the kingdom is primary, Christians are also to be praying for "common good things" too.[125]

On the other side of the Declaration of Independence, Edwards Jr. preached on deliverance from temptation with "some things especially tempted to in the present day."[126] In this sermon, Edwards addresses various vices which entice, but notes that a heart which is "dead in sin—[desires] no holy acts." Bellamy and Edwards Sr. reverberate in a brief subpoint on the voluntary nature of free agents.[127] Sinners who have no heart for the good ("disposed to sin, [that is,] no heart to good") are still accountable. He asks rhetorically if "a man literally dead [is] excusable," and answers, "utterly inexcusable voluntary—consents to it—chooses."[128] Perhaps to illustrate voluntary choice in hard times, Edwards Jr. addressed the need for Sabbath attendance in spite of the war ("our congregation [is] too thin").[129] His last use of this text produced a very practical multi-generational message exhorting dependency upon God in all kinds of temptation at every season of life.[130]

The Lord's Prayer provides a good look at the ability of Edwards Jr. to be a practical preacher. He was aware of the stress of his people due to famine or economic hardship during the war, and he strove to serve his people. In this way, he was an able pastor, and able to address needs. Edwards

---

[124] His congregation had seen "by experience–of late [we have experienced famine. The] fields of corn [are withered] and suffering—pastures burnt up [and the] cattle pinched." Edwards Jr., "Vol. 211," 2.

[125] Jonathan Edwards Jr., "Vol. 305. July 25, 1773 Mat. 6.11," *Jonathan Edwards and Calvin Chapin Papers,* Beinecke Rare Book and Manuscript Library (Box 1, Folder 2), 1–4, 1.

[126] "1) Distrust of God, 2) Murmurings against God, 3) Profaneness 4) A renunciation of the righteous cause, [and] 5) Injustice—extortion. Jonathan Edwards Jr., "No. 552. March 8.1778. Mat. 6.13," *Jonathan Edwards and Calvin Chapin Papers,* Beinecke Rare Book and Manuscript Library (Box 1, Folder 2), 8.

[127] Bellamy, *True Religion Delineated,* 103–106. Jonathan Edwards Sr, *Freedom of the Will,* in *Works of Jonathan Edwards,* Vol. 1, ed. by Paul Ramsey (New Haven, CT: Yale University Press, 1970), 295–301.

[128] Edwards Jr., "No. 552.," 3.

[129] Edwards Jr., "No. 552.," 5.

[130] Jonathan Edwards Jr., "[Unnumbered] Feb. 6. 1791. Mat. VI.13," *Jonathan Edwards and Calvin Chapin Papers,* Beinecke Rare Book and Manuscript Library, Yale University (Box 1, Folder 4), 1–6.

Jr. also sees the Church, as Stephen Holmes puts it, "one particular and important part of the single history of redemption and creation by which God brings about His single purpose: all else that exists reveals God's glory to the church, which glorifies God in knowing and delighting in what He has revealed."[131] This interest in a pure church drove New Divinity students of Edwards Sr. to prioritize a credible confession of salvation experience before admittance to the Lord's Table.

God's Superior Kingdom (Matt 6:19-33)

Just prior to the Revolutionary War, Edwards Jr. preached a sermon from Matthew 6:19-21 at a time when the American economy was very strong. In good times, sermon application that disassociates wealth from covetousness is easier. For example, illustrations of rich men like Abraham and David who loved God come easily. In his sermon, wealth is not the issue; rather, "it is to set our hearts so on earthly things as— supreme good—above Spirit."[132] Yet covetousness and idolatry have deadly consequences, so Edwards Jr. shows how God "desires the soul—formed for noble purposes—to glorify and enjoy God."[133] In a later sermon (1787), delivered a few years after the Continental Dollar's collapse, Edwards Jr. is more free to contrast treasure in heaven to that which has the risk of "melting away to nothing."[134] Those who seek security and happiness in heaven will experience a greater security and happiness generated out of "a right according to the gospel."[135]

---

[131] Stephen Holmes, *God of Grace and God of Glory: An Account of the Theology of Jonathan Edwards* (Edinburgh, Scotland: TandT Clark, 2000), 197.

[132] Jonathan Edwards Jr., "Vol. 276. Feb. 28. 1773. Mat. 6. 19, 20, 21.," *Jonathan Edwards and Calvin Chapin Papers,* Beinecke Rare Book and Manuscript Library, Yale University (Box 1, Folder 2), 1.

[133] Edwards Jr., "Vol. 276.," 4.

[134] "We in these times had experienced this kind of treasure." Jonathan Edwards Jr., "No. 988. April 15. 1787. Mat. VI. 20," *Jonathan Edwards and Calvin Chapin Papers,* Beinecke Rare Book and Manuscript Library (Box 1, Folder 3), 4.; In an accounting ledger for the White Haven Society's School Accounts the treasurer notes in 1781 that Continental Money received in 1778 just three years later is equal at "forty for one," in "White Haven Society's School Accounts Committed to the Care of Jeremiah Atwater, 1770–1802," *The United Church Papers, Series 1,* New Haven Museum (MSS 9, Box 1, Folder K).; During the Revolution, the Continental Congress issued fiat money in the tens of millions to finance the war without a solid plan to finance the currency. Within a short period of time these bills, along with many of the states who printed their own, depreciated to nearly nothing. Farley Grubb, "State Redemption of the Continental Dollar, 1779–90," *The William and Mary Quarterly,* vol. 69, no. 1 (2012): 147–80.

[135] Edwards Jr., "No. 988.," 2. The gospel is the gateway to happiness: in particular, "by a compliance with the gospel and—and by any progress in holiness." This begins by faith in

From Matthew 6:33, Edwards Jr. issued another reminder of the human "propensity to covetousness" (within a few months preaching Matt 6:19–21 in February 1773).[136] The sense of ultimate and infinite happiness is a just motivation to pursue "that great Being, who made [everything, who] up holds [and]governs—on whom [we] depend to his kingdom."[137] Those who pursue God's kingdom, instead of wealth, find "the end for which [they are] created" and find just "how gracious God [is. He] provided a kingdom in which alone [we are] happy."[138] Twenty-two years later in a sermon "To the Young People," he concisely stated that "what is of great value and importance should be sought first."[139] In other words, whatever has the greatest value will not only bring the greatest joy but also has the promise of the greatest reward. Seeking entrance into the kingdom of God is to seek a place in "the true church [and] to seek this is to seek heaven."[140]

The Invitation and Warnings of Christ (Matt 7:12–28)

In the last major section of the SM, Edwards Jr. develops his father's doctrine of benevolence into a powerful argument for abolition. In that he uses benevolence to advocate for the end of slavery is an important link to his father. Edwards Jr. will argue that private affection must not fall short of considering enslaved people who exist under God's moral government. The Golden Rule is an important display of one's benevolence to God through the care of humanity. On the Golden Rule, first preached a month before the issue of the Stamp Act in March 1774, could Edwards

---

Christ, reconciliation to God, by repentance, by love to men, by forgiveness of enemies, and improvement of our talents for God. Edwards Jr., "No. 988.," 2–3.

[136] Jonathan Edwards Jr., "Vol. 308 August 15. 1773 Mat. 6.33.," *Jonathan Edwards Jr. Papers (Sermons)*, Hartford Seminary Library (Box 166, Folder 2733), 1. Edwards Jr. also connects covetousness with an "inconsistency with piety—v. 24.," "vanity v. 27," and "the example of birds and lilies v. 26 [-] 30." Edwards Jr., "Vol. 308," 1.

[137] Edwards Jr., "Vol. 308," 3.

[138] Edwards Jr., "Vol. 308," 8.

[139] Jonathan Edwards Jr., "[Unnumbered] March 1795. Mat. VI. 33.," *Jonathan Edwards Jr. Papers (Sermons)*, Hartford Seminary Library (Box 169, Folder 2753), 3.

[140] Edwards Jr., "[Unnumbered] March 1795," 1. Also see Edwards Jr.'s brief notes prepared for several itinerate locations through the year 1800, in which he concludes, that the church is the kingdom of God by comparing Matthew 7:28 with Matthew 21:43, Mark 1:15; 9:1, Luke 17:21, and Rev 12:10. Jonathan Edwards Jr., "[Unnumbered] Octr. 10. 1798. Mat. VI. 33.," *Andover Newton Miscellaneous Personal Papers Collection*, Yale Divinity Library (Box 168, Folder 13), 1, 4.

have been aware of just how relevant his illustration of rulers and subjects would be? Perhaps if king and subject were to trade places, they both might better understand the effects of "mildness—severity" in the application of submission to justice.[141] In the concluding thoughts, Edwards left an open door for further development as he concludes that since Christ's rule summarized the law and the prophets it also reflects "the justice of God."[142]

The introduction and outline of the sermon from 1774[143] formed the backbone for his 1791 sermon[144] from the same text, preached before an anti-slavery society. This sermon is probably one of the most consequential sermons in American History. Unbeknownst to Edwards Jr., the published version of this sermon[145] ("The Injustice and Impolicy of the Slave Trade, and of Slavery") would fall into the hands of Owen Brown's son John (of Harper's Ferry), thus causing Edwards Jr. to be responsible, although indirectly, for the start of the Civil War.[146]

Edwards Jr. asks his listeners to imagine if they would "be willing, that the Africans or any other nation should purchase us, our wives and children, transport us into Africa and there sell us into perpetual and absolute slavery?"[147] After surveying the cost in human life which is required for slavery to exist, Edwards Jr. attacks various arguments for slavery. Toward

---

[141] Jonathan Edwards Jr., "353. Feb. 27. 1774. Mat. 7.12.," *Jonathan Edwards Jr. Papers (Sermons)*, Hartford Seminary Library (Box 166, Folder 2734), 4.

[142] Edwards Jr., "353," 4.

[143] Edwards Jr., "353.," 1–4.

[144] Jonathan Edwards, "The Injustice and Impolicy of the Slave Trade, and of Slavery," *The Works of Jonathan Edwards, D.D., Late President of Union College. With a Memoir [...]*, ed. Tyron Edwards, vol. 2 (New York: Dayton and Newman, 1842), 75–97.

[145] According to Joy Craun this sermon went through five reprints by 1854; see Joy Craun, "We Are Them: The Golden Rule as a Theological Impetus in the Anti-Slavery and Abolitionist Movement," *Online Journal* 9, no. 1 (April 4, 2019): 25–48.

[146] See note 10 above. At one time Abraham Lincoln had referred to Harriet Beecher Stowe as the little woman who started "this big war." Ironically, and contrary to Stowe's caricature of Edwards Jr. and Samuel Hopkins as pre-occupied with metaphysical abstractions, they did much to create an abolitionist spirit in New England ahead of the Civil War. Indeed, maybe Lincoln ought to have expressed gratitude to the New Divinity theologians. For example, Owen Brown was persuaded of abolitionism after reading a published sermon of Jonathan Edwards Jr. on the matter. Owen Brown's account of reading Jonathan Edwards Jr.'s sermon is preserved in *John Brown Liberator of Kansas and Martyr of Virginia: Life and Letters*, 4th edition; ed. by F. B. Sanborn (Cedar Rapids, IA: The Torch Press, 1910), 11. Also see James P. Byrd, "We Can If We Will: Regeneration and Benevolence" in *After Jonathan Edwards: The Courses of the New England Theology*, ed. Oliver D. Crisp and Douglas A. Sweeney (New York: Oxford University Press, 2012), 63.

[147] Edwards Jr., "The Injustice and Impolicy," 75–76.

the end, Edwards Jr. displays his great rhetoric ability. He argues from the lesser crime, in which Americans were willing to fight Great Britain "in her attempt to enslave America" (loss of a small part of property), to the greater crime of enslaving Africans (loss of all property and autonomy).[148] Edwards Jr. concludes with optimism that just thirty years earlier (1750s–60s), none considered slavery to be evil.

In this regard, Edwards Jr. is significantly different from his father with respect to slavery. Edwards Sr. was undoubtedly wrapped up in the culture of his day. For example, in a theological brief for the Hampshire Association (1741), Edwards Sr. argued for "a narrow definition of 'neighbor'—as limited only to those of the same religion and in close proximity, or to those identified typologically (and racially) as the new 'children of Israel.'"[149] Perhaps Edwards Jr. was aware of his father's growing uneasiness with the slave trade as Kenneth Minkema has proposed.[150] In spite of the fact that his father's female slave Venus was treated well, the Hampshire brief on slavery seems to indicate a shifting stance in general toward trade. If sensing a change in his own father over a decade, then perhaps this led Edwards Jr. to conclude that within fifty years (1840s–50s) public opinion would finally tip and slave-owning might be "as shameful [...] as to be guilty of common robbery or theft."[151]

In a sermon published as "The Broad Way" (1768) from Matthew 7:13,[152] Edwards Jr. highlights the gravity of the gate metaphor because of an absent 'middle way.'[153] If the narrow way is missed in this life, they must necessarily go through the broad way to destruction.[154] The broad way is easy to find

---

[148] Edwards Jr., "The Injustice and Impolicy," 89.

[149] Kenneth P. Minkema, "Jonathan Edwards's Defense of Slavery," *Massachusetts Historical Review*, vol. 4 (2002), 38.

[150] Minkema, "Defense of Slavery," 42.

[151] Edwards Jr., "The Injustice and Impolicy," 92–93.

[152] Jonathan Edwards, "The Broad Way," in *JEW2*, 412–427.

[153] In another sermon on this text he will call it "an alarming/mortifying doctrine/that the way to heaven/is narrow." Jonathan Edwards Jr., "No. 1095. July 19. 1789. Mat. 7.13, 14.," *Jonathan Edwards and Calvin Chapin Papers*, Beinecke Rare Book and Manuscript Library (Box 1, Folder 4), 1.

[154] In the latest development of this text, Edwards Jr. essentially describes the gates in the same way with a slight variation. "The way and gate [is] not essentially different [as]both mean the character necessary to life [of] the one in the metaphorical sense naturally precedes the other way first—the gate that opens into heaven." Jonathan Edwards Jr., "[Unnumbered] June 1. 1794. Mat. VII. 13,14," *Jonathan Edwards and Calvin Chapin Papers*, Beinecke Rare Book and Manuscript Library (Box 1, Folder 4), 1. The image of the gate leading to heaven was

"for all by nature already in that way; [...] Yea, further, this gate is so wide, that it can be easily found in the dark."[155] In the third point, Edwards briefly examines the proportion of those who will pass through this broad gate; however, the following year he will devote eighty-eight pages in a series, spread over two months, to the phrase "And few there be that find it" (Matt 7:14).[156] That his father begins *Religious Affections* with a reference to this verse is more than coincidence.[157]

Edwards Jr. determines that the greatest obstacle and hindrance to finding the narrow gate "is the individual's own heart, and the opposition which arises within."[158] However, this obstacle is not insurmountable. In the later long sermon (Matt 7:14), he begins with Adam and passes through redemption history through the eighteenth century's extraordinary out pouring of the Spirit noting along the way how relatively few truly find life.[159] But is man to blame? Edwards Jr. answers yes with a brief reiteration of his father's *Freedom of the Will;*[160] therefore, none can blame their inherited depravity.[161]

---

developed six years earlier as "The gate, the gate of heaven [that which is] called a city. What hath foundation, the holy city, the new Jerusalem [and] all cities have a way or ways leading to them." Edwards Jr., "No. 1095.," 2.

[155] Ibid., 414.

[156] Jonathan Edwards Jr., "Volume 59. May and June 1769. Mat. 7.14," *Jonathan Edwards and Calvin Chapin Papers,* Beinecke Rare Book and Manuscript Library (Box 1, Folder 1), 1–88. This sermon series may have pushed the unrequited minority in opposition to Edwards Jr.'s pastorate in New Haven over the edge for its unusual length and focus on key New Divinity doctrines. The formation of the Fair Haven Church would occur just three months later.

[157] Edwards Sr., *Religious Affections,* 83.

[158] Edwards Jr., "The Broad Way," 417.

[159] "[I]t has pleased God frequently at different times and in different places in an extraordinary manner, to influence the minds of men and awaken them to attention to divine truth. But can it be truly said that in these times of awakening, the greater part even of those who were the subjects of some degree of illumination, have been brought to the inheritance of life? Thence have indeed been great numbers, who have professed the Christian faith: but what reason do we have to believe that the greater part of them have ever found life?" Edwards Jr., "Volume 59," 47. Edwards also borrows the illustration of a child who hates his parents from Bellamy as being blamable on its own merit. Edwards Jr., "Volume 59," 57–58. Cf. Bellamy, *True Religion Delineated,* 112–114.

[160] Edwards Jr. advocates strongly for "the freedom of our own will; and whatever we do, whether of good or evil we do freely and voluntarily. [... No one] is under constraint so to act, as to miss of life. [We are under ...] no constraint at all to live wickedly." Edwards Jr., "Volume 59," 54.

[161] "What is your depravity? Is it not a temper of enmity and rebellion against God? And is this temper a mere calamity? So there no wickedness and guilt therein? And are we not to blame

Twenty-eight years later, from this same text Edwards Jr. with a greater pointedness identifies the Spirit's "regenerative and decisive influence" which is necessary to overcome "native depravity."[162] Edwards Jr. also proposes, like his father and Bellamy,[163] a postmillennial return of Christ will occur after a broad out-pouring of the Spirit.[164] Later on for another audience, he urges compassionately to "be reconciled to God—repent [and] believe" for this was the only way to "secure an entrance," while not neglecting "the use of means by the unregenerate," as means would make entrance "more probable."[165]

In a sermon from Matthew 7:20, Edwards Jr. instructs his listeners on the need to examine the kind of fruit people produce. It is necessary to evaluate character in others and themselves.[166] External acts of obedience display what is "internal—mental— inaccessible."[167] While outward display is necessary for Christian profession, nevertheless, "profession [is] part of the fruit [which is] not mere profession [rather] both [works and profession are necessary] together."[168] Edwards reaches back to an earlier context of the SM to qualify his statement on the analysis of one's own heart. Because

---

upon the account of it?—What if we were born with it; how does that lessen or remove our guilt and blame?—I would illustrate this by an example or two. When we see a man who is of a remarkable perverse, forward malicious temper of mind; and always was of that temper, was born with it, do we not always determine him to be to blame for that temper? Do we at all excuse him from blame, because he was born into the world?" Edwards Jr., "Volume 59," 84–85.

[162] "Only [the] Spirit" can give "the love of heaven the spiritual good." Edwards Jr., "June 1. 1794.," 2–3.

[163] "Days, and months, and years, will hasten along, and one revolution among the kingdoms of the earth follow upon another, until the fulness of time is come; till all things are ripe for the event; and when the ministers of Christ will accomplish, in reality, what St. John saw in his vision.—"I saw an angel fly in the midst of heaven, having the everlasting gospel to preach unto them that dwell on the earth, and to every nation, and kindred, and tongue, and people."—And then shall it come to pass, that the veil of ignorance, which hath so long spread over all nations, shall be destroyed, (Isa. xxv. 7,) and [. . .] Babylon shall fall, Satan be bound, and Christ will reign, and truth and righteousness universally prevail, a thousand years." Joseph Bellamy, *The Works of Joseph Bellamy*, vol. 1 (Boston: Doctrinal Tract and Book Society, 1850), 554–555. Also see C. C. Goen, "Jonathan Edwards: A New Departure in Eschatology," *Church History* vol. 28, no. 1 (1959): 25–40.

[164] Edwards Jr., "Volume 59," 62–73. Cf. Edwards Jr., "No. 1095.," 4.

[165] Edwards Jr., "No. 1095.," 8.

[166] Jonathan Edwards Jr., "No. 917 Oct. 23. 1785. Mat. 7.20," *Jonathan Edwards and Calvin Chapin Papers*, Beinecke Rare Book and Manuscript Library (Box 1, Folder 3), 1.

[167] Edwards Jr., "No. 917.," 1.

[168] Edwards Jr., "No. 917.," 2.

of man's sin nature, the potential to "argue in a circle" is great. In other words, a person's capacity to evaluate himself is dependent, to begin with, upon his having "a good heart."[169] Since he does not have a good heart, he cannot evaluate properly. Therefore, the church needs to be evaluating one another.

From the following verse, Edwards concludes his teaching from the SM by emphasizing that true religion alone has consistency of profession and fruit.[170] Building on his earlier exegesis of The Lord's Prayer, Edwards Jr. interprets that "generally—the gospel churches" reflect the kingdom of heaven ("on earth [as] in heaven").[171] In two versions of this text, he develops the church-kingdom metaphor around the King, his laws, and his subjects. Because Christ embodies "every qualification of a king," he is worthy to rule over man as he has also "suffered in our nature."[172] His laws are plain, perfect, and suited to the glory of God. But not all professors of religion are true subjects. In *Religious Affections,* his father described the seal of the Spirit by a similar sovereign-subject metaphor:

> That which is called the witness of the Spirit (Romans 8), is elsewhere in the New Testament called the seal of the Spirit [...] alluding to the seal of princes, annexed to the instrument, by which they advanced any of their subjects to some high honor and dignity, or peculiar privilege in the kingdom, as a token of their special favor.[173]

It is possible that Edwards Jr. adapts this metaphor for his purposes to illustrate true subjects as those who "love God" and "lead a holy life."[174] Examination of the heart is critical as externals "may be without any real religion."[175] The religion of the heart does not consist in self-preservation

---

[169] Edwards Jr., "No. 917.," 3.

[170] Jonathan Edwards Jr., "No. 870. Octr. 1784. Mat. 7. 21.," *Jonathan Edwards and Calvin Chapin Papers,* Beinecke Rare Book and Manuscript Library (Box 1, Folder 3), 1.

[171] Edwards Jr., "No. 870.," 1. Cf. Edwards Jr., "Vol. 211.," 1–2.

[172] Edwards Jr., "No. 870.," 2.

[173] Edwards Sr., *Religious Affections,* 230–231.

[174] Edwards Jr., "No. 870.," 7.

[175] Edwards Jr., "No. 870.," 8. In another manuscript on the same text used as late as August 3, 1800, he says, a person may have a perfectly orthodox confession; however, "may be alienated in/heart." Jonathan Edwards Jr., "[Unnumbered] July 15. 1792. Mat. VII. 21.," *Andover Newton Miscellaneous Personal Papers Collection,* Yale Divinity Library (Box 168, Folder 10), 2.

or a "natural compassion [or] natural affection"; rather, "obedience must proceed from sincere and supreme love to God."[176]

Conclusion

Edwards Jr.'s last canonical manuscript from the SM (Matt 7:21)[177] is appropriately drafted on a folded *Proposal for Printing by Subscription [...] A Treatise Concerning Religious Affections* (Jan. 1787). The proposal states that his father's treatise "is the best to discriminate between true and false affections in Religion, of any thing that has ever appeared since the first promulgation of Christianity." That this manuscript is preserved on a proposal for *Religious Affections* bears tribute to how the elder Edwards's undying concern that the true church would have a "relish" for "true religion" carries over to the younger Edwards.[178]

But even more significantly, this last sermon was prepared during the beginning stages of the Second Great Awakening, in which the Colebrook Church experienced significant growth during Edwards Jr.'s last pulpit ministry (1796–1799).[179] These SM manuscripts show a rich textual dependence by Edwards Jr. upon Bellamy and his father. Through six major divisions in the SM Edwards Jr.'s demonstrates a consistency with his father thinking on the Spirit's role in producing true piety. While these sermons were considered chronologically, they do span his entire thirty-year pulpit ministry—and demonstrate a remarkable consistency of concern for true religion. That the emphasis or style of sermon did not change dramatically between the beginning and end of his career is an important point to consider. He had been counselled to change his approach, but instead of changing approach, he remained consistent in his style and content. This point is important because toward the end of his ministry, he also saw the fervent response to

---

[176]Edwards Jr., "July 15. 1792.," 3.

[177]Jonathan Edwards Jr., "[Unnumbered] Augt. 28. 1796. Mat. VII. 21.," *Jonathan Edwards and Calvin Chapin Papers*, Beinecke Rare Book and Manuscript Library (Box 1, Folder 4), 1–4; On reverse is a proposal for a reprinting of *Religious Affections* (from Carroll and Patterson of New York).

[178]Both of these words are lifted from this very manuscript. Edwards Jr. recognizes that in the visible church a Judas may exist "among us" and that "not all such the/subjects of true religion—/this necessary/otherwise not prepared accord/ing to divine con/stitution/nor relish." Edwards Jr., "Augt. 28. 1796.," 2.

[179]Two years after this sermon, church records indicate that since the beginning of his ministry in 1795 that Edwards admitted twenty-seven new members, so that by 1799 the membership had nearly tripled in size to over sixty members. Ferm, *Edwards the Younger*, 151.

his preaching at the beginning of the Second Great Awakening. Rather than a demarcation from his father, the younger Edwards demonstrates he is a faithful inheritor of his father's theology, in conversation with Bellamy and Hopkins. Edwards Jr. did not contribute to the decline of piety; rather, he also shared a relish that true religion would flourish in the congregations he ministered to in Connecticut.

Chapter 4

A Received Edwardsean Pneumatology

The First Great Awakening occurred during Jonathan Edwards's early pastoral ministry in the 1730s and 1740s. Over this decade religious fervor grew from a localized renewal to a more broadly known and shared experience. The local revivals that occurred, for example, in Stoddard's ministry were not as widely known as those that occurred under Edwards Sr.'s ministry. This exposure came through the publication of *A Faithful Narrative* (1737). People in Boston and as far away as England and Scotland were now aware of revivalism in New England.[1]

This publicity gradually brought critique. For example, in Boston, pastors like Charles Chauncy openly questioned reports from the western frontier, and in time put his thoughts into print. Even before Chauncy published *Seasonable Thoughts on the State of Religion* (1743), Edwards Sr. was also beginning to question the excesses himself and responded to those excesses publicly.[2] The experiences of the previous decade moved Edwards Sr. to write *Religious Affections* (1746). This book was to be a tool for spiritual evaluation with its marks of genuine spirituality. William Breitenbach de-

---

[1] Isaac Watts was concerned that Edwards Sr. might have been exaggerating his account and requested some secondary witnesses and testimony in another edition. John Wesley owned a copy and "provided one of the models for the revivals he hoped to promote." George M. Marsden, *Jonathan Edwards: A Life* (New Haven, CT: Yale University Press, 2003), 172–173.

[2] Charles Chauncy, *Seasonable Thoughts on the State of Religion in New England* (Boston: Rogers and Fowle, 1743); Jonathan Edwards Sr., "Some thoughts Concerning the Present Revival of Religion in New England," in *The Works of Jonathan Edwards*, Vol. 4, ed C.C. Goen (New Haven, CT: Yale University Press, 1972). See also Marsden, *Jonathan Edwards*, 280–281.

scribes *Religious Affections* as "the most important work in the development of the 'new' divinity."[3]

This brief background is necessary to appreciate the vision for genuine renewal placed into Edwards Sr.'s successors. Wanting to be in step with the Spirit's reviving work, while defending traditional Calvinism, Edwards's students sharpened their mentor's thinking on the Spirit. For example, in Edwards Jr.'s assessment of his father's legacy he describes their continuity with him in this way:

> But according to Mr. Edwards, and those who adopt his views on the subject, regeneration consists in the communication of a new spiritual sense or taste. In other words, a new heart is given. This communication is made, this work in accomplished, by the Spirit of God. It is their opinion, that the intellect, and the sensitive faculties, are not the immediate subject of any change in regeneration.[4]

The emphasis on "the communication of a new spiritual sense or taste" stands in contrast to his father's debate with Charles Chauncy. Chauncy emphasized "an enlightened mind" rather than "raised affections."[5] The New Divinity continued this debate into the revolutionary age with additional tools provided by Edwards Sr: *Freedom of the Will* (1754), *Original Sin* (1758), and *The Nature of True Virtue* (1765).

These additional volumes provided the biblio-philosophical categories for his successors to articulate a theology of the Spirit and navigate the pressures of rationalism in the revolutionary era. In *Freedom of the Will* Edwards Sr. parsed the difference between natural and moral ability.[6] For New Divinity successors, these categories of distinction were helpful tools to call for response, while looking for the evidence of the Spirt as described in *Religious Affections*. *Original Sin*, on the other hand, provided a framework to understand the limits of moral ability as a result of genetic depravity.[7] Yet,

---

[3] William Breitenbach, "Piety and Moralism: Edwards and the New Divinity," in *Jonathan Edwards and the American Experience*, ed. Nathan O. Hatch and Harry S. Stout (New York: Oxford University Press, 1988), 183.

[4] Emphasis original. *JEW1*, 490–492.

[5] Charles Chauncy, *Seasonable Thoughts*, 327.

[6] Jonathan Edwards Sr., *Freedom of the Will*, in *The Works of Jonthan Edwards*, Vol. 1 ed. Paul Ramsey (New Haven, CT: Yale University Press, 1957), 157–162.

[7] Jonathan Edwards Sr., *Original Sin*, in *The Works of Jonathan Edwards*, Vol. 3 ed. Clyde A. Holbrook (New Haven, CT: Yale University Press, 1970), 370–371.

to assess the communication of divine virtue by the Spirit, the regenerated person will be known by benevolence. While not the entire emphasis of *The Nature of True Virtue,* benevolence became a kind of litmus test of true religion.[8] Edwards Sr.'s students sharpened their mentor's thinking in such a way that subsequent readers would at times mischaracterize their position on the third person of the Trinity's role in regeneration.

For example, in the October 1850 edition of the *Biblical Repertory and Princeton Review,* Charles Hodge questioned Edwards Amasa Park's commitment to a received Edwardsean theology. This article was written in response to the widely acclaimed Andover Convocation sermon preached earlier that year by Park. In Hodge's analysis, New England Theology, as represented by Park, was an interrelated web of theological deductions that led back to a prioritization of the human will.[9] Consequently, Hodge was concerned that the doctrine of regeneration by the Holy Spirit was at risk of being lost due to mismanagement by Edwards's theological heirs. Hodge was worried. He argued that "the Scriptures nowhere tell men they can regenerate themselves,

> but expressly declare that the natural man cannot discern the things of the Spirit of God, so that blessed Agent, in leading men to a knowledge of themselves, uniformly convinces them of their entire happiness, i.e. that they cannot of themselves repent, believe, or even thing any good thought. It is not a surprise, therefore, that the doctrine of adequate power, or that men 'can by their own strength turn themselves unto God,' is repudiated as anti-Christian no less by Romanists than by Protestants.[10]

---

[8] Edwards Sr. contrasts inferior kinds of self-love that tend to mimic a benevolence but do not consist "in a sense and relish of the essential beauty of virtue, consisting in a being's cordial union to Being in general, from a spirit of love to Being in general." Jonathan Edwards Sr., "The Nature of True Religion," in *The Works of Jonathan Edwards,* Vol. 8, ed. Paul Ramsey (New Haven, CT: Yale University Press, 1989), 612.

[9] Charles Hodge, "Review of The Theology of the Intellect and that of the Feelings. A Discourse before the Convention of the Congregational Ministers of New England, in Brattle Street Meeting House, Boston, May 30th, 1850 by Edwards A. Park," *The Biblical Repertory and Princeton Review,* vol. 22, no. 1–4 (1850): 655.; Charles Hodge, "Review of Remarks on the Princeton Review, vol. 22, no. 4., 7 by Edwards A. Park," *The Biblical Repertory and Princeton Review,* vol. 23, no. 1–4 (1851): 308–312

[10] Charles Hodge, "Unity and Diversity of Belief even on Imputed and Involuntary Sin; with Comments on a Second Article in the Princeton Review relating to a Convention Sermon," *The Biblical Repertory and Princeton Review,* vol. 23, no. 4 (Philadelphia: Wm. H. Mitchell, 1851): 680–683.

While provocative, Hodge's use of the phrase "regenerate themselves" is an indirect reference to Charles G. Finney's adaptation of Nathanael Emmons's sermon "Duty of Sinners to Make Themselves a New Heart."[11]

Park replied to Hodge and addressed the accusation of theological mismanagement. He asserted continuity between the elder and younger Edwards. According to Park, the Princeton theologians were attempting to "draw a line of demarcation between the elder Edwards, Bellamy, on the one side, and the younger Edwards, Emmons, West, on the other." Hodge, said Park, could not arbitrarily divide them between faithful and unfaithful adherents of Edwards. Instead, he claimed that the "commune vinculum [common bond]" between the two groups was Samuel Hopkins.[12] In other words, according to Park, Hodge could not claim an essential difference between the older and younger Edwards with regard to the "nature of sin" and "a natural power of choosing right and wrong" because Hopkins held both groups together.

Park is correct because Edwards Jr.'s connection to his father's theology began in Samuel Hopkin's home over the winter of 1765–1766. Jonathan Edwards Jr. did not only commit himself to understand his father's theology, but also to honor his father's legacy.[13] A brief overview of the elder Edwards's theology of the Spirit is necessary in order to appreciate the common bond between father and son's thinking on the Spirit, and to address subsequent claims of theological mismanagement. This chapter will first present a short summary of Edwards Sr.'s pneumatological legacy in conversation with older and newer interpreters of Edwards. In this review, I will show how Edwards Sr.'s trinitarian model affected how he understood the work of the Spirit in

---

[11] Nathanael Emmons, "Duty of Sinners to Make Themselves a New Heart," in *The Works of Nathanael Emmons,* vol. 5., ed. Jacob Ide (Boston: Crocker and Brewster, 1842), 122–131; Charles G. Finney, "Sinners Bound to Change Their Own Hearts," in *Sermons on Various Subjects* (New York: Benedict and Co. Printers, 1834), 3–28.

[12] Edwards A. Park, "New England Theology," *Bibliotheca Sacra* 9, no 33 (1852): 175. The two groups alluded to were those of the Exercise Scheme and the Taster Scheme. The key question which divided the two groups rested on the role of the Holy Spirit to either create a new taste or to prompt a new successive pattern of holy exercises in the soul.

[13] Edwards Jr. was very conscientious of his father. In his personal journal, Edwards Jr. upbraids himself for failing to follow his father's last bit of spiritual advice to him before he died. Jonathan Edwards Jr., "Diary," *Jonathan Edwards Papers,* Beinecke Rare Book and Manuscript Library (Gen MSS 151, Box 24, Folder 1357), 1–19, 16. Later, in a letter to his grandmother, he speaks of his desire to honor his parent's legacy. Jonathan Edwards Jr. to Esther Stoddard Edwards, 1765 April 12. MS, one leaf. *Shepard Family Collection,* Special Collections, Yale Divinity Library.

redemption. Then, in the various written remains of Edwards Jr., I show how Edwards Sr.'s thoughts surface in his son.

Jonathan Edwards Sr.'s Pneumatological Legacy

Park's description of the relationship between the groups as *commune vinculum* can also be used to describe an emphasis in Edwards Sr.'s thinking about the Spirit. W. Ross Hastings has suggested that "union is a significant driving force in Edwards's Trinitarian theology" along with Robert W. Caldwell.[14] According to Edwards, in his unpublished "Discourse on the Trinity," the Holy Spirit is the living affection or volition arising out of the mutual love and delight of the Father and Son. As infinite repetition of this exercise, the Holy Spirit is that mutual self-repetition of affection and volition.[15]

Kyle Strobel describes this bond of union in which each member of the Trinity participates as "personal beatific-delight."[16] He arrives on this by reading Edwards's thinking on the Trinity as progressively taking shape over time. He recommends this approach rather than pitting two versions of Edwards against himself.[17] The two versions, often pitted against each other, are the psychological view (Western or Augustinian) or social view (Eastern). Instead, Strobel argues for an ontological view in which to some degree both models are incorporated to "highlight the key features of religious affection as the very life of God."[18] This new approach is not entirely unanticipated by others.

Amy Plantinga Pauw, for example, observed that Edwards had a "high toleration for theological tension" as he could not only conceive of the triune

---

[14] "I wish to make the modest proposal that union is a significant driving force in Edwards's Trinitarian theology, if not its overarching trope, and that his theology essentially tells a 'from eternity, to eternity' story of *three unions in the Spirit: the eternal union within the Trinity of the Father and the Son in the Holy Spirit, the union in history of the human and divine natures of Christ by the Spirit, and the union of the saints with God by the Spirit.*" Emphasis original. W. Ross Hastings, *Jonathan Edwards and the Life of God: Toward an Evangelical Theology of Participation* (Minneapolis: Fortress Press, 2015), 2. Also see Robert W. Caldwell, *Communion in the Spirit: The Holy Spirit as the Bond of Union in the Theology of Jonathan Edwards* (Eugene, OR: Wipf and Stock, 2006).

[15] Jonathan Edwards Sr., "Discourse on the Trinity," in *Writings on the Trinity, Grace, and Faith*, Vol. 21, ed. Sang Hyun Lee (New Haven, CT: Yale University Press, 1957–2008), 121.

[16] Kyle Strobel, *Jonathan Edwards's Theology: A Reinterpretation*, T&T Clark Studies in Systematic Theology 19 (New York: Bloomsbury T&T Clark, 2013), 65–71.

[17] Strobel, *Jonathan Edwards's Theology*, 69.

[18] Strobel, *Jonathan Edwards's Theology*, 70.

deity as the permutations of its own highest ideal, but also to incorporate Eastern and Western metaphysics. Edwards enjoyed alternating between a society of persons and essential unity within the Trinity whenever he thought useful for his theological purposes. Whereas Strobel sees a synthesis in these approaches to the Trinity, Pauw sees these two approaches held in tension. McClymond and McDermott also recognize this tendency in Edwards and move in the same direction of Strobel but without commitment to a full synthesis. They observe that "Edwards used both the psychological and social analogies for the Trinity in a synthetic way that put more weight on the latter, and at the same time restored honor to the Spirit."[19]

By stressing the Holy Spirit who is, as Sang Lee has noted, not just a bond of love but an active, full-fledged person,[20] Edwards Sr. desired to elevate the significance of the Third Person. Though, by accenting the role of the Holy Spirit as the "thing purchased"[21] in the atonement, Edwards knowingly created his own problem of apparent inconsistency. Scripture, demurred Edwards in "Discourse on the Trinity," is absent of any apparent direct affection toward the Spirit by the Father and Son.[22] Yet, he was willing to overlook this potential problem for the sake of glory of the Spirit in the work of redemption, which was "the price, and the thing bought with that price [...] and therefore 'tis the same glory, and an equal glory."[23]

Pauw also proposes that Edwards's dual use of a psychological and social model served his desire to do theology narratively instead of systematically.[24] Pauw specifically identifies Peter van Mastricht's *Theoretico-practica Theologia* as Edwards's source for a social trinitarian framework when Mastricht said that "the holy Trinity consists in the most perfect fellowship and communion of the divine persons, when the infinite perfection of God, by reflecting as it were from person to person, grows immeasurably strong, so also from the

---

[19] McClymond and McDermott, *The Theology of Jonathan Edwards*, 198.

[20] Sang Hyun Lee, "Editors Introduction," in *Writings on the Trinity, Grace, and Faith*, vol. 21, ed. Sang Hyun Lee (New Haven, CT: Yale University Press, 1957–2008), 18–19.

[21] "If we suppose no more than used to be supposed about the Holy Ghost, the concern of the Holy Ghost in the work of redemption is not equal with the Father's and the Son's, nor is there an equal part of the glory of this work belongs to him. [...] To be the love of God to the world is as much as for the Father and the Son to do so much from love to the world; and to be [the] thing purchased was as much as to be the price: the price, and the thing bought with that price, are equal." Edwards Sr., "Discourse on the Trinity," 137–138.

[22] Edwards, "Discourse on the Trinity," 140.

[23] Edwards, "Discourse on the Trinity," 140.

[24] Pauw, *The Supreme Harmony*, 10–15.

unity and communion of the saints."[25] Adriaan Neele also notes that "the communion and economy of the Three Persons thus draws one's attention throughout [the theology of God]."[26] Remarkably, though, Van Mastricht also employed Augustine's psychological model to ascribe the inherent unity within the Godhead as a counterbalance to a social analogy.[27] Van Mastricht's sympathy with the Eastern position, which will be developed below, allowed both Edwards Sr. and himself to formulate the Holy Spirit's role as the communicator of the grace of Christ and love of the Father.[28]

If the trajectory of older (Pauw) and more recent scholarship (Strobel) is correctly moving along a trajectory of some sort of combination or synthesis of models, then aspects of this thinking ought to be able to be found subsequently in Edwards Sr. The combination of these models can be seen in how Edwards Sr. speaks of the regenerating work of the Spirit. In regeneration, humanity by necessity is a social participant in loving union of God. In other words, the Holy Spirit communicates the internal psychological delight of the Trinity in a social way to humanity. This communication, according to Strobel, is an emanation of the "beatific mutual delight" in humanity which elicits a "remanation" in the subject creating union.[29] Thus, the affections of humanity become excited in ways that, Edwards Sr. and his successors described as, yet misunderstood by Charles Hodge, choosing to "make himself a new heart." This movement of the Spirit and response of man are simultaneous acts—that is, two sides of the moment that Strobel describes as emanation and remanation. The emanation and remanation is the process of creating union by the Holy Spirit in regeneration.

To describe the work of the Holy Spirit as a bond of union, while still portraying him as unique person in the Godhead, Edwards Sr. used different words as metonymy for the Holy Spirit. In this way, the third person of the Trinity is said to appropriate attributes in the process of regeneration. Peter Reese Doyle observes that love, holiness, fullness, and glory are among

---

[25] Pauw, *The Supreme Harmony*, 36; Petrus van Mastricht, *Theoretical-Practical Theology*, Vol. 2, trans. Todd M. Rester (Grand Rapids: Reformation Heritage Books, 2019), 525.

[26] Adriaan Neele, *Petrus van Mastricht (1630–1706) Reformed Orthodoxy: Method and Piety*, vol. 35 in Brill's Series in Church History, ed. by Wim Janse (Boston: Brill, 2009), 253.

[27] Pauw, *The Supreme Harmony*, 44–46. Peter van Mastricht also followed Augustine's psychological model to ascribe an inherent divine unity of essence as counterbalance. Van Mastricht, *Theoretical-Practical Theology*, Vol. 2, 522. Pauw, *The Supreme Harmony*, 74–75, also Van Mastricht, *Theoretical-Practical Theology*, Vol. 2, 517, 522.

[28] Neele, *Petrus van Mastricht*, 269.

[29] Strobel, *Jonathan Edwards's Theology*, 12–20.

Edwards Sr.'s favorite substitute words to describe the work of Spirit in the creation of union.[30] Doyle is not alone in this observation as Robert Caldwell also recognizes Edwards's tendency to see the Holy Spirit as the person who brings an infinite perfection to the intra-trinitarian relations and imparts these perfections *ad extra* to humanity. Caldwell observes that the Holy Spirit is often described as divine love who brings to perfection the bond of union through the *intensification* of holiness, excellency, happiness, fullness, and grace.[31] Intensification is another way to describe what Strobel proposed as "mutual beatific delight." That is, the increase of the honor that exists *ad intra* emanates *ad extra* with humanity and "remanates" back to himself creating union.

As much as these accents of the divine nature are communicable to one another *ad intra,* there is a creative work carried out by the Holy Spirit to bring a "communion" and a "partaking" to humanity *ad extra.*[32] Edwards Sr. seems to have picked up on this communion theme in van Mastricht's *Theoretico-practica Theologia* to practically articulate the equality of the Spirit *ad intra.* Specifically, van Mastricht says that "the *ad extra* operations, on account of the fact that they flow from the essence, are undivided, and they are worked only in a mode or order that is diverse."[33] This qualification about the undivided nature of the Trinity *ad extra* does three very important things. First, it retains the unity inherent in the psychological model because it retains the internal 'psychology' which consists of, what Strobel called, "mutual beatific delight." Thirdly, by acting economically to replicate this internal delight *ad extra* in humanity reveals elements of the social model. In other words, the internal operations and motivations of the Trinity do not change when communicated to humanity by the Holy Spirit to draw us to the Father through the Son. Van Mastricht says in the same context that "the end" by which the Trinity acts in our salvation is so that "by every effort we might embrace the communion of the most holy Trinity."[34] The way van

---

[30] Peter Reese Doyle demonstrates from one passage in "Charity and its Fruits" how these four categories tend to resurface in Edwards's writings to describe the person and work of the Holy Spirit. *Jonathan Edwards on the New Birth in the Spirit: The Life, Times, and Thought of America's Greatest Theologian* (Durham, England: Torchflame Books, 2017), 102–115.

[31] Caldwell, *Communion in the Spirit,* 49–54.

[32] Caldwell, *Communion in the Spirit,* 54–55.

[33] Petrus van Mastricht, *Theoretical-Practical Theology,* Vol. 2 trans by Todd M. Rester (Grand Rapids: Reformation Heritage Books, 2019), 506.

[34] Petrus van Mastricht, *Theoretical-Practical Theology,* Vol. 2, 522–23. Adrian Neele also recognizes this reception by Edwards. Neele, *Petrus van Mastricht,* 276–277.

Mastricht describes this movement toward humanity is inherently aligned with both a psychological and a social model and bears a similarity with Edwards Sr.'s thinking about regeneration.

The bond of union in the Trinity was meant to be shared with his creation. This mystical union occurs through the gift of the Holy Spirit provided through Christ's atonement. According to Caldwell, Edwards views this union as occurring through illumination and infusion.[35] As two sides of the same coin, spiritual perception is caused by the presence of the Spirit. Edwards Sr. says in *The Threefold Work of the Holy Ghost,* an exposition of John 16:8, that "although Jesus Christ prepares the way for man's salvation by his righteousness and sufferings, yet 'tis the immediate work of the Holy Ghost actually to make men partakers of that salvation; 'tis he that doth the finishing stroke."[36] In this same discourse, he describes the Spirit as dwelling in believers "as a principle. [...] as it were a principle of nature; thereby, they are of a new nature, and 'tis by this means they are partakers of the divine nature."[37] This principle, according to Edwards Sr. occurred through "physical infusion."[38] In *Charity and Its Fruits,* this physical infusion is described as "a principle of life which acts."[39] In other words, within the natural capacity of a person, the only thing that changed was the moral disposition due to the presence of the Holy Spirit.[40] This presence of the Holy Spirit is what triggers the start of communion with the triune God.

---

[35] Caldwell, *Communion in the Spirit,* 104–108. See also, Caldwell's discussion of spiritual sight. Caldwell, *Communion in the Spirit,* 142–155.

[36] Jonathan Edwards, "The Threefold Work of the Holy Ghost," in *Sermons and Discourses: 1723–1729, Works of Jonathan Edwards Online,* vol. 14, ed. Kenneth P. Minkema (New Haven, CT: Yale University Press, 1957–2008), 377.

[37] Edwards, "The Threefold Work," 384.

[38] McClymond and McDermott recognize that physical infusion may be misunderstood as referring to the material, when in actuality, physical refers to "the change of nature (Greek, phusis) that came about through the agency of the Spirit." Michael J. McClymond and Gerald R. McDermott, *The Theology of Jonathan Edwards* (New York: Oxford University Press, 2012), 269–270.

[39] Jonathan Edwards, "Charity and Its Fruits," in *Ethical Writings, Works of Jonathan Edwards Online,* vol. 8, ed. Paul Ramsey (New Haven, CT: Yale University Press, 1957–2008), 298.

[40] "Therefore it follows that saving grace in the heart, can't be produced in man by mere exercise of what perfections he has in him already, though never so much assisted by moral suasion, and never so much assisted in the exercise of his natural principles, unless there be something more than all this, viz. an immediate infusion or operation of the Divine Being upon the soul. Grace must be the immediate work of God, and properly a production of his almighty power on the soul." Jonathan Edwards, "Treatise on Grace," *Writings on the Trinity, Grace, and Faith, The Works of Jonathan Edwards,* vol. 21, ed. Sang Hyun Lee (New Haven, CT: Yale University Press, 1957–2008), 165.

This presence is a regenerative act which is wholly a result of the physical infusion of the Holy Spirit.

Remarkably, and controversially, Edwards famously stated in his *Treatise on Grace* that "[w]e are not merely passive in it, nor yet does God do some and we do the rest, but God does all and we do all. God produces all and we act all."[41] What is less often quoted is the broader context in which Edwards Sr. reflects upon the work of the Holy Spirit. Edwards Sr. continues:

> For that is what he produces, our own acts. God is the only proper author and fountain; we only are the proper actors. We are in different respects wholly passive and wholly active. There the same things are represented as from God and us. So God is said to convert, and men are said to convert, or turn. God makes a new heart, and we are commanded to make us a new heart. God circumcises the heart, and we are commanded to circumcise [our hearts]. Not merely because we must use the means in order to the effect, but the effect itself is our act and our duty.[42]

In this broader context, Edwards Sr. picks up the conundrum of the command, in the words of Hodge, to "regenerate themselves."[43] Remarkably Edwards Sr. collapses infused grace (presence of the Holy Spirit) into the visible response (the doing) of the will.[44]

In "A Divine and Supernatural Light" Edwards expands on this apparent contradiction as the work of the Holy Spirit as a "vital principle [...] which] acting in the soul of a godly man, exerts and communicates himself there in his own proper nature. Holiness is the proper nature of the Spirit of God. The Holy Spirit operates in the minds of the godly, by uniting himself to them, and living in them, and exerting his own nature in the exercise of their

---

[41] Edwards, "Treatise on Grace," 251.

[42] Edwards, "Treatise on Grace," 251.

[43] Edwards, "Treatise on Grace," 251. One can see how a Charles G. Finney might capitalize on Edwards's intellectual dexterity; however, Edwards might prefer to err on the side of God's sovereignty, whereas Finney seems to prefer error on the side of human responsibility.

[44] "And in this case, not only is it true, that it is easy for a man to do the thing if he will, but the very willing is the doing; when once has willed, the thing is performed; and nothing else remains to be done." Edwards Sr., *Freedom of the Will*, 162.

faculties."⁴⁵ This exercise of a believer's moral faculties to respond to the gospel manifests as the operation of the Holy Spirit. Thus, the Holy Spirit continues to indwell and move a believing soul to delight and enjoy God.

A lot more could be said about Jonathan Edwards Sr.'s theology of the Spirit. I have focused specifically on old and new research that focuses on Edwards's thinking about the Spirit in relationship to the Trinity and his work of regeneration. By focusing on the influence of van Mastricht, I have attempted to show how Edwards Sr. found resources to articulate two theological models of trinitarian relations in a singular way. Edwards Sr. appears to have been able to see a synthesis of a psychological model and the social model. This unique way of viewing competing ideas about the Trinity is also apparent in the process of regeneration. Regeneration is also described as a duplex in that "God does all and we do all." This capacity to synthesize regeneration and conversion as distinct but complementary unity is Edwards Sr.'s legacy of the Spirit in his followers.

This intellectual ability to bring two tensions together, and the limits of communication, has caused some like Charles Hodge to misunderstand Edwards Sr.'s intentions. Instead of two separate competing interests (divine sovereignty and human freedom) in regeneration, there is, rather, a simultaneous interest in divine excellence that occurs by the indwelling presence of the Holy Spirit. When God "commends to man his own excellence" by the Spirit, man takes delight in and responds to God in such a way that both interests are satisfied at once. Like Edwards Sr.'s thinking on the Trinity, the work of the Holy Spirit in regeneration follows in the same logical way.

McClymond and McDermott describe Edwards Sr.'s trinitarianism as "original in a number of ways."⁴⁶ Yet, as Pauw and Strobel have demonstrated, Edwards Sr. had found resources in van Mastricht. This intellectual aptitude to unify what others tend hold in tension is a characteristic of both the older younger Edwards. As noted in his biography, the younger Edwards held his father in very high esteem. Thus, the younger Edwards had also perused Van Mastricht not just once, but according to Edwards Amasa Park, seven times.⁴⁷ Thus, when Charles Hodge accused the successors of Edwards of theological mismanagement, he did not realize how Edwards

---

⁴⁵Jonathan Edwards, "A Divine and Supernatural Light," *Sermons and Discourses, 1730– 1733, The Works of Jonathan Edwards*, vol. 17, ed. Mark Valeri (New Haven, CT: Yale University Press, 1957–2008), 411.

⁴⁶McClymond and McDermott, *The Theology of Jonathan Edwards*, 197.

⁴⁷Park, "New England Theology," 191.

Sr.'s articulated a duplex of trinitarian models as one, nor how regeneration consists of a unified act of the Spirit and humanity.

The Younger Edwards's Common Bond

Jonathan Edwards Jr. does reflect a common bond with his father's theology of the Holy Spirit; however, this continuity is often overlooked because of a greater interest in the uniqueness of his moral governmental theory of the atonement.[48] As noted earlier, this tendency is further exacerbated by a long-standing decline narrative. Yet, this is beginning to change, due to a reexamination of Edwards Jr.'s unpublished sermons and interest in mentorship. In the following in-depth analysis of Edwards Jr.'s writings, continuity can be found with his father's pneumatology thinking. This survey will examine the younger Edwards's questions and answers for students, his theological writing, and his sermons.

Mentoring Preachers

The younger Edwards, like his father, continued the practice of bringing apprentices into his close acquaintance for the purpose of advancing the Edwardsean theology. Among his pool of ministerial aspirants are some significant preachers, theologians, and educators whose contributions in New England society outlived themselves.[49] Rhys Bezzant recognizes that often

---

[48] Cooley, Daniel W. and Douglas A. Sweeney. "The Edwardseans and the Atonement," *A New Divinity: Transatlantic Reformed Evangelical Debates during the Long Eighteenth Century*, ed. Mark Jones and Michael A. G. Haykin, 109–125. Reformed Historical Theology Series, vol. 49, ed. Herman J. Selderhuis (Gottigen, Germany: Vandenhoeck and Ruprecht Verlage, 2018): 122. Oliver Crisp, "Non-Penal Substitution," *International Journal of Systematic Theology*, vol. 9, no. 4 (October 2007), 415–433; Oliver Crisp, "Penal Non-Substitution," *Journal of Theological Studies*, vol. 59, no. 1 (April 2008), 140–168; Oliver Crisp, "The Moral Government of God: Jonathan Edwards and Joseph Bellamy on the Atonement," *After Jonathan Edwards: The Courses of the New England Theology*, ed. Oliver D. Crisp and Douglas A. Sweeney (New York: Oxford University Press, 2012), 78–90; S. Mark Hamilton, "Jonathan Edwards on the Atonement," *International Journal of Systematic Theology* 15, no. 4 (Oct. 2013), 394–415.; S. Mark Hamilton, "Jonathan Edwards on the Election of Christ," *Neue Zeitschrift für Systematische Theologie und Religionsphilosophie* 58, no. 4 (2016), 525–548.; S. Mark Hamilton, "Jonathan Edwards, Anselmic Satisfaction and God's Moral Government," *International Journal of Systematic Theology* 17, no. 1 (Jan. 2015), 46–67.; S. Mark Hamilton, "Re-thinking Atonement in Jonathan Edwards and New England Theology," *Perichoresis* 15, no. 1 (2017), 85–99. S. Mark Hamilton, "Jonathan Edwards, Anselmic Satisfaction and God's Moral Government," *International Journal of Systematic Theology* 17, no. 1 (Jan. 2015), 46–67.

[49] Timothy Dwight (President of Yale), Samuel Austin (President of the University of Vermont), Jedidiah Morse (Father of American Geography), Edward Dorr Griffin (Minister of Park Street

the first draft of Edwards's books and sermons filtered through his students,[50] and so we ought to expect that in the printed works of his students are aspects of Edwards Sr. Edwards Jr. made theological preservation a display of his filial loyalty by adapting his own version of the theological questions for students out of his father's ninety.

These questions, which are a largely overlooked resource for Edwardsean studies, were composed by father and son to facilitate meaningful conversation with students in their study.[51] Both sets of questions begin with the existence of God and conclude with ecclesiology. For the most part they follow the basic outline of the *Westminster Confession*[52] with just one notable exception. Both father and son start with necessity of God's existence and attributes, whereas the *Confession* begins with special revelation.[53] While impressive already at ninety questions, the younger Edwards added two hundred and twenty-three to his father's and thus rounding it out to a weighty three hundred and thirteen. A comparison of these questions reveals, not that Edwards Jr. added "New Divinity" content as the editors suggested,[54] but rather the additional questions systematize his father's theology in greater detail. The character of the expansion itself indicates a robust reception of his father's theology in general.

One might wish for the opportunity to sit and discuss these questions with Edwards Sr., or his son for that matter, but the next best thing has recently become more available. One of Edwards Jr.'s students had taken the

---

Church in Boston, and President of Williams College), Samuel Nott (Pastor in Norwich, CT and brother of Eliphalet Nott, President of Union College). See Robert L. Ferm, *Jonathan Edwards the Younger 1745–1801: A Colonial Pastor* (Grand Rapids: Eerdmans, 1976), 87.

[50] Bezzant, *Edwards the Mentor*, 120.

[51] Jonathan Edwards and Jonathan Edwards Jr., "The Theological Questions of President Edwards, Senior, and Dr. Edwards, His Son (1822 Questions)," in *Church and Pastoral Documents, Works of Jonathan Edwards*, vol. 39 (New Haven, CT: Yale University Press, 2008).

[52] Jonathan Edwards Center, ed. "Editor's Introduction," in Jonathan Edwards and Jonathan Edwards Jr., "Theological Questions."

[53] The confessional Charles Hodge, in his paper war with Edwards Amasa Park, would opine the Edwardseans for founding their theology on virtue ethics rather than the historical safety-net of scriptural confessionalism. Charles Hodge, "Review of The Theology of the Intellect and that of the Feelings. A Discourse before the Convention of the Congregational Ministers of New England, in Brattle Street Meeting House, Boston, May 30th, 1850 by Edwards A. Park," *The Biblical Repertory and Princeton Review*, vol. 22, no. 1–4 (1850): 642.

[54] In the editor's introduction, Edwards Jr.'s additional questions are said to be those which "pertain to late eighteenth-century controversies and issues dear to the New Divinity." Jonathan Edwards Center, ed. "Editior's Introduction," in Jonathan Edwards and Jonathan Edwards Jr., "Theological Questions."

time to write out the three hundred and thirteen answers and had collected them in a notebook. Maltby Gelston's notebook, titled *A Systematic Collection of Questions and Answers in Divinity,* is a carefully written compilation of the answers to those questions asked of him in Edwards Jr.'s study.[55] Recently, this collection has also been published as *New England Dogmatics.*[56] This notebook not only holds the answers to the questions, but also has a valuable appendix of supplemental additions and corrections provided by Jonathan Edwards Jr.

While each student of Edwards Jr. would have answered these questions in their own style and capacity, because Gelston's copy appears to have been corrected by Edwards Jr. it is a reliable resource for a reception of Edwards Jr.'s thinking on a variety of theological topics. For our purposes we will limit discussion to those that are relevant to the Holy Spirit. These questions are very useful for an understanding of how Edwards Jr. processed his own doctrine of the Spirit and can be compared with his father. In appendix six, I include a list of those questions that are relevant to discussion below.

As previously indicated, Edwards Jr. modeled his expanded questions off his father's list. For example, when his father penned three questions directly relating to the Trinity,[57] Edwards Jr. expanded them to twelve.[58] On the Holy Spirit, Edwards Sr. has five questions;[59] however, his son generates eighteen to fill out his father's five on such pneumatology topics of redemption, regeneration, sanctification, and assurance.[60] An analysis of these questions will show the consistency of a received Edwardsean pneumatology in his son. Since these answers had passed by the eyes of Edwards Jr. himself,

---

[55] Maltby Gelston, *A Systematic Collection of Questions and Answers in Divinity,* Yale University Manuscript and Archives Division (Misc. MSS Collection, MS 354, Series III. E–G, box 5, f. 499). Wesley Carl Ewert, *Jonathan Edwards The Younger: Theological Questions and Answers of Maltby Gelston,* vol. 2, (PhD diss., Hartford Theological Seminary, 1953). A microfiche copy of the original is also held at the Hartford Seminary Library.

[56] *New England Dogmatics: A Systematic Collection of Questions and Answers in Divinity by Maltby Gelston (1766–1865),* ed. Robert L. Boss, Joshua R. Farris, and S. Mark Hamilton (Eugene, OR: Pickwick Publishers, 2019). The answer to Question 154 is missing in Boss, Farris, and Hamilton's work but can be found in Wesley Carl Ewert's two volume dissertation. Wesley Carl Ewert, *Jonathan Edwards The Younger: Theological Questions and Answers of Maltby Gelston,* vol. 2, (PhD diss., Hartford Theological Seminary, 1953). A microfiche copy of the original is also held at the Hartford Seminary Library.

[57] Edwards Sr.'s. Questions. 9–11; hereafter, we will be abbreviated as Sr. Qs.

[58] Edwards Jr.'s. Questions. 62, 67–69, 71–79; hereafter, we will be abbreviated as Jr. Qs.

[59] Sr. Qs. 50–52, 61–62.

[60] Jr. Qs. 177–191, 228–229, 271–272.

and have specific additions and corrections, Gelston's answers can be taken as consistent with Edwards Jr.'s own thinking on pneumatology. So, we should use these answers then, to reconstruct a systematic understanding of Edwards Jr. on the Spirit. In the systematic analysis of these questions, I will draw general parallels between father and son. But, most importantly, I will highlight how Edwards Sr.'s synthetic understanding of the trinitarian relations was likewise applied by his son in the person and work of the Holy Spirit to regeneration.

Trinitarian Relations[61]

In those questions which deal directly with Christology,[62] Edwards Jr. argues against the creatureliness of Christ on the basis of infinite evil of sin. A finite being could not support an "infinite load" which justice required.[63] In faithfulness to his father's questions, regarding the infinite character of the Godhead, he demonstrates that the atonement must also be of infinite value. While the focus of this question tends toward Anselm's argument that Christ had to be both God and man so that the atonement would have infinite value, he also implies Christ's divinity was necessary to provide "gifts of the spirit to his people."[64] In other words, the trinitarian relations manifest an infinite quality, and thus the Spirit is of infinite quality. Christ is said to be "the object of their [Father and Spirit] supreme delight and highest enjoyment."[65] This focus directly corresponds to his father's description.[66] While the *infinite* nature of Christ is articulated in anticipation of the distinctive governmental atonement theory,[67] the *infinite* nature of the godhead participating in infinite relationship intends to bring humanity into a common bond through the infinite character of the Spirit. This emphasis on the infinite is a definite reception of Edwards Sr. In *Discourse on the Trinity,* he says:

> When we speak of God's happiness, the account that we are wont to give of it is that God is *infinitely* happy in the enjoyment of

---

[61] Sr. Qs. 9–11 and Jr. Qs. 62–63, 67–69, 71–79.

[62] Jr. Qs. 62–63, 67–69.

[63] Jr. Qs. 63, Gelston, *A Systematic Collection,* 109.

[64] Gelston, *A Systematic Collection,* 108–109.

[65] Gelston, *A Systematic Collection,* 109–110.

[66] Edwards Sr., "Discourse on the Trinity," 121.

[67] Jr. Qs. 152–158, 171–175.

himself, in perfectly beholding and *infinitely* loving, and rejoicing in, his own essence and perfections. And accordingly it must be supposed that God perpetually and eternally has a most perfect idea of himself, as it were an exact image and representation of himself ever before him and in actual view.[68]

The Holy Spirit moves toward the elect to bring them into relationship with the infinite "mutual beatific delight" so enjoyed by the Trinity. Furthermore, the gifts of the Spirit is an emanation bringing humanity into union with Christ so that He is also "the object of their supreme delight and highest enjoyment."[69]

Questions 67–69 continue to pursue Christology; nevertheless, they are related to the topic of the Spirit also. For example, later in Question 73 on "the tripartite distinction in the deity from eternity," recognition is paid to how this question was answered already in the necessary distinctions required by the eternal generation of the Son.[70] This answer indicates that the inter-trinitarian relations of the Spirit must also be of the same nature as Father and Son. Specifically, since a distinction between Father and Son exists prior to the work of redemption, therefore a distinction between Father, Son, and Holy Spirit is also required.[71] Thus the eternality of the Spirit is evident based upon the relation to the Father and to the Son that "exclude[s] the idea of time and to intimate that his existence, as Son, was without beginning or from eternity."

This distinction of timelessness is a necessary nuance to distinguish the Son's independence yet in a way not to imply a bringing into existence. Timelessness, or eternality, eases a tendency to view denominations as sequential generations within the Godhead. With time sequences a moot point, then denominations of first, second,[72] and therefore, third are of no pressing concern. While the term generation is a human construct, it is merely a way for humanity to carry out discourse regarding the "eternal constitution" of the Trinity. Edwards Jr.'s observation seems to be built upon his father's observation that the infinite character of each person is found in

---

[68] Emphasis added. Edwards Sr., "Discourse on the Trinity," 113, 116, 131.

[69] Gelston, *A Systematic Collection*, 109–110.

[70] Gelston, *A Systematic Collection*, 122.

[71] Question 66. Gelston, *A Systematic Collection*, 112.

[72] Question 68–69. Gelston, *A Systematic Collection*, 115–116.

the infinite "end of the other two in their acting *ad intra*."⁷³ By looking for the respect and honor of one another, the good that is enjoyed becomes "the end," which eternally never ends.

Question 71 directly asks how "the personality of the Holy Ghost" may be proved. This personality distinction is proved from the "three that bear record in heaven" (1 John 5:7), the baptismal formula in Matthew 28:19, and benedictions. Yet, moving toward the unity of the three persons (Question 72), he argues that since the Holy Spirit is said to proceed from the Father (John 15:26) he must have a definite personality. Further along these lines, Christ himself claimed to proceed from the Father (John 8:24), requiring an essential oneness of the Son and the Holy Spirit.⁷⁴ This description of Spirit and Son as a double procession from the Father is very similar to his father's explanation in *Discourse on the Trinity*. Specifically, his father says,

> All three are persons, for they all have understanding and will. There is understanding and will in the Father, as the Son and the Holy Ghost are in him and proceed from [him]. There is understanding and will in the Son, as he is understanding and as the Holy Ghost is in him and proceeds from him. There is understanding and will in the Holy Ghost, as he is the divine will and as the Son is in him.⁷⁵

In this description by Edwards Sr., he provides each person with understanding and will; however, to guard against independent gods, describes this understanding and will as proceeding from each other in perichoresis.

Edwards Jr.'s student got part of this question wrong because he did not describe perichoresis. He wrongly suggested that mere procession from the Father was sufficient to prove the deity of the Spirit; in the supplement, he was corrected by Edwards Jr.⁷⁶ Edwards Jr. appropriately illustrates his

---

⁷³"So the Son has his peculiar glory, though the Son as it were depends on the Father, as the Father is as it were his principle. Yet in other respects the Father depends on him as his object. The Father has good, and though the Son receives the infinite good, the Holy Spirit, from the Father, the Father enjoys the infinite good through the Son. He is the end of the other two in their acting *ad intra*, and also in his acting ad extra, in all they do in redemption and their distinct economical concerns." Jonathan Edwards Sr., "On the Equality of the Persons of the Trinity," in *Writings on the Trinity, Grace, and Faith*, Vol. 21, ed. Sang Hyun Lee (New Haven, CT: Yale University, 1957-2008), 146.

⁷⁴Question 72. Gelston, *A Systematic Collection*, 120–121.

⁷⁵Edwards, *Discourse on the Trinity*, 134.

⁷⁶Supplement Question 72. Gelston, *A Systematic Collection*, 352.

student's error with three erroneous analogies. He then goes on to caution against mere procession because it may be an indication of singularity; thus, the student must observe that plurality cannot be proved by procession. The following illustrations are also said to miss the mark: "The Indian illustrated the Trinity by three branches from one stump, St. Patrick by three clover leaves from one stock, and a woman by folding her apron in to three parts."[77] The student's answer does improve as he continues writing. He guards against the potential of deducing "three Supremes," each having "all-power" (that is exercises of the will) and "allknowledge" independently. If this independence was the case, then adoration would have to be paid to all three and therefore a validation of tritheism. Nevertheless, Edwards Jr. was looking for a more robust explanation which included perichoresis like his father.

Regeneration[78]

The elder Edwards's first question[79] on the Holy Spirit's role in redemption is repeated in his son's list. The second question,[80] which defines regeneration, is divided into two[81] so that regeneration and conversion might be distinguished. The third question,[82] "Whence arises the necessity of it [regeneration]?" is broken out into twelve questions[83] with a characteristic thoroughness, leaving almost nothing to mystery.

The work of the Holy Spirit in redemption is described as "making application" of that which Christ has "obtained," but not limited to this act. For salvation to occur, there must be "a termination in real conversion."[84] This observation brought Edwards Jr. to make a clear-cut distinction between regeneration and conversion. But before he moves into the second question, he asserts in brief that justification and sanctification, as well as "various exercises of grace" are part of the Spirit's duty in redemption.[85] Drawing out

---

[77] Gelston, *A Systematic Collection*, 383.

[78] (Sr. Qs. 50–52; Jr. Qs. 177–191, 199).

[79] (Sr. Qs. 50–51).

[80] (Sr. Qs. 51).

[81] (Jr. Qs. 178–179).

[82] (Sr. Qs. 52).

[83] (Jr. Qs. 180–191).

[84] Gelston, *A Systematic Collection*, 241.

[85] Gelston, *A Systematic Collection*, 242.

of the deep well of Peter van Mastricht, Edwards Sr. has been seen to follow van Mastricht over Calvin in this sharp distinction.[86] Ironically though, Edwards Sr. does not distinguish between regeneration and conversion in his theological questions. While Edwards Sr. does not distinguish between the two, in this instance, Edwards Jr. demonstrates his effort to preserve his father's thinking by dividing the two questions, as it were, for him. Later in Question 179, Edwards Jr. will show again his desire to preserve his father's thought by showing that conversion is something continuing throughout one's lifetime.

Regeneration[87] is defined as "an effect produced by the operation of the Holy Ghost in which there is an effectual change of the temper and disposition of the heart. In consequence of this, a foundation is laid for the exercise of holy and gracious affections, such as the subject of this change never before experienced." In the clarifying follow-up question,[88] regeneration is described as "the actual implantation of a principle [and is ...] but one act, and produced but once in life;" whereas, conversion[89] is "the exercise and flowing out of the principle into various acts, and these acts are ascribed to him who is the subject of them [and ...] consists of a great variety of acts, and continues through life."[90] If Gelston fairly represents his mentor, then Edwards Jr. indeed remains faithful to his father's nuanced position articulated in *Treatise on Grace*. Yet, it is important to note that the use of the words "exercise and act" is at the heart of the taste-exercise controversy of which Edwards Amasa Park referred to in his debate with Charles Hodge. Those who followed Nathanael Emmons in the exercise scheme may have set the stage for a collapse of the Edwardsean distinction in the later theology of Charles Finney; however, in this systematic presentation, Edwards Jr. demonstrates a duplex of "God does all and we do all."

Edwards Sr.'s short question[91] "Whence arises the necessity of it?" suggests a short answer. To this short question, however, Edwards Jr. develops

---

[86] John Calvin, *Institutes of the Christian Religion*. 2 vols. ed. Richard A. Bailey and Gregory A. Wills (Wheaton, IL: Crossway Books, 2002), 3.24; Peter van Mastricht, *Treatise on Regeneration*, 1769; reprint (Morgan, PA: Soli Deo Publications, 2002), 26–27, 31.

[87] (Jr. Qs. 178).

[88] (Jr. Qs. 179).

[89] (Jr. Qs. 179).

[90] Gelston, *A Systematic Collection*, 243–244.

[91] (Sr. Qs. 52).

an additional twelve questions[92] to coach his students through the intricacies of the human heart, starting with native blindness and concluding with the logic required in his father's question of necessity[93] and free agency.[94] Questions 180–181 show "native blindness" to be a symptom of depravity. While symptomatic, this blindness is fairly and frequently represented as criminal.[95] Blindness necessarily requires divine illumination.[96] Illumination is said not to be some "new truth conveyed to the understanding," rather in the process of regeneration the heart becomes affected to appreciate the truth. This affective turn very much corresponds to Edwards Sr.'s entry in his *Miscellanies* on "Conversion." A person's mental faculty may have access and ability to understand truth; however, an illumination must occur "causing such an alteration with respect to the mind's ideas of spiritual good."[97] In other words, the Holy Spirit is the energy which enlivens the heart to engage the faculty of understanding. Just as love is a visible corollary of light, so knowing is a result of illumination.[98] The heart, according to Edwards Jr., is "a faculty of the mind on the nature of which praise, or blame is found."[99]

Remarkably, these questions expand to take in those relating to the perception of spiritual beauty and glory.[100] For example, Question 184 reveals that the ability to see spiritual beauty is "peculiar to the Christian" based on 1 Corinthians 2:14–15; however, this is also evidentially true as there are many unregenerate people who nevertheless "possess an understanding, or pure intellect, far superior to some of the most eminent Christians. A man may reason accurately and have a clear and extensive speculative knowledge of divine truths without having the least taste or relish for them."[101] Accordingly, the perception of spiritual beauty will not cause a person to become

---

[92] (Jr. Qs. 180–191).

[93] (Sr. Qs. 52; Jr. Qs. 190).

[94] (Jr. Qs. 191).

[95] Gelston, *A Systematic Collection*, 243–244.

[96] (Jr. Qs. 182).

[97] Jonathan Edwards, "284. Conversion" in *The "Miscellanies." The Works of Jonathan Edwards*, vol. 13, ed. Harry S. Stout (New Haven, CT: Yale University Press, 1957–2008), 381.

[98] Gelston, *A Systematic Collection*, 245–246.

[99] Gelston, *A Systematic Collection*, 246.

[100] (Jr. Qs. 184–187).

[101] Gelston, *A Systematic Collection*, 248.

proud or hard-hearted.[102] In branching off, as these questions appear to do, instead they demonstrate that Edwards Jr. desired to preserve his father's legacy of the Spirit, which appear in *Religious Affections* and *Nature of True Virtue*.

Edwards Jr. recognized that the exercise of the heart is an indication of an implanted taste or a relish by the Holy Spirit. The next question[103] addresses the possibility that the sight or appreciation of moral beauty may fall short if it is not coupled with love for moral beauty. In other words, a regenerate person who has an implantation of the Holy Spirit will not only see "the beauty and excellency of divine things [but] will also love and delight in them."[104] Evidently, when faith occurs through implantation, according to his father, "a spiritual taste and relish of what is excellent and divine" accompanies the Spirit.[105] The unregenerate are devoid of this spiritual taste, and a necessary infusion of the Holy Spirit must occur so that the mind can move beyond nominal ideas of divine things. The Spirit "spiritualizes" the unregenerate with a "heavenly temper" for divine things.[106] Gelston proceeds to explain how the ability to see beauty of divine things is not attainable by natural understanding; however, "to determine wherein [the taste or will] differs from the exercise of action" will not be easy.[107]

This answer recorded in Gelston's notebook may shed light on how the move toward a non-nuanced psychology of the will would gradually come so easily in subsequent generations. With the coming nineteenth century individualism and romanticism, Charles Finney would strongly state that

> in morals and religion [...] the willing is the doing. The power to will is the condition of obligation to do. [...] it is absurd and sheer nonsense to talk of an ability to do when there is no ability to *will*. Every one knows with intuitive certainty that he has no ability to do what he is unable to will to *do*. It is, therefore, the

---

[102] Gelston, *A Systematic Collection*, 249.

[103] (Jr. Qs. 184).

[104] Gelston, *A Systematic Collection*, 249–250.

[105] Jonathan Edwards Sr., "Faith," in *Writings on the Trinity, Grace, and Faith, in Works of Jonathan Edwards*, vol. 21, ed. Sang Hyun Lee (New Haven, CT: Yale University Press, 1957–2008), 417.

[106] Jonathan Edwards Sr., "A Spiritual Understanding of Divine Things Denied to the Unregenerate," in *Sermons and Discourses: 1723–1729, Works of Jonathan Edwards*, vol. 14, ed. Kenneth P. Minkema (New Haven, CT: Yale University Press, 1957–2008), 78–81.

[107] Gelston, *A Systematic Collection*, 250.

vilest of folly to talk of a natural ability to do anything whatever, when we exclude from this ability the power to *will*. If there is no ability to will, there is and can be no ability of the Edwardsean school is no ability at all... and nothing but an *empty name, a metaphysico-theological* FICTION.[108]

The inability of Charles Finney to hold Edwards's nuanced premise that "God does all and we do all" found in *Treatise on Grace* caused him to collapse Edwards's position into something more acceptable to the Jacksonian era. Charles Hodge rightly had concerns about Finney's claim to Edwards Sr.; however, Hodge was wrong about Edwards Jr.'s claim to his father. Edwards Jr., like his father, unequivocally asserts that "to have a taste and inclination for holiness, or spiritual glory, must presuppose the existence of a holy principle."[109]

While a taste must presuppose a movement of the will toward divine things, nevertheless, Edwards Jr. concludes that all moral beings (whether regenerate or not) are under obligation to be holy by necessity. Question 185 asks: "Is it a matter of duty to all men to see the spiritual glory of divine objects?" Even though his answer is brief, an impowered ability to do, can be derived out of his understanding of native blindness. Blindness does not exempt a person from responsibility as "all moral beings are under obligation to exercise a holy principle." In this regard, that moral aptitude or capacity to appreciate spiritual beauty is present.

The next two questions discuss to what degree any faculty of the mind is influenced by regeneration, or conversely, if mere light of truth has any bearing on regeneration.[110] To these questions, Edwards Jr. recognizes that if regeneration affected other aspects of the mind, then a definite class of superior intellectuals would be apparent among the regenerate; however, this is not the case for it is the heart that is under influence of regeneration. In other words, no new faculty of the mind is given to the regenerate. Regeneration is not produced by the light of truth, just as a description

---

[108] Emphasis original. Charles G. Finney, *Lectures on Systematic Theology, Embracing Lecutres on Moral Government, The Atonement, Moral and Physical Depravity, Natural, Moral, and Gracious Ability, Repentance, Faith, Justification, Sanctification, Etc.* (Oberlin: James M. Fitch, 1846), 13–14.

[109] Gelston, *A Systematic Collection*, 250.

[110] (Jr. Qs. 186–187).

of "the taste of any of the productions of nature could not be excited by describing the nature and properties."[111]

If regeneration be not an addition of a new faculty of the mind, then what exactly is this new heart given? In other words, "What do you mean by the physical operation of the Spirit in regeneration?"[112] Helpfully, Edwards Jr. reveals that the physical operation of the Spirit is applied to man's moral nature, which is "represented as being by nature dead."[113] With regard to means of grace, they provide an avenue of opportunity for the mind, but the actual change is produced "by the immediate operation of the Spirit." Since the operation of the Spirit is immediate, man must necessarily be passive in the process of regeneration.

The following question[114] explores the difference between active or passive regeneration. While not explicitly stated as such here, "active regeneration" tends to be associated with conversion and "passive regeneration" as actual regeneration. This nuance can be observed when he says that in "the moment he is regenerated, he may be active." Further, regeneration is said to be nearly impossible to discover as a point in time; however, when "he puts forth holy exercises," then one may deduct a prior regenerative activity of the Holy Spirit has occurred.[115] Previously in an earlier question,[116] he clarified the difference between regeneration and conversion.

Finally, after an exhaustive approach to the question of regeneration, Edwards Jr. returns to his father's third question,[117] which queries what might cause the necessity of regeneration. This question is expanded into two.[118] Necessity for regeneration is caused by total depravity.[119] This depravity, according to Gelston's notebook, is not passive but actively "opposed to every holy exercise and inclined to evil continually. [...] Unless, therefore, he be regenerated, he never can be happy."[120] Interestingly, the following

---

[111] Gelston, *A Systematic Collection*, 252.

[112] (Jr. Qs. 188).

[113] Gelston, *A Systematic Collection*, 253.

[114] (Jr. Qs. 189).

[115] Gelston, *A Systematic Collection*, 254.

[116] (Jr. Qs. 179).

[117] (Sr. Qs. 52).

[118] (Jr. Qs. 190–191).

[119] (Jr. Qs. 190).

[120] Gelston, *A Systematic Collection*, 255.

question[121] was misunderstood by Gelston, and his mentor corrected his answer with this short supplemental answer: "This question was misunderstood. It respects the acts of the soul. They are doubtless free."[122] Gelston had supposed that the physical operation of the Spirit, like the creation of Adam's soul indicated necessity rather than free agency; however, as is the case with his father's work *Freedom of the Will* the human soul is considered naturally free. The physical operation of the Spirit plants a new principle of affections out of which the soul freely does what it wants to do based on new affections.

Common and Special Grace[123]

This question clarifies theological jargon. All grace is said to be an operation of the Holy Spirit; however, special grace is the implantation of a new principle and the subsequent production of "new and holy exercises."[124] A specific and essential difference exists between the two as common grace is more general. Those movements of "awakening, convincing and reforming the sinner" may be classified as common.[125] While not directly related to his father's questions, this clarification is consistent application of his father's thoughts in *Treatise on Grace*.[126]

---

[121] (Jr. Qs. 191).

[122] See Supplement. Gelston, *A Systematic Collection*, 385.

[123] (Jr. Qs. 199).

[124] Gelston, *A Systematic Collection*, 265.

[125] Gelston, *A Systematic Collection*, 265.

[126] "[T]he phrase, *common grace,* is used to signify that kind of action or influence of the Spirit of God, to which are owing those religious or moral attainments that are common to both saints and sinners, and so signifies as much as common assistance; and sometimes those moral or religious attainments themselves that are the fruits of this assistance, are intended. So likewise the phrase, *special* or *saving* grace, is sometimes used to signify that peculiar kind or degree of operation or influence of God's Spirit, whence saving actions and attainments do arise in the godly, or, which is the same thing, special and saving assistance; or else to signify that distinguishing saving virtue itself, which is the fruit of this assistance. These phrases are more frequently understood in the latter sense, viz. not for common and special assistance, but for common and special, or saving virtue, which is the fruit of that assistance: and so I would be understood by these phrases in this discourse." Edwards, Sr., "Treatise on Grace," 153–154.

Sanctification by the Spirit[127]

Questions 61–62 are repeated by Edwards Jr. exactly, however, with addition of Scripture verses to guide a desired answer. The intent of these questions is to examine the extent of human responsibility considering the Holy Spirit's sanctifying influences. To some degree, these questions may exist to discover how much their students had absorbed his father's *Treatise on Grace*. In particular, the answer given to the first question[128] demonstrates, again, the prior work of the Holy Spirit is necessary to influence the acts of man with "a new and holy principle." These acts consist of the two great commandments written upon their hearts.[129]

Remarkably, the second question[130] deals directly with the bone of contention between Charles Hodge and Edwards Amasa Park. By directing the answerer to explain the apparent conflict latent in the command to circumcise one's heart in Ezekiel 18:36, Edwards Jr. demonstrates an awareness of how controversial his father's position on the influences of the Holy Spirit might be.[131] Rather than reframing his father's position on pneumatology in *Treatise on Grace*, he passed it along to his own students. Gelston's lengthy answer is worth hearing:

> If volition be an act of our minds, however, it be produced, it still is ours. Nothing more is necessary to make the volition wholly ours, than for us to will to put forth an act. If we were operated upon, as a machine is by mere natural powers, volition would be no duty. But this is not the case. We are influenced by arguments and motives. It is our duty, therefore; to be influenced by the most proper motives. This appears from the express command of Scripture. "Circumcise therefore, the foreskin of your heart, and be no more stiff-necked." Deut. 10:16. Here, those who are spoken to are commanded to do this, as if the act were their own, which also fully implies a duty. The same however, is said to be done by God. "And the Lord thy God will circumcise

---

[127] (Sr. Qs. 61–62; Jr. Qs. 228–230).

[128] (Jr. Qs. 228).

[129] Gelston, *A Systematic Collection*, 287.

[130] (Jr. Qs. 229).

[131] "God circumcises the heart, and we are commanded to circumcise [our hearts]. Not merely because we must use the means in order to the effect, but the effect itself is our act and our duty." Edwards Sr., "Treatise on Grace," 251.

their heart, and the heart of thy seed." [Deuteronomy] 30:16. "Cast away from you all your transgressions, whereby ye have transgressed, and make you a new heart, and a new spirit!" Ezek. 18:31. "A new heart also will I give you, and a new spirit will I put within you, and I will take away the stony heart out of your flesh, and I will give you an heart of flesh." [Deuteronomy] 36:26. From these different passages, it appears evident, that the same things are a duty and performed by those who are the subjects of the duty, as their own personal act; and yet are also said to be performed by God.[132]

This extended quotation shows Edwards Jr.'s filial duty to his father's understanding of the will having natural capacity and thus a moral responsibility to respond. It also shows how Edwards Jr. described the Spirit's role in regeneration like his father. This displays the continuity of both Edwardses on the divided aspects of regeneration, which are yet nevertheless unified, creating union with the Triune God.

The Spirit and Assurance[133]

In this series of questions, beginning with the perseverance of the saints, a conscientiousness about the Spirit's possessiveness is what makes assurance of faith possible. In the leading question,[134] the major proof of perseverance is the continuance of "the implanted principle in regeneration," which is none other than "the indwelling of the Holy Spirit as a sanctifier."[135] Assurance of one's election[136] is said to come about due to the observance of the effects of grace. By this, a person might know that "he is actually possessed of grace."[137] The last two questions in this series reveal that in Edwards Jr.'s view both the witness of the Spirit[138] and the seal of the Spirit[139] are essentially the same. The witness of the Spirit is not immediate;

---

[132] Gelston, *A Systematic Collection*, 288–289.

[133] (Jr. Qs. 266–272).

[134] (Jr. Qs. 266).

[135] Gelston, *A Systematic Collection*, 321.

[136] (Jr. Qs. 270).

[137] Gelston, *A Systematic Collection*, 326.

[138] (Jr. Qs. 271).

[139] (Jr. Qs. 272).

rather, it is mediated as if by the impression of a seal upon the Christian by those "several graces which are produced" by the Holy Spirit.[140] The distinction between mediate and immediate, again, reveals his father in the background. Edwards Sr. "had not patience with those enthusiasts who limited the testimony of the Spirit to inward, invisible, 'impractical' flashes of assurance."[141] Rather the Holy Spirit gives a temper and progressively sanctifies a person over time so that this quality comes to be viewed as "an evidence in favor of that man's good estate as infallible as the seal upon a deed is of the authenticity of that deed."[142] Edwards Jr.'s puritan ancestors might simply have called this assurance "a clear title."

These questions, which were reviewed by Edwards Jr. with his student, demonstrate a theological patriarchy. In several places, he expanded the number of questions to ensure that his father's thinking be preserved on regeneration, conversion, and sanctification. Yet, fundamental to his understanding, is the work of the Holy Spirit it create union with regenerate humanity. This close reading of Edwards Jr. of his father's theology could be missed by subsequent theologians. Due to frustration with the antics of a Charles Finney to persuade response to gospel invitation, Charles Hodge had thought he found a weakness in Edwards Sr.'s successors. While some of Edwards Sr.'s successors were less capable of holding theological tensions together, nevertheless Edwards Jr. was capable. The union Edwards Sr. found within the Trinity was thus applied in the work of regeneration by the Spirit. Edwards Jr. can be found to have shared these formulations with his students. Even in published sermons, which we will now examine, a received pneumatology can also be found.

Published 'Occasional' Sermons

While a pastor in New Haven, he published a lengthy response (1789) to the Universalism found in Dr. Charles Chauncy's *The Salvation of All Men* (1782). After his relocation to Colebrook in 1796, he submitted a *Dissertation Concerning Liberty and Necessity* (1797) in response to Samuel West's *Essays on Liberty and Necessity* (1795), written to refute Edwards Sr.'s

---

[140] Gelston, *A Systematic Collection*, 328.

[141] Conrad Cherry, *The Theology of Jonathan Edwards* (1966; repr., Indianapolis, IN: Indiana University Press, 1990), 144. Also see, Jonathan Edwards, "Charity and Its Fruits," in *Ethical Writings, Works of Jonathan Edwards*, Vol. 8, Ed. by Paul Ramsey (New Haven, CT: Yale University Press, 1957–2008), 168–170.

[142] Gelston, *A Systematic Collection*, 328.

Dissertation on the Freedom of the Will (1754). Both of these larger works demonstrate his inherited genius, yet this section will focus on the lesser known occasional sermons. So called occasional sermons were designed for potential publication and were a familiar staple through New England on fast days, thanksgiving days, and election days.[143] These sermons more directly touch on his received theology of the Spirit than the treatises. The earliest of these sermons originated at the beginning of his ministry. *Grace Evidenced by Its Fruits* (1769) was evaluated in the previous chapter; however, this sermon will now be considered for its systematic value in pneumatology. The second sermon, *All Divine Truth Profitable* (1792), was occasioned as an ordination sermon for Dan Bradley. The last two sermons were prepared for General Association meetings. The first for the Congregational churches of Connecticut in 1786 (*Christ Our Righteousness*) and second in 1794 (*God the Author of All Good Volitions and Actions*). This section will note the shared thinking on the Spirit by both father and son in these four occasional sermons, as well as a brief article in the *New York Theological Magazine*[144] on "The Promise of the Holy Spirit."

"Grace Evidenced By Its Fruits"

Prepared and preached early in Edwards Jr.'s ministry in New Haven, *Grace Evidenced By Its Fruits* bears the most similarity to *Religious Affections* on the basis several borrowed metaphors.[145] Not considered to this point, however, is how Edwards Jr. sees with his father an "infused grace" as the bond of union created by the Holy Spirit. This union is created by "a principle of divine grace." Following the pattern of empiricism, Edwards Jr. recognized how an infusion of grace will produce evidence so that others will see the splendor of the Spirit in "holy practice."[146] Edwards Sr. wrote that "if God should take away his Spirit out of the soul, all habits and acts of grace would of themselves cease as immediately as light ceases in a room when a candle is carried out."[147] Like his father, Edwards Jr. sees that the life of God is

---

[143] Harry S. Stout, *The New England Soul: Preaching and Religious Culture in Colonial New England* (New York: Oxford University Press, 1986), 27–31.

[144] *The New York Theological Magazine* was a periodical, established in 1795 by Dr. Worcester, a graduate of Dartmouth College.

[145] Please see the earlier discussion in chapter 3 for a detailed explanation of the parallels to *Religious Affections*.

[146] *JEW2*, 388.

[147] Edwards Sr., "Treatise on Grace," 196.

necessarily activity, energy, and power, so that by virtue of infusion of this divine nature, the Holy Spirit must have an observable effect. In this way, Edwards Jr. recognized the work of the Holy Spirit to produce a moral necessity by virtue of its "native tendency" toward holiness.[148] Edwards Jr. repeatedly highlighted this as an exercise of power producing a "continued series of visible and gracious fruits."[149] This "implanted" power of godliness necessarily produces fruit which are evident.[150] In dealing with the "great Christian grace [of] faith," Edwards Jr. noted a dispositional change toward truth and Christ himself as a "cordial consent." This affective change is foundational, which turns a person towards a gracious trust and love to God.[151] Throughout the remainder of the sermon, he showed how the Holy Spirit produces fruit by the bond of union created by infused grace.

"Christ Our Righteousness"

Thirteen years later Edwards Jr. prepared *Christ Our Righteousness* from 1 Corinthians 1:30 for the General Association of Connecticut. In this sermon, the Holy Spirit as bond of union is no less essential than it was in his early years of ministry. While the majority of the sermon deals with aspects of imputation, Edwards Jr. revealed his understanding of "a two-fold union which exists between Christ and believers." He termed these as *vital* and *relative*: a vital union is both real and affective; however, the second is consequential. This distinction makes clear that the vital union with God himself is also "the cordial and mutual love which subsists between Christ and all true believers. [...] He has the very spirit of Christ."[152] The use of the word *subsist* is particularly apt to describe the bond of union which exists between Father and Son as the mutual love of the Holy Spirit.

Both Oliver Crisp and Kyle Strobel recognize that "the big picture of Edwards [Sr.]'s soteriology is organized around God's movement in the Son and Spirit to call his people into his own life."[153] This makes the second distinction of a *consequential* or "relative union" important in Edwards

---

[148] *JEW2*, 388–389.

[149] *JEW2*, 391.

[150] *JEW2*, 392.

[151] *JEW2*, 393–394.

[152] *JEW2*, 259.

[153] Oliver D. Crisp and Kyle C. Stobel, *Jonathan Edwards: An Introduction to His Thought* (Grand Rapids, MI: Eerdmans, 2018), 121.

Jr.'s thinking on the work of the Spirit to create union. This description is also parallel with the non-imputation of righteousness described in his moral government theory of atonement. In other words, this relative union, which grants the resources of righteousness, is based upon association with Christ in saving union. In this distinction, one might easily miss the fine nuance on how Edwards Jr. employed the bond of union with God by the Spirit. In this case, even the application of righteousness to humanity is based upon the trinitarian relations being shared in union with humanity. Thus, Edwards Jr. is arguing that a vital union is created with humanity out of the bond of love within the Trinity. Yet, nonetheless, a believer is "as entirely distinct from Christ as from God the father or from the Holy Spirit."[154] In other words, a prior union with the Holy Spirit does not remove distinctiveness of the believer; rather, they are treated *as if* they are one. This is an important distinction when considering Edwards Jr.'s thinking on the atonement;[155] however, it shows that this application of righteousness in justification is built upon a prior understanding of intertrinitarian relations. This trinitarian nuance is fundamental to Edwards Jr.'s understanding of union and is precipitated on his father's understanding of Spirit bond of union. In other words, a bond of union does not erase distinction of person, nor does the bond of union by the Spirit do so in redeemed humanity.

"All Divine Truth Profitable"

All Divine Truth Profitable was preached at the ordination of Dan Bradley, a graduate of Yale College, on January 11, 1792 in Hamden, CT. Shortly afterward, Bradley and his wife Eunice migrated to Whitestown, NY (New Hartford near Utica in Oneida County) as a missionary-pastor in the Mohawk Valley.[156] In this sermon, Edwards Jr. challenged Bradley, as one of the first ministers of the congregational denomination in that region to "take care how he sowed," for out of a profitable doctrine he would have influence on all the neighboring settlements for generations.[157] In this lengthy sermon, Edwards Jr. spells out ten divine truths which are profitable, two of which

---

[154] *JEW2*, 261.

[155] See discussion of "as if" in terms of a legal fiction in penal theories of atonement. Crisp, "Non-Penal Substitution," 422–431.

[156] Donald Lines Jacobus, "Rev. Peter Buckley," in *The Buckley Genealogy* (New Haven, CT: Tuttle, Morehouse, and Taylor, 1933), 529.

[157] *JEW2*, 119. Ironically, according to a family genealogy, Bradley led his people to form a Presbyterian church in New Hartford, NY. He resigned after three years to take up farming, but not before performing a remarkable fifty weddings. This according to the New

are directly applicable to a received pneumatology. These two leading doctrines are *"the divine existence and character and the mode of the divine subsistence."*[158]

During the long eighteenth century, the Trinity was deemed to be unprofitable in the practice of piety, as the ancient doctrine was the source of much turmoil in the church. Yet, in this sermon, Edwards Jr. finds that the Trinity, like his puritan forefathers is the "object and foundation of all piety; and the stronger will be the motive to the inward emotions" should this doctrine be embraced.[159] First, Edwards Jr. examined the biblical evidence for Christ's divinity. Then, he argued the divinity of the Holy Spirit on the basis of the Spirit's divine epitaph in the baptismal formula and the evangelical blessing.[160] But is are these merely modalistic statements? By highlighting the problems inherent in Sabellianism, he focused on the need for doctrinal clarity on the Trinity. Clarity on the Trinity, according to Edwards Jr., is necessary for a confidence in Christ's mediatorial efficacy, and by necessary extension, the power of regeneration by the Holy Spirit.[161]

Underneath the head of "Regeneration," Edwards Jr. showed that due to total depravity, the Holy Spirit is necessary for any and all holiness. In fact, he contended that there are "no natural or stated connection between any exercises, doings or strivings of the natural man and true holiness."[162] While espousing the same view as his father, Edwards Jr. came to it indirectly by addressing the Sandemanian view of a "bare belief of the bare truth."[163]

Hartford Presbyterian Church Records. Kathy Last, "New Hartford Presbyterian Church Marriages," transcribed by the Daughters of the American Revolution. n.d. Accessed July 5, 2020. http://oneida.nygenweb.net/towns/newhartford/NHmarriages.htm.

A further irony, is that the New Hartford Presbyterian Church would host Charles Finney as a visiting revivalist during the 1820s and 30s creating the legendary "burned-over district."

[158] Emphasis Original. *JEW2*, 98–101.

[159] *JEW2*, 99. Puritan Lewes Bayly's (d. 1631) influential *Practice of Piety* was one of the most reprinted works on spirituality and influential in John Bunyan's spiritual development. This book begins with about sixty pages devoted to the Trinity. See Philip Dixon, Nice and Hot Disputes: The Doctrine of the Trinity in the Seventeenth Century (London: T&T Clark, 2003), 6–11.

[160] *JEW2*, 99.

[161] Ibid., 100–101, 109.

[162] Ibid., 110.

[163] Michael A. G. Haykin, "Andrew Fuller and the Sandemanian Controversy" in *'At the Pure Fountain of Thy Word': Andrew Fuller as an Apologist*, ed. Michael A. G. Haykin (Carlise, England: Paternoster Press, 2004), 226. Edwards Jr. describes Sandemanism as "the bare light and motives exhibited in the gospel," in "Remarks on the Improvements Made in Theology by his Father, President Edwards," in *JEW1*, 491.

Edwards Jr. emphatically denied that regeneration is simply having in one's possession "proper information" or even a "supernatural and merely intellectual light" apart from holy affection. The light necessary cannot come through the intellect but passes into the heart through "the immediate influence of the Holy Spirit."[164]

On the whole, Edwards Jr. is charitable of what this immediate influence might consist. In his charitable approach, he outlined three ways of looking at regeneration, which are within the main of the supernatural influence of the Holy Ghost to produce "holy acts, emotions or affections in the heart."[165] While conscious of a variety of ways the same truth could be articulated, he revealed his position by arguing that "a *physical* influence" (or, in his father's vocabulary, infusion), is not less inconsistent with liberty.[166] A master of definition, Edwards Jr. also differentiated regeneration from conversion.[167] To both Edwardses, regeneration occurs on the passive subject; whereas, in the act of conversion a man is active. In his father's *Treatise on Grace*, regeneration and conversion are the two agreeing acts by which "God is the only proper fountain; we only are the proper actors. We are in different respects wholly passive and wholly active."[168] Both Edwardses recognize the tension and found a unity in them.

"God the Author of All Good Volitions and Actions"

Edwards Jr. very directly argued that the Spirit is the immediate cause of new affections and actions in a sermon preached two years later. *God the Author of All Good Volitions and Actions* (1794) was preached before the General Association, where he stated that "all morally good dispositions are implanted in the heart in regeneration." Out of Philippians 2:13 Edwards Jr.

---

[164] *JEW2*, 111.

[165] These three ways to articulate regeneration fall upon a spectrum: 1) an implanted principle in the heart that has existed much prior to the observation of affections, 2) immediate observable affections in consequence of implantation, 3) no new principle is implanted; however, the Holy Spirit immediately produces affections. Ibid., 110.

[166] Emphasis original. *JEW2*, 111–113. Edwards Jr. describes his father's articulation of regeneration as a tightening up of what had been a fairly loose understanding of the process of salvation. But, all in all, "regeneration consists in the *communication of a new spiritual sense or taste*. In other words, a new heart is given. This communication is made, this work is accomplished, by the Spirit of God," in Remarks on the Improvements Made in Theology by his Father, President Edwards," *JEW1*, 491.

[167] *JEW2*, 110.

[168] Edwards, "Treatise on Grace," 251.

argues that God's working is not only that of simple goodness of heart, but that which is sufficient "to do" according to his good pleasure. This is not simply arbitrary unpredictability, rather, while God is absolutely supreme, he always acts consistently with the general good of his "moral system" and the ends for which he has created the world.[169] Apart from this explicit allusion to the Holy Spirit being implanted in regeneration, the rest of the sermon discusses how the "implanting" of the Spirit does not destroy agency, freedom, or accountability. Freedom of the will, of course, is a topic relevant to Spirit's work of regeneration.

"The Promise of the Holy Spirit"

In an article submitted to the *New York Theological Magazine*, Edwards Jr. describes what a person means when they ask for the Holy Spirit in Luke 9:13. Most simply, according to Edwards Jr., the Father responds to the implanted desires of the Spirit which reside in the human heart. To arrive at this conclusion, in this short piece, he depicted regeneration from the opposite but complementary perspective of conversion. Edwards Jr. began by making the case that God is in truth ready to give his Holy Spirit to the unregenerate provided that the object of the request is "to be sanctified, to be made holy, to be delivered from the dominion and from the love of sin, and to become the subject of the love of holiness and true virtue."[170] He observed that a person is wholly to blame should they ask with impure motive and thus not receive the Holy Spirit. A person remains unconverted because he does not have appropriate desires and therefore evidences his unregenerate heart. By asking out of a selfish desire, they are asking without a sincere love to God, true repentance, and ultimately, a lack of faith.[171] So, from the equal but opposite perspective articulated by his father's *Treatise on Grace*, there is no conversion because there has been no implanting of the Holy Spirit. While unstated in the article, the necessary conclusion would be that the Father must give what is asked for, which is, a new spiritual sense or taste for God himself through the gift of the Holy Spirit. In this short, and pithy article, Edwards Jr. reinforces his father's perspective on physical implanting of the Holy Spirit as prerequisite to the exercise of holy desire.

---

[169] *JEW2*, 349–350.

[170] *JEW2*, 469.

[171] *JEW2*, 470–471.

Unpublished Weekly Sermons

Jonathan Edwards Jr.'s consistency with his father's pneumatology is most readily seen in the unpublished weekly sermons before his people in New Haven and Colebrook. Through the years, Edwards Jr. stayed consistent in how he thought about the person and work of the Holy Spirit, as this section will demonstrate.

"2 Peter 2:22, August 1766"

The earliest extant sermon by Edwards Jr., prepared under the guidance of Joseph Bellamy in Bethlehem, CT during August 1766, indirectly refers to the Spirit's work to create an appetite for virtue and holiness. In comparing hypocrites to pigs and dogs (2 Peter 2:22), Edwards showed how natural it is for unbelievers to "act out their very nature in sinning [...]" as

> they feel an entire complacency in sin considered in itself, so that nothing can please them better; they are also in their very element while they are practicing all manner of wickedness, and every abominable thing. They have not taste, bias, or inclination for virtue and holiness; but their whole souls are corrupted; they run greedily in the way of sin, without any disrelish toward it, but with an entire and absolute relish, and satisfaction.[172]

Yet, most do not act out and refrain from "all kinds of open sins," not because they lack a "taste and inclination for them,"[173] rather, something outside is keeping them from their natural disposition. Toward the end of the sermon, he concludes "the necessity of true grace; or something beyond these external reformations, legal repentance and terrors of conscience, viz. repentance towards God; and faith towards our Lord Jesus Christ, or what is meant by the general scriptures name charity or love; universal love of God and his creatures."[174] In his article in *William and Mary Quarterly*, Mark Valeri misses the significant spiritual conclusion at the end of this very sermon suggesting that moral law is Edwards Jr.'s main focus.[175] Yet, in

---

[172] Jonathan Edwards Jr., "Sermon 3. 2 Peter 2.22.," *Jonathan Edwards Jr. Papers (Sermons)*, Hartford Seminary Library (Box 165, Folder 2725), 7.

[173] Edwards Jr., "Sermon 3. 2 Peter 2.22.," 9.

[174] Edwards Jr., "Sermon 3. 2 Peter 2.22.," 28–29.

[175] Mark Valeri, "The New Divinity and the American Revolution," *The William and Mary Quarterly*, vol. 46, no. 4 (Oct 1989), 754, n23.

actuality, these are metonymy to describe the influences of the Holy Spirit. Rather than lead his listener to moralism, Edwards Jr. is drawing the listener to respond to the conviction of the Holy Spirit. In a helpless position of spiritual depravity, "true grace" or "charity or love" is critically necessary, and the invitation to respond to the conviction of the Spirit is given in the application of the sermon.

"Philippians 1:18, January 1767"

Prior to his installation in New Haven, Edwards Jr. filled the pulpit as a potential candidate, preaching from Philippians 1:18 on the following theme: "That when Christ is preached, it is ground of joy to all good men."[176] After pointing out how the preaching of the gospel is the foundation on which joy is brought to desperate people, he developed how happiness is "proportionally increased" as one observes that the "true interest of others [is] promoted." He argues that the "general principle of benevolence" is meant to be universally shared and enjoyed proportionally, that is on an ever-increasing scale by intellectual beings.[177] This scalable joy through the preaching of the gospel is not only "according to the divine constitution," but also a necessary prerequisite to "the transcendent beauty and excellency, and glory of all these [...] to all holiness."[178]

Edwards Jr. followed his father in describing how the knowledge of Christ is communicated. This knowledge is spiritual and is communicated by the Holy Spirit through preaching as a "saving understanding." Specifically, this saving understanding "is the same thing, [as] a principle of holiness or true virtue."[179] After accumulating a variety of Scriptural proofs, he concluded that

> the true knowledge of Christ and his gospel, or true wisdom and holiness, being such an excellent, precious, beatific endowment, no wonder if benevolent principle reigning in the hearts of all good men, which seeks and rejoices in the happiness of all intelligences; no wonder, I say, that this principle is gratified, and so they made to rejoice in the prospect of such bliss to men in the

---

[176]Jonathan Edwards Jr., "Sermon V. Phil. 1.18 Composed at Princeton, Jan. 1767.," *Jonathan Edwards Jr. Papers (Sermons)*, Hartford Seminary Library (Box 165, Folder 2725), 3–4.

[177]Edwards Jr., "Sermon V. Phil. 1.18," 10.

[178]Edwards Jr., "Sermon V. Phil. 1.18," 12.

[179]Edwards Jr., "Sermon V. Phil. 1.18," 14.

preaching of Christ as the necessary and proper mean for that end. Surely a man, whose nature it is to rejoice in the happiness of others when he has a prospect of their becoming possessed of the greatest, and only true happiness, that is to be enjoyed upon the earth, will rejoice with exceeding joy.[180]

While the Spirit is not named directly here in this sermon, the words *endowment* and *benevolent principle* describe the regenerative work and evidence of the Holy Spirit who alone provides true wisdom, holiness, and a beatific vision of joy and happiness.

While Edwards Jr. could at times descend into metaphysics, as this sermon demonstrates, he does so only to develop the overall message in relationship to "the benevolent principle." This *benevolent principle* is a categorical term, which not only refers to the characteristic of divinity, but also refers to the Holy Spirit. In the Improvement section of the sermon, he states that "if we have one spark of that true, generous, noble-Spirited benevolence, in which all true virtue primarily and essentially consists, or in other words, [then] we have the least degree of holiness or true grace in our hearts."[181] Edwards Jr. also states that the Holy Spirit is "conferring upon men the greatest and only true happiness to be enjoyed on earth; of conferring upon them eternal happiness hereafter, and of advancing the glory of God."[182] In the exhortation, he encourages those who have been indwelt by the Spirit, to "indulge your benevolent souls to the full. Rejoice in the Lord, rejoice in the Lord always" as the gospel is preached.[183]

"Revelation 22:17, October 15, 1769"

After his installation in New Haven, and just a few weeks after the church he inherited split, he preached from the last clause of Revelation 22:17 "And whosoever will, let him take of the water of life freely."[184] In this sermon, he proposed that if the referent of "water of life" could be determined, then the meaning of the verse would be unlocked. Noted earlier in the context is

---

[180] Edwards Jr., "Sermon V. Phil. 1.18," 16–17.

[181] Edwards Jr., "Sermon V. Phil. 1.18," 28.

[182] Edwards Jr., "Sermon V. Phil. 1.18," 26–27.

[183] Edwards Jr., "Sermon V. Phil. 1.18," 32.

[184] See appendix 2 for a full transcript of this sermon. Jonathan Edwards Jr., "Volume 79. Rev. 22:17 [Last Clause] Oct. 15, 1769," *Jonathan Edwards Jr. Papers (Sermons)*, Hartford Seminary Library (Box 165, Folder 2728).

the pure river of life proceeding out of the throne of God and of the Lamb. Moving on from this observation, Edwards Jr. used *analogia Scripturea* from John 7:37–39 and Isaiah 44:3 to solve his advertised riddle.[185] From both of these texts, he concluded that the water of life refers specifically to the Holy Spirit who is "the grand and highest blessing, or rather, as the sum of all the blessedness bestowed on true saints." From Luke 11:13 the Spirit is described as the "grand gift," that is "the great reward," bestowed upon the Son to be given to "whosoever will" ask.[186]

This exegesis is not necessarily original, but the parallelism to his father's exegesis is clear. Edwards Jr. used his father's superlative 'the sum of all blessedness'[187] as a descriptive reference for the Holy Spirit.[188] However, in spite of this potential common phrase, Edwards Jr. showed continuity with his father in that described the Holy Spirit as "the spiritual good which Christ hath purchased, consisting not only of divine communications in this world; but especially in the inconceivable and unutterable joys of the world to come."[189] Note how the Spirit who is "the sum" is stated to be that which is purchased by Christ. The association of Spirit with "the thing purchased" is nearly identical to how his father referred to the Spirit in the *Discourse on the Trinity*.[190]

Further into this sermon, partaking of the Holy Spirit is said to be a measure of how "he is communicated in the world of light. In this consists

---

[185] Edwards Jr., "Volume 79," 2–3.

[186] Edwards Jr., "Volume 79," 4.

[187] In England Edwards Jr.'s friend John Ryland uses this phrase as well in his exegesis of Luke 11:13. According to Michael Haykin, "[t]here is a similarity of tone between [Ryland] ... Whitefield and Griffiths" as well. See "'The Sum of All Good': John Ryland, Jr. and the Doctrine of the Holy Spirit," *Churchman*, Vol. 103, No. 4 (Oct 1989): 332–353, 341.

[188] "The Spirit of God is the chief of the blessings, that are the subject matter of Christian prayer; for it is the sum of all spiritual blessings; which are those that we need infinitely more than all others, and are those wherein our true and eternal happiness consists. That which is the sum of the blessings that Christ purchased, is the sum of the blessings that Christians have to pray for; but that, as was observed before, is the Holy Spirit: and therefore when the disciples came to Christ, and desired him to teach them to pray (Luke 11), and he accordingly gave them particular directions for the performance of this duty." Jonathan Edwards Sr., "An Humble Attempt," in *Apocalyptic Writings, Works of Jonathan Edwards*, vol. 5, ed. Stephen J. Stein (New Haven, CT: Yale University Press, 1957–2008), 347.

[189] See note 85 above. Edwards Jr., "Volume 79," 5–6; in another sermon on Ezekiel 18:21 he equates Christ and Spirit as purchasing the pardon. Jonathan Edwards Jr., "Vol. 170., Ezek. 18.21., June 30, 1771," *Jonathan Edwards and Calvin Chapin Papers*, Beinecke Rare Book and Manuscript Library (Box 1, Folder 1), 1–8, 6.

[190] Edwards Sr., "Discourse on the Trinity," 137–138.

the joys of heaven."[191] In other words, while the same kind of pleasure and enjoyment is communicated, nevertheless it must be to a "lesser degree" due to the indwelling principle of sin.[192] Edwards Jr. expounded his doctrine as "eternal life, with its joys, and foretastes of it in this world are freely offered to everyone who will accept of them [them]." Through the remainder of the sermon, he argued along the lines of the Edwardsean doctrine of moral and natural necessity and calls for response to the gracious call of the gospel from the heart.

"John 3, Various Dates"

Early on in his ministry, Edwards Jr. seemed to be concerned that his flock was unaware of the supernatural work of the Holy Spirit in regeneration. So, he developed several sermons from John 3.[193] In an early 1770 sermon from John 3:6 he distinguished the new birth as necessarily distinct from the depravity inherent in the flesh. From Romans 8:7 he defined the new birth in contrast to the carnally minded. Spiritually minded people have by necessity "a temper of holiness" implanted within.[194] Since the human condition prior to new birth is one of spiritual deadness, "the first thing is a principle of life [which] then follow *actions*."[195] Following his father's earlier articulation of Spirit implantation, Edwards Jr. described the divine act of regeneration as that which is necessary to all other acts as the principle of life.[196] "The principle of life" is another Edwardsean catchphrase for the Holy Spirit's regenerative work; however, it comes from the deep reservoir of the old puritans.

In the 1770 version of the sermon from John 3, Edwards Jr. quoted at length from John Flavel, Samuel Willard, and Joseph Alliene, but first he argued that the principle of life produces temperamental changes. First,

---

[191] Edwards Jr., "Volume 79," 10.

[192] Edwards Jr., "Volume 79," 11.

[193] (1) Jonathan Edwards Jr., "Volume 95. Joh. 3.6., Feb. 18, 1770," *Jonathan Edwards Jr. Papers (Sermons)*, Hartford Seminary Library (Box 165, Folder 2728), 1–31.; (2) Jonathan Edwards Jr., "Volume 147. Joh. 3.5., Feb. 3, 1771," *Jonathan Edwards Jr. Papers (Sermons)*, Hartford Seminary Library (Box 165, Folder 2730), 1–9; (3) Jonathan Edwards Jr., "Vol. 189., Joh. 3.8., Sepr. 22. 1771.," *Jonathan Edwards Jr. Papers (Sermons)*, Hartford Seminary Library (Box 166, Folder 2731), 1–8.

[194] Edwards Jr., "Volume 95," 1–3. Also, in Edwards Jr., "Volume 147," 5.

[195] Edwards Jr., "Volume 95," 4.

[196] See earlier discussion on physical infusion and the "principle of life which acts" from his widely quoted *Charity and Its Fruits*. Edwards Sr., "Charity," 298.

sinners are reconciled in their minds toward "the brightest glories" of God. Those qualities of God which ought to attract had formerly "disgusted" him like holiness and truth.[197] Out of the awareness of God's holiness comes a sensitivity toward his own sinfulness. This process of growing humility causes a person to "desire nothing so much as to be delivered from it [iniquities]—not only from the punishment but [also] the power of it."[198] The principle of life creates the conditions "whereby the mind is prepared to receive and close with Christ." The conditions for conversion to occur necessitate a birth of life, that is, the implanted principle of life.

Three quotes from John Flavel occurring in this sermon are derived from the 1754 edition of *The Whole Works of the Reverend Mr. John Flavel [...] in Two Volumes*. Out of this immense collection, Edwards Jr. refers to "Sermon 5: Opening that Work of the Spirit more particularly, by which the Soul is enabled to apply Christ." By quoting the primary doctrine of Flavel's sermon, which references "the supernatural principle of life," Edwards Jr. showed that he stands in line, not only with his father's "Divine and Supernatural Light" but also with the Puritans.[199] Edwards Jr. reasoned on the basis of Flavel's argument that cause and effect in nature demonstrate a spiritual cause and effect. Reflecting on this argument, Edwards Jr. proposed that some might suppose then that on the basis of justification "in time" that death might perchance short-circuit the regeneration process of those for whom Christ died. Edwards Jr. showed that Flavel puts to silence this object by saying regeneration is more a "priority of nature, than of time, the nature and order of the work requiring it to be so."[200] In other words, regeneration is more about change of the heart's nature, than it is of time sequence.

To Flavel is added Samuel Willard's prestige as "an eminent divine of the last century, who lived at Boston."[201] Willard, who had served as the acting president of Harvard and pastor of Boston's Third Church, produced *A Compleat [sic] Body of Divinity in Two Hundred and Fifty Expository Lectures*

---

[197] Edwards Jr., "Volume 95," 3.

[198] Edwards Jr., "Volume 95," 5.

[199] "Doct. That those souls which have union with Christ, are quickened with a supernatural principle of life by the Spirit of God in order thereunto." Edwards Jr., "Volume 95," 22. See John Flavel, "Sermon V: Opening that Work of the Spirit more particularly, by which the Soul is enabled to apply Christ," in *The Whole Works of the Reverend Mr. John Flavel, Late Minister of the Gospel at Dartmouth in Devon, in Two Volumes* (Glasgow, Scotland: John Orr, 1754), 178–183, 179.

[200] Edwards Jr., "Volume 95," 9–10; Flavel, "Sermon V," 182.

[201] Edwards Jr., "Volume 95," 10–11.

on the Assembly's Shorter Catechism. On the thirty-first question, "What is Effectual Calling," Edwards Jr. points to life creates the conditions "whereby the mind is prepared to receive and close which the necessity of a change "wrought, by creating a new principle of saving grace in the will and affections."[202] This regenerating work of the Holy Spirit restores the mind so that the will "closes in with that light [...]. He never gives a new Understanding, but a new Will with it." This process is "infused at once."[203]

By quoting Willard, Edwards Jr. maintained that the immediacy of regeneration is created by the supernatural light of the Holy Spirit. Light by itself is not sufficient as some would suggest the process of conviction is enough; however, conviction is insufficient to produce a saving faith, no matter how helpful. To this point, Edwards Jr. illustrated the problem by showing how Sandemanians taught that one is "regenerated by light [in a way which is] not by the immediate agency of God." Edwards Jr. then moves to describe the difference between active and passive conversion, again from Willard. "Thus is the work wrought in the Soul which belongs to passive conversion and by it the grace of faith, together with all other graces is implanted in the man." This Edwards Jr. characterized as passive regeneration; whereas, active conversion is the result.[204]

Moving from the distinction between passive regeneration and active conversion, he claimed the need to distinguish these two from one another as regeneration is necessarily instantaneous.[205] Many fall into the error of describing regeneration as "a gradual thing" in which a person is awakened and then "by and by enter into covenant, and then all done. But when [were they] converted?"[206] According to Edwards Jr., either extraordinary experience or protracted conviction over two or three months does not constitute

---

[202] Edwards Jr., "Volume 95," 22–23.

[203] Edwards Jr., "Volume 95," 24. Edwards Jr. crosses out the words "without the Spirit" after regeneration. So, we should understand immediate agency of God as a reference to the Holy Spirit's work. Also, In this quotation, Edwards Jr. footnotes these as coming from pages 155 and 156 of Willard's Body of Divinity; however, in actuality, they come from pages 455 and 456. This mistake is repeated several times by not fully making a numerical four. Samuel Willard, *A Compleat [sic] Body of Divinity in Two Hundred and Fifty Expository Lectures on the Assembly's Shorter Catechism* (Boston: Green, Kneeland, and Elliot, 1726).

[204] Edwards Jr., "Volume 95," 9–10.; Willard, *Body of Divinity,* 456.

[205] In another sermon about a year later: "The immediate effect—these exercises—in this operation of God reconciled. [With the enmity slain then a new world [comes] into view. [You are then able to see] everything in a new light [because] a new eye [is] given [...] all [gospel and Christ are seen] in a most glorious light" Edwards Jr., "Volume 147.," 2–3.

[206] Edwards Jr., "Volume 95," 25–26.

conversion or regeneration. Conviction can occur over months or years; however, "the other [regeneration/conversion occurs] in a moment."[207] Returning to Flavel, Edwards Jr. builds his case to a crescendo by saying that "this infusion of spiritual life is done instantaneously; as all creation work is. [...] Even as it in the infusion of the rational soul, the body is long ere it be prepared and molded, but when it is prepared and ready, it is quickened with the Spirit of life in an instant."[208] Earlier in the sermon, and along similar lines, Joseph Alleine's *An Admonition to Unconverted Sinners* is appealed to as support for a *divine* light necessary for regeneration. "Without the application of the Spirit in regeneration we can have no saving interest in the benefits of redemption."[209]

In the *Improvement* section of his sermon, Edwards Jr. offered the following pithy line for his parishioners to take home and ponder: "faith [is] a vital act [which] supposes a vital principle."[210] This assertion, which he had defended throughout the sermon, follows his father's observation that vital act and vital principle are necessarily complementary. Without directly saying so, Edwards Jr. is presenting key points from his father's philosophical treatise *The Freedom of the Will*. According to Paul Ramsey, Locke began the process of deconstructing the divide between understanding and the will, whereas Edwards Sr. "abolished" the divide.[211] In other words, the will and the understanding cannot ever really oppose one another in regard to the same perception of thought. This philosophical 'non-distinction' ought to be born in mind when considering Charles Hodge's claim that the heirs of Edwards had distorted Edwards. In one respect, Hodge's claim is correct regarding certain heirs like Charles Finney. Finney had indeed minimized the philosophical nuance of the vital principle necessary in regeneration.

By collapsing the divide initiative in favor of human psychology, Finney tipped the argument in favor of human self-sufficiency. Yet, on the other hand, Hodge's claim that the heirs of Edwards wrongly represent their mentor is overstated due to Edwards's observation of how humanity responds to divine light. A divine and supernatural light 'physically infused' may

---

[207] Edwards Jr., "Volume 95," 26.

[208] Edwards Jr., "Volume 95," 26–27.; Flavel, "Sermon V," 181.

[209] Joseph Alleine, *An Admonition to Unconverted Sinners; in a Serious Treatise* (London: Millar, Law and Cater; and Wilson, Spense, and Mawman, 1793), 57.; quoted from an earlier but unknown edition of Alleine in Edwards Jr., "Volume 95," 11–12.

[210] Edwards Jr., "Volume 95," 29. See similar in Edwards, *Religious Affections*, 201.

[211] Jonathan Edwards, *Freedom of the Will* (1754), in *Works of Jonathan Edwards*, vol. 1, ed. Paul Ramsey (New Haven, CT: Yale University Press, 1957–2008), 50.

indeed be observable in the conversion of a human soul. In other words, Edwards's heirs, especially his namesake, who were well-versed in *Religious Affections* and *Freedom of the Will,* were articulating along the lines of their theological mentor.[212] Familiarity with these works caused them to posit divine sovereignty as necessarily prior to the observable human response. This means that the Holy Spirit was "a vital principle" necessary so that the human will might move toward response.

Yet, according to Edwards Jr., this moral necessity does not displace human responsibility or "duty to repent and believe."[213] To show this unabating responsibility, he argued from the opposite starting point that the will is still free. Edwards Jr. shows how a drunkard will not do what he doesn't want to do. In other words, he will not break off drunkenness because he chooses otherwise which on the one hand demonstrates depravity, and on the other, ought to cause him to move toward "self-abasement." Instead of humility and contrition, his innate depravity increases actual and felt guilt.[214] Felt guilt, instead of producing humility increases pride, exacerbating actual guilt. Choosing to remain a drunkard or a sluggard increases the need for "true light."[215]

About a year later, Edwards Jr. prepared another message from his earlier exegesis of John 3. This sermon accents the principle of grace necessary to cause one to be born again of the Spirit. After describing a new temper imbedded in a person, he maintained that this does not occur "from instruction and cultivation." Light is not enough, nor the "common influences of the Spirit."[216] Edwards Jr. heightened the need for response to conviction while at the same time paying recognition that conviction is a kind of common grace. Conviction, as a common grace, ought not be confused with a special grace which is "positively by the supernatural agency of God—sending his Holy Spirit to act, live and abide." To show that this positive movement is more than common, he showed from John 1:13 and 1 John 3:9 that from time to time the Scriptures will interchange the agency of new birth between God and the Holy Spirit, thus elevating

---

[212] In another sermon, from this text, he described the Holy Spirit along the lines of those biblical metaphors in *Religious Affections* such as a fountain and a fire. To these examples, the Holy Spirit's vital action is described as "a principle of grace—or a foundatation of holy exercises and affections." Edwards Jr., "Volume 147.," 2.

[213] Edwards Jr., "Volume 95," 30.

[214] Edwards Jr., "Volume 95," 30–32.

[215] Edwards Jr., "Volume 95," 31.

[216] Edwards Jr., "Volume 147.," 5.

the new birth above that of common grace.[217] So, from this difference, he pointed to the special work of the Spirit as significantly different from the gradual conviction of the Spirit. The special work of Spirit implantation is an instantaneous "turning point."[218] In his doctrinal *Improvement*, he highlighted the necessity of the Holy Spirit in order to persevere and produce fruit. The divine nature dwells so that "all the exercises of grace [are] fruits of the Spirit [and must be] all by the gift of the Sprit."[219]

Many years later (June 1800), and toward the end of his life, Edwards Jr. returned to John 3 to preach the necessity of regeneration again.[220] This late manuscript demonstrates that through his nearly thirty-year pulpit ministry Edwards Jr.'s basic understanding of the Spirit's work remained consistent. For example, in noting what the phrase born again means, he was emphatic that it must be more than reformation of morals, nor simply the awakening conviction of the Spirit. Joy in religious activity is insufficient as new birth has to be an "essential change of the heart."[221] This essential change of heart moves a person from depravity to sanctification, from sin to holiness, so that the heart is submissive and filled with love for God whom they can now perceive.[222] The agent of regeneration is clearly ascribed to the Holy Spirit: "God by his Holy Spirit [...] is the efficient cause [that] confers no new faculty, but a disposition to use aright the faculties already [possessed]." Like his earlier sermon, nearly thirty years earlier, he preserved his position on how Spirit's action is a necessary consequence so that "the man himself becomes active [and] actively turns to God" in repentance, reconciliation, and faith.[223]

Conclusion

Wanting to be in step with the Spirit's reviving work, while defending traditional Calvinism, Edwards's students sharpened their mentor's thinking on

---

[217] Edwards Jr., "Volume 147.," 5–6.

[218] Edwards Jr., "Volume 147.," 6.

[219] Edwards Jr., "Volume 147.," 8.

[220] Jonathan Edwards Jr., "[No number] At Schenectady, Wednesday at The Hill, June 1800, John III.7.," *Andover Newton Miscellaneous Personal Papers Collection, Jonathan Edwards, Jr.*, Yale Divinity Library (RG 295, Box 168, Folder 4): 1–8.

[221] Edwards Jr., "At Schenectady," 2.

[222] Edwards Jr., "At Schenectady," 1–2.

[223] Edwards Jr., "[No number] At Schenectady," 4.

the Spirit. The wide variety of evidence collected in the areas of systematic theology, occasional sermons, as well as weekly sermons demonstrate that Edwards Jr.'s was a faithful inheritor of his father's pneumatology. Through the mentoring of theologians like Maltby Gelston, Edwards Sr.'s legacy can be seen as lasting into at least the early nineteenth century. While Edwards Sr. wrote several treatises, which advanced his pneumatologically focus, Edwards Jr.'s major writings on atonement and the will, often distract scholars from the common bond that does exist between father and son in their thinking on the Holy Spirit. While there were adaptations of Edwards Sr.'s pneumatology by later revivalists like Charles Finney, yet Hodge's claim that Edwards Jr. broke the flow of the Edwardsean tradition on regeneration cannot be maintained. Edwards Sr.'s thinking on the Spirit shows up in the younger Edwards's mentoring of preachers, theological writing, and pulpit ministry. Edwards Jr. is himself a forgotten Edwardsean resource.

Chapter 5

Conclusion: In Step with the Spirit

THE EDWARDSEAN INFLUENCE upon his "New Divinity" followers was extensive. The emphasis on the Spirit in Edwards Sr.'s writings was shared broadly throughout New England. The New England Theology preserved by men like Jonathan Edwards Jr. became a repository for the reformed ministers to participate in the political conflict with Britain. Gradually, a desire for the glory of God and benevolence also sowed seeds for the coming abolition movement.[1] Even in "Old England" prominent evangelical Calvinists like Andrew Fuller, John Ryland, William Carey, and John Erskine had expressed an appreciation for the New England Theology.[2] In a letter on March 16, 1787 to his friend, John Ryland Jr. across the sea, Edwards Jr. spoke of the influence of his father and Dr. Bellamy's writings in his state:

> I believe a majority of the ministers in Connecticut, mean to be on the plan of my father and Dr. Bellamy: and most of the young ministers and students in divinity are inclined to that plan. There have been several places during the late war, and since

---

[1] New Divinity leadership of Edwards Jr. and Samuel Hopkins did much to create an abolitionist spirit in New England ahead of the Civil War. Unbeknownst to Jonathan Edwards Jr., a fateful passing of a sermon to Owen Brown, the father of John Brown, would cause Edwards Jr. to be responsible, although indirectly, for the start of the civil war. Owen Brown was persuaded of abolitionism after reading a published sermon of Jonathan Edwards Jr on the matter. Brown's account of reading Jonathan Edwards Jr's sermon is preserved in his own words. John Brown, *John Brown Liberator of Kansas and Martyr of Virginia: Life and Letters,* 4th edition; ed. by F. B. Sanborn (Cedar Rapids, IA: The Torch Press, 1910), 11.

[2] In England the "New England Theology" was called "The American Theology." Edwards Amasa Park, "The New England Theology," *Biliotheca Sacra* 9 (1852), 174–175.

the war, general religious Awakenings, which have terminated in the hopeful conversion of a goodly number.[3]

In this brief excerpt is found not only a picture of Edwards Jr. attempt to keep in step with his father's divinity, but also a sincere desire for the Holy Spirit to be poured out on New England again. Within a few years, he would participate along with Timothy Dwight and others, in the early rains of the Second Great Awakening in the late 1790s.

Through this research, Edwards Jr. seems to be vindicated a faithful inheritor of his father's pneumatology, not only in his mentoring, but also in his occasional and weekly sermons. Both men were thoroughly sensitive to the Holy Spirit in their youth and both became prominent scholars. Both father and son were men who were devoted to the religion of the heart, even though they were both gifted with such a strong intellect. When Tryon Edwards recounts that his grandfather's "preaching became less metaphysical and argumentative, and more experimental and tender,"[4] he likely alludes to the pastoral struggles he had with Ebenezer Beardeslee in New Haven. Yet, the evidence demonstrates that a transition to Colebrook did not necessarily change the style or content of his preaching. Indeed, multiple manuscripts bear record of their provenience in New Haven and their reuse in Colebrook. While certainly a person's disposition in preaching can change with a new context and a fresh audience, the primary documents show a remarkable consistency throughout his twenty-nine years of preaching. His doctrinal content and dependence upon the Holy Spirit seemed to have remained the same.

Much of the mid-nineteenth century biography of Edwards Jr. tends to be skewed toward the mood of the nation in the mid-nineteenth century. Nathan Hatch showed how the nineteenth century moved to embrace a Jacksonian philosophy of individualism. This shift produced strong fractures in the old clerical authority that Edwards Jr. would have assumed.[5] The seeds of this anti-clericalism were very present in Edwards Jr.'s own White Haven Church in the generation that preceded him and bloomed again in his own ministry. Coupled with the pressures of a post-Revolution inflationary

---

[3] Jonathan Edwards Jr., letter to John Ryland Jr., March 16, 1787, *Edwards Family Correspondence, Jonathan Edwards 1745–1801 Outgoing Letters,* Beinecke Rare Book and Manuscript Library (GEN MSS 152 Box 1, Folder 3), 4–5.

[4] Tryon Edwards, "Memoir," in *JEW1*, xxxii.

[5] Nathan Hatch, *The Democratization of American Christianity* (New Haven, CT: Yale University Press, 1989), 208–209.

crisis and a westward land boom, these and other pressures affected every church in Connecticut. Edwards Jr. was not exempt from these issues. Loss and suffering, especially early in one's life, can also contribute to one's personality. Pushing through the trauma of the frontier violence, loss of nuclear family to the pox, and his young wife to drowning could impress upon on others a kind of austerity. Yet, in spite of these challenges, those who knew him well understood that he battled the perfectionist tendency and that he was yet affable and gentle.

There is much more work that can be done in the comparative theology of Edwards Jr. Since his personal mission seems to have been to preserve his father's legacy, a case could be made that he did not change his father's view of penal atonement theory to a great degree. In particular, more study could be done to discover how Edwards the younger refined his father's trinitarianism and atonement theory so as to safeguard the historic Calvinistic penal substitution theory from the reaches of antinomianism and incipient Arminianism. The younger Edwards, like his father, was more than capable of holding two seemingly contradictory elements in view and reconciling them in a way that others after could not. And while this volume cannot begin to explore this method in atonement thinking, the potential for further study is now justified.

Again, while Edwards Jr. is more well-known for his governmental atonement theory, or his apologetic works against Universalism, these should not distract scholars from the younger Edwards's concern for the Spirit which *pervades* his unpublished sermons. Specifically, this research has attempted to show that Edwards Jr. was a worthy successor, contrary to the inherited caricature, in the reception of an Edwardsean pneumatology. If not the direct object of his effort in the printing press, the younger knew how necessary the Spirit was for true religion to flourish in his congregation and in his own theological production.

APPENDIX 1

THE NATURE OF EDWARDS JR.'S SERMON MANUSCRIPTS

The older established method[1] of verse-by-verse exposition through paragraphs was not Edwards Jr.'s typical approach; rather, he characteristically arranged a sermon around a single verse text or phrase and on the rare occasion strung two or three verses together. In reference to his father's sermonic pattern Owen Strachan observes how Edwards Sr. characteristically "focused his attention on a single phrase or sentence in the Bible." In his otherwise excellent essay, Strachan neglects to mention the more prominent mentor behind Edwards Sr.'s style.[2] Following the recommendations of Peter van Mastricht, both father and son produced dense expositions of otherwise very sparse texts.

A small slice of text would be selected each week, and an exposition of the next passage or verse on the following week was rare. Normally several seasons would pass before he would touch upon the same chapter, let alone the next verse. One notable exception occurred during his first year

---

[1] In Harry Stout's *The New England Soul*, a survey of five generations (1600–1776) of sermons in New England, he describes how preachers would economize their study for two to three speaking engagements in a week by the 'sermon series.' That is, "instead of selecting scattered texts that would vary widely in theme and subject matter from week to week, they preferred to take a chapter or book of Scripture for long-term study, a verse at a time. Sometimes a single verse could occupy their attention for many weeks." Harry S. Stout, *The New England Soul: Preaching and Religious Culture in Colonial New England* (New York: Oxford University Press, 1986), 34.

[2] Owen Strachan, "Of Scholars and Saints: A Brief History of the Pastorate," in Kevin J. Vanhoozer and Owen Strachan, *The Pastor as Public Theologian: Reclaiming a Lost Vision* (Grand Rapids: Baker Academic, 2015), 69–93, 84.

in New Haven in May and June 1769. During these months, he prepared an extended discourse consisting of eighty-eight pages from "Matt 7:14 Last clause; *And few there be that find it*" (see Figure D). In spite of the week-to-week series Edwards Jr. did not change his text. This length was also atypical as most of his full manuscripts were less than forty bound pages, and his note-form sermons were often shorter than a dozen pages.

Toward the end of his second year of regular preaching (1770), Edwards developed the habit of marking a line in the center of his page, jotting brief phrases to the left and right side of the line. If his notes were more than a quarto folded in half (making four pages), an insert was stitched into the center to add more pages. On occasion a thought might come to him, and not wanting to forget it, he would attach a slight scrap of paper with a tiny metal pin with the addition.[3] The vast majority of his manuscripts from 1770's through 1801 are in note form (see figure D). Donald Weber is probably correct when he suggests that this tendency arose from a desire to be connected to the "extemporaneous mode of his New Light forebears who took their identity from the evangelical method of brief, shorthand notes."[4] While Weber may rightly conclude a desire to walk in the footsteps of his forebears, more likely however, is Edwards Jr.'s desire to follow the paradigm of his father's favorite systematic theologian and pulpit instructor.[5]

Edwards Jr. had, according to Edwards Amasa Park, read through Peter van Mastricht's *Theoretical-Practical Theology* seven times.[6] The preface to the 1698 edition of Mastricht's theology gave instruction to preachers to organize their sermons to be organized with just a few universal principles. These few would be able to be carried home in one's memory to be discussed with their families. Furthermore, these principles would provide ease of memory for the preacher and be the bones on which application may hang.[7]

---

[3] For an example of an addition with a metal pin see Sermon 5 on Phil. 1.18 composed at Princeton January 1767 and then preached throughout the next year in seven different towns, *Jonathan Edwards Jr. Papers (Sermons)*, Hartford Seminary Library (Box 165, Folder 2725), 36–37.

[4] Weber, "The Edwardsean Legacy," 52.

[5] "For divinity in general, doctrine, practice and controversy, or as an universal system of divinity, [Mastricht's Theoretical-Practical Theology] is much better than [Francis] Turretin or any other book in the world, excepting the Bible, in my opinion." Jonathan Edwards to Joseph Bellamy, January 15, 1746/7, in *Works of Jonathan Edwards Online, Letters and Personal Writings*, Vol. 16, ed. by George S. Claghorn (New Haven, CT: Yale University Press, 1957–2008), 217.

[6] Edwards Amasa Park, "The New England Theology," *Biliotheca Sacra* 9 (1852), 191.

[7] Peter van Mastricht, *Theoretical-Practical Theology: Prolegomena*, vol. 1., trans. by Todd M. Rester, ed. by Joel R. Beeke (Grand Rapids: Reformation Heritage Books, 2018), 3–5.

Most of Edwards Jr.'s sermons follow a three-stage progression. First, he begins with a text, providing its context and meaning. Out of this brief introduction and exegesis he proposes his Doctrine. After this first major section called the Doctrine, the Improvement followed providing the lock-proof argument demonstrating the consistency of the doctrine with the text. In listening to the Improvement, the hearer was left with a need to apply the text to their lives. This concluding application was typically called the Examination.

With van Mastricht as his guide, each section of his sermon flowed through the paradigm of "The Best Method of Preaching." A modern reviewer of Edwards Jr.'s sermon notes will observe the absence much introduction except the immediate context development. Edwards Jr. follows Mastricht's recommendation to produce an introduction "derived from the coherence of the text."[8] Edwards Jr. was also religiously faithful to select short texts typically a verse or part of a verse. Mastricht advised preachers not to pick too long of a text. A lengthy text may not allow a proper argumentation, or a defense of the doctrine proposed.[9] Edwards Jr. consistently took time to define key words out of which his doctrine will be argued and applied to his church. This might properly be called exegesis. In the majority of Edwards Jr.'s sermons he uses a two-point our three-point outline to exegete his Doctrine. From the doctrinal statement is the Improvement (what van Mastricht calls the argument).[10] The improvement is "the rationale of the deduction or consequence" so plainly rendered that the hearers are compelled to agree that the doctrine is "the word of God." To make the connection from doctrine to the word of God may be carried out by appeal to parallel or equivalent passages and confirmed through reason.[11] Occasionally Edwards Jr. will sprinkle in apologetic argumentation, or what van Mastricht calls *eclentic*, taking care to not overtax his listeners.[12] From the Improvement Edwards Jr. moves into the application phase of the sermon called the Examination or Exhortation. Among the variety of options provided by van Mastricht, surprisingly and contrary to caricature of a harsh, metaphysical preacher, Edwards Jr. uses the exploratory or hortatory uses more frequently than the rebuking approach. "The ingredients of the

---

[8] Van Mastricht, *Theoretical-Practical Theology*, 7.

[9] Van Mastricht, *Theoretical-Practical Theology*, 6.

[10] Van Mastricht, *Theoretical-Practical Theology*, 11.

[11] Van Mastricht, *Theoretical-Practical*, 11–15.

[12] Van Mastricht, *Theoretical-Practical Theology*, 16–17.

exploratory use: motives, signs, and affections"[13] are such that may be used by the Holy Spirit to cultivate a taste for virtue.

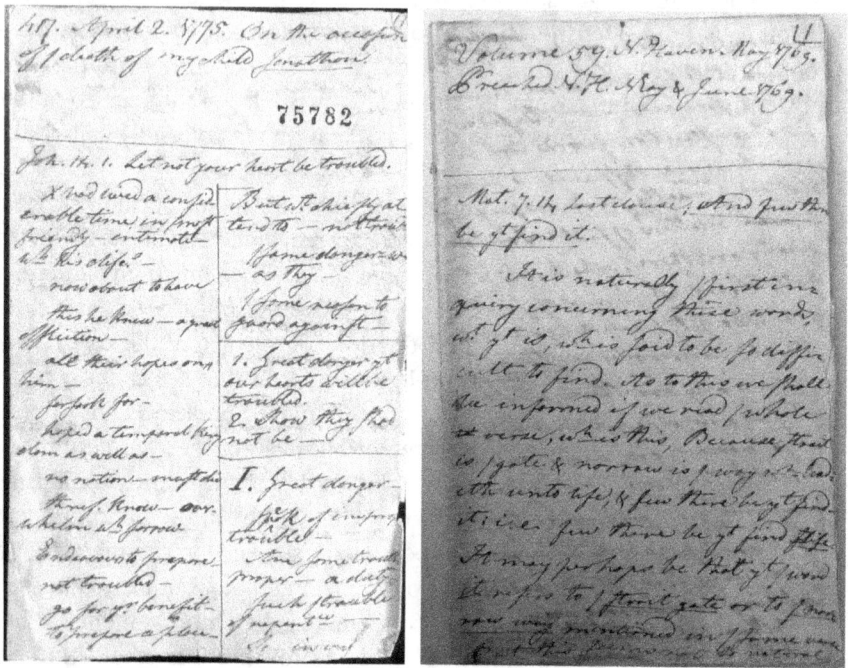

Figure D: Example of a partial note manuscript (courtesy of the Hartford Seminary Library) and a full note manuscript (courtesy of the Beinecke Rare Book Library)

---

[13]Van Mastricht suggests the following approaches in the application phase of the sermon depending on the need: consolatory, rebuke, exploratory, and hortatory. Van Mastricht, *Theoretical-Practical Theology*, 18–28.

APPENDIX 2

SERMON 79 (REV. 22:17): A TRANSCRIPT

Jonathan Edwards Jr., "Volume 79," *Jonathan Edwards Jr. Papers (Sermons)*, Hartford Seminary Library. Box 165, Folder 2728. Transcript permission by the Hartford Seminary Library, 77 Sherman St., Hartford, CT 06105–9509.

Volume 79. New Haven Oct. 1769. Preached Oct. 15, 1769 [in] New Haven. Oct. 1769, Rev. 22:17 (Last Clause)

Rev. 22:17 [last clause] And whosoever will, let him take of the water life freely.

 This chapter in which our text is contained is the last chapter in the whole Bible and doubtless it is of great importance that we take careful notice how a book so serious, so instructive and so replete with divine truth, as the Bible is, concludes. And if we read the whole of this chapter we shall find that it contains, besides some severe and awful threatenings, many gracious promises and precious encouragements to weary and heavy laden broken-hearted sinners. Among others, our text is in this view especially worthy of our notice. The whole verse is this; "And the Spirit and the bride say come. And let him that heareth say come. And let him that is athirst come: And whosoever will let him take the water of life freely

 All that needs to be explained in these last words in order to the right understanding of them, is the water of life. If we can find out what the inspired writer intended by these words, the whole will be plain. In the first place, it will not be amiss to observe that in these words, he doubtless refers to what he had just before said in the first verse in the chapter which is as follows: *And he showed me a pure river of water of life, clear as crystal, proceeding out of the throne of God and of the lamb.* This is the water of life of which we are often invited in our text to partake. But inquiry still remains, what is meant by this pure river of water of life proceeding out of the throne of God and of the lamb. And for a solution of this inquiry, I shall refer you to two passages of Scripture. The first is John 7:37–39. "In the last day,

> *[that great day of the feast, Jesus stood and cried, saying, If any man thirst, let him come unto me, and drink. He that believeth on me, as the scripture hath said, out of his belly shall flow rivers of living water. (But this spake he of the Spirit, which they that believe on him should receive: for the Holy Ghost was not yet given; because that Jesus was not yet glorified.)"]*

Here we are expressly told that by living water, which seems to be of the same import with what in our text is expressed by the words water of life, is intended the Holy Spirit. The other text is in Isaiah 44:3 For I will pour water

> *["upon him that is thirsty, And floods upon the dry ground: I will pour my spirit upon thy seed, And my blessing upon thine offspring"]*

Here again water and the Spirit seem to be used as signifying one and the same thing. But the Spirit may be is spoken of in Scripture as being the grand and highest blessing, or rather, as the sum of all the blessedness bestowed on true Saints.

Luke 11:13. If ye then being evil, know how to give good gifts unto your children; how much more shall your heavenly father give the Holy Spirit to them, that ask him. The meaning of this seems to be as if it had been Said, how much more does your heavenly father know how to bestow all Spirit gifts on them, that ask him. Again, the Spirit is the grand gift which God gave to his Son Jesus Christ as we read in John 3:34. For he whom God hath sent speaketh the words of God. For God hath not given the Spirit by measure unto him. Again, we read Heb. 1:9. Thou hast loved righteousness, and hated iniquity; therefore, God even thy God hath anointed thee with the oil of gladness above thy fellows: Which words are spoken of Christ. And in them we are told what is the great reward which the father bestows on the Son for his love of righteousness and hatred of iniquity expressed in his life and death; and that is, that he anointed him with the oil of gladness. But oil it is well known, under the Mosaic dispensation was used as a type and Symbol of the Holy Spirit. So that in this text we are taught that the grand reward bestowed upon Christ for his faithful obedience to his father in his painful life, and ignominious death, which comprehended all the joys and blessedness to which he was exalted; consisted in the plentiful bestowment of the Holy Spirit.

If then these things be so; if water in our text, and in all such like passages in the Bible signifies the Holy Spirit and if the Holy Spit bestowed to believers comprehends all the spiritual good which is ever given to them; yea all that good which was given as a reward to Christ himself for his obedience and death; then the meaning of our text is plain, viz. this; Whosoever will, let him come and freely take to himself abundantly of all that spiritual good which Christ hath purchased, consisting not only of divine communications in this world; but especially in the incommunicable and unutterable joys of the world to come. This I apprehend to be the true sense of our text, which exhorts to take the water of life freely.

DOCTRINE

Eternal life, with its joys, and the foretastes of it in this world are freely offered to everyone who will accept of them. In speaking on this doctrine, I shall endeavor 1) to show what eternal life is, and what its joys, and the foretastes of it in this world are. 2) What it is to accept of these things. 3) That they are freely offered to the acceptance of all.

FIRST. What eternal life [is], its joys and foretastes are.

As to this I would observe that eternal life is not merely to live forever, or to continue forever in existence. For in this sense all mankind good and bad, shall enjoy eternal life. All will necessarily exist forever; nor will it be possible for them to cease from their existence. Many will indeed seek death; many will wish not to be; but death shall forever flee from them.

But eternal life may be considered as consisting of two things, deliverance from misery, and enjoyment of positive holiness. The misery from which we are therein delivered is dreadful and inconceivable. The representations given of it in Scripture are most striking to the imagination. The place wherein the wicked are to be tormented is represented to be a lake of liquid fire and brimstone. This is the place that God hath prepared for the execution of his enemies. Tophet is ordained of old: the pile thereof is fire and much wood; and the breath of the Lord like a stream of brimstone doth kindle it. Even God himself with all his omnipotence will exert himself for the punishment and most awful destruction of his enemies. He will make bare his arm for their of his enemies. Tophet is ordained of old: the pile thereof is fire and much wood; and the breath of the Lord like a stream of brimstone doth kindle it. Even God himself with all his omnipotence will exert himself for the punishment and most awful destruction of his enemies. He will make bare his arm for their destruction; he will whet his glittering sword, and his hand shall take hold on vengeance; yea he will make all his arrows drunk in their blood. Neither will his eye pity them, or his hand spare them. But he will pour out upon them the vials of his wrath, and the cup of his fury even to the very dregs.

This misery not only consists in suffering the divine wrath and displeasure but at the same time the soul is wholly sunk in sin and wickedness: and no small part of these sufferings proceeds from this wicked temper in of the suffers hearts. Hence, we read in Scripture of the worm that dieth not, as well as of the fire that is not quenched. The soul that suffers this destruction is wholly given up to its own wicked lusts and affections, to its enmity against God which immediately breaks out into rage and blasphemy. And this perhaps appears to be the most dreadful part of this sufferings to one who is under the influence of a holy taste and temper of the mind. The soul who suffers this destruction is also to be entirely banished from all friendly intercourse with the deity or with any holy beings whatsoever. And is to be left in the company of none but those, who exactly resemble himself in character and outward circumstances.

But eternal life consists not only in being delivered from these evils but also in being admitted to the greatest positive enjoyments. These enjoyments consist in being admitted into the immediate presence of God in being admitted to see kind as he is, and to behold his glory; in loving and being beloved of G; in praising and glorifying him, and in this way having communion with the father and his son Jesus Christ. And not only with these but also with the saints and angels in glory. In short eternal life consists in being perfectly conformed to God in the temper and frame of our mind, and in all those acts and exercises which are implied in and consequent upon it: this is what is meant by being made partakers of the Holy Spirit in that perfect measure in which he is communicated in the world of light. In this consists the joys of heaven; this is to drink of the pure river of water life, clear as crystal, proceeding out of the throne of God and the lamb; which in Ps. 36:8 is called the river of God's pleasures. See the place: They shall be abundantly satisfied with the fatness of thy house: and thou shalt make them drink of the river of thy pleasures.

As we observed of the destruction of the wicked that they will be delivered up to their own wicked lusts and affections, and that therein will a great part of their misery consist so I would observe concerning the salvation of the righteous that it will in a great measure consists in being made perfectly holy themself and in being entirely delivered from sin whether in themself or others. And the very excellency and glory of the heavenly state is that will it is of such a stateperfect holiness, where no sin ever will or can enter.

Thus, I have endeavoured briefly to unfold what we are to understand to be meant by eternal life and its enjoyments. Now although these enjoyments are chiefly and most eminently to be had in the world to come; yet God is pleased to give to his saints some foretastes of them in this world. And these foretastes are of the very same kind, though less in degree, with those which are to be had in heaven itself: they consist in some degree of the communication of the same Spirit and same blessedness which is called (in our text by the name of the water of life.)

According to the originally proposed we come now to consider,

SECOND. What it is to accept of eternal life, its joys and foretastes. Now this methinks cannot be difficult for us to understand, if we consider what it is to accept of any other good when freely offered to us. Let us take a Scripture example, See Luke 11:11–12 If a son shall ask bread of any of you that is a father, will he give him a stone? or if he ask a fish, will he for a fish, give him a serpent? Or if he ask an egg, will he give him a scorpion? Now to apply this to the case before us, I ask what is it to accept of bread, when we stand in great need of it, and it is freely offered to us? In what manner and with what temper does the hunger child accept that bread which he had most earnestly asked of his father? Does he accept it with coldness, with indifferency and lukewarmness, as if he hardly know whether it were best to accept it at his father's hands or no?

Or does he accept it in such a manner and with such a temper as plainly indicates great haughtiness of Spirit and that he really thinks within himself that his father is greatly obliged to him for taking it, and not he to his father for giving it? Or is he want to accept and eat it without any relish of it or satisfaction in the participation? I say, is this the way and this the temper which with an hungry child is wont to accept of bread at the hand of his father? The contrary of this you all know to be fact: you all know that such a child in want to accept the bread given it, with eagerness, with joy and delight, with a thorough relish of it, as according to its proper nature a good: and not only so, but he is also want to accept it with humility, being sensible of his dependence on his father; and also with gratitude and thankfulness, being fully sensible of the good bestowed upon him. Now by this example, we are taught by our Lord himself who spoke as never man spoke, what it is really and truly to accept of eternal life.

For he himself brings this example to illustrate this very point as you may see in the following verse, If ye then being evil, know how to give good gifts unto your children: how much more shall your heavenly father give the holy Sp. to them that ask him? By this he plainly teaches us, that to ask for the Sp. in the gift of which consists the good and blessedness of eternal life, in the same manner in which a child asks bread of his parent; and to accept it with the same temper, with which the child accepts the bread when it is given, is the very asking and accepting of the true saint. And whosoever accepts it, or which in the same thing, is ready to accept it in this manner, shall certainly be admitted to the enjoyment of it.

But perhaps some may be ready to say, if this be the true acceptance of eternal life, even that to which the inheritance is promised; if this be all that is necessary in order to have a sure title to eternal life, then doubtless I have it and not only I but also most men under the gospel. Fear who is there of such who do not desire eternal. life as eagerly as the hungry child desires bread, and who is not as ready to accept it? If then these things be so, it seems that we may set our hearts at ease and be sure of eternal happiness. But to this I would briefly answer. Although most men who enjoy the light of the gospel have some very earnest desires respecting eternal life yet if they be examined they will be found to be very different from those which a child when hungry has for food. Such a child not only desires a deliverance from the pain and disagreeable sensation of hunger; but also has a clear idea of the good to be enjoyed in the participation of wholesome food and in this view he correctly desires it. But the case is very different with respect to those desires which most men under the gospel have respecting eternal life. For if the matter be searched to the bottom, they will be found not to desire eternal life in a view of the true Spirit good to be enjoyed in it, but quite in another view as a means of escaping misery and in general of obtaining happiness. They are perhaps in a measure sensible that they are exposed to eternal misery; and they have heard that the gift of the Holy Spirit is necessary in order to escape. Therefore in this view, they in some sense desire it. But to desire the Spirit in this manner is very different from the manner in which an hungry child desires food. For he desires food because it is good and for its own sake desirable, agreeable to the exhortation of the wise man; My son eat thou honey because it is good, and the honeycomb because it is sweet to thy taste.

Again men in general under the gospel have heard that there is great happiness to be enjoyed in the gift of the Holy Spirit and happiness in general they desire. But as to that peculiar kind of happiness which there is to be had in Spiritual enjoyments, of this they are entirely ignorant and have no taste or relish for it. In this then there is another essential difference between these desires of the Spirit and those with which the hungry child desires its proper food. For the child not only desires good in general, but that peculiar kind of good which is to be had in eating its proper food. And if sinners did thus desire the gift of the Spirit and were ready to accept of it with this temper, it is not to be doubted, but that God would fulfill his promise and bestow it upon them, and make them heirs of eternal life.

But this brings me to the consideration of our third general head, which is,

THIRD. That eternal life with its joys and foretastes are freely offered to the acceptance of all. The way is now perfectly prepared for all to come to the enjoyments of these infinitely good things that will. Observe the words of our text (whosoever will let him come and take of the water of life freely). The way into the most holy is opened by Jesus Christ. Had he not entered in once for all and offered up his own blood for an atonement: had he not thus led the way before us; we must for ever have been excluded. Had he not been appointed to be our redeemer, all access to the father would have been for ever shut. For no works of righteousness wrought by us; nor any prayers, cries or tears; no sacrifices of beasts; not thousands of rams nor ten thousand of rivers of oil, would have been sufficient to make an atonement for our sins. In this miserable and wretched condition must we have forever remained and perished had not the son of G. undertaken to make an atonement But he had compassion on us and freely offered himself to become our surety and propitiation and not only he, but the father also had compassion on us and commissioned his son for the great work to which he offered himself. And he who knew no sin became sin for us in order that we might become the righteousness of God and God gave his only begotten Son that whosoever believeth on his name might not perish but have everlasting life. And now, since Christ has become incarnate, and suffered and died, the father is become entirely well pleased for his righteousness sake; an atonement is made; the divine wrath is appeased; God is become reconcilable to sinners, yea even to the most guilty and vile and a pardon of all sins, justification in the sight of God a title to eternal life, to its joys and foretastes are freely offered to all who will of accept of them. And thus, the way is entirely prepared a wide door is opened, and all thing on the part of God are ready: every obstacle is removed. God can now consistently with his own honour and the dignity of his government give eternal life to all who will accept of it. And this he offers to do freely, i.e., without money and without price. God requires no price for such an infinite good as eternal life of those who will accept of it on the terms offered in the gospel. All that he requires of them is, to come for all things are ready. Thus, having spoken upon the several heads of discourse at first proposed, nothing remains but some

IMPROVEMENT

FIRST. Hence, we may learn the only reason why any of mankind are not saved. The only reason is, that they will not accept of salvation or eternal life as it is freely offered to them in the gospel. Were they willing to accept it upon the terms of the gospel, they would certainly and infallibly be saved. For God is all ready to save them. He is naturally full of goodness and compassion and delights not in the misery of his creatures: but he delights in their good; in their happiness; in their salvation. And from his goodness and mere mercy and because he delights not in their ruin, he was influenced to provide a way for your escape. Yea he has provided this way, although it cost him as it were infinitely dear. And he by his life and death has removed every obstacle out of the way, which would otherwise prevent his acceptance of the sinner. Since then, every obstacle on the part of God is removed out of the way, the only thing which prevents the salvation of the sinner is his not accepting, or not coming to God in the way proposed. And this is the true and only reason which prevents the salvation of all those of mankind who finally perish. This is the only reason even with the greatest of sinners. For God is equally wiling in this way to accept of the greatest sinners as of the least. Sinners are wont to flatters and to justify themselves in their own eyes, by this consideration; that they on their part are exceedingly desirous of salvation, and altogether ready to accept of it if G. would but bestow it upon them: but that this he is not willing to do; that he is determined upon their final and eternal ruin; although they are ready to comply with any reasonable terms of salvation. Thus, by their own self, flatteries they cast all the blame of their ruin upon themselves God and utterly clear and justify themselves. But this is entirely contradictory to the truth. It is contradictory to the whole tenor of the gospel, which everywhere invites and calls upon sinners to return to their rightful sovereign, and promises them eternal salvation as a reward. How contrary it is to our text and a thousand other texts that might be mentioned? How contrary to facts? to the giving of his son, and all that God has done to make all things ready for the return of the sinner? May we not justly argue that since he has given us his only begotten Son, how shall he not with him also freely gives us all things?

SECOND. Hence also we may born the exceeding greatness and freeness of the grace of the gospel. What ground had we to expect any merely at the hand of God after we had apostatized from him? Was it a light thing that we had offended and rebelled against the king of heaven, a being infinitely great and glorious, our creator and rightful proprietor? Had we any reason to believe that he would ever pass over our grievous offence? Might he not most justly have forever rejected us? And what else could we reasonable have expected at his hand? But behold, when we had the greatest reason to expect wrath and indignation, what a most wonderful display of mercy and this not confined in the offer to this or that man or to a few particulars but extended to all who will accept of it. Nor is it offered only to those who are small sinners; but is equally offered to the greatest. And all this free! all without money and without price! What a wonderful and rich display of mercy is this!—O the depth of the riches both of the wisdom and knowledge of God! how unsearchable are his judgments and his ways past finding out!

THIRD. I would briefly improve this in a way of exhortation to all.

EXHORTATION

Here you see, my dear friends and brothers is eternal life with all the joys and blessedness of it, freely offered to you? And will you not accept of it? Will you not catch at the offer? You do certainly all of you dread misery and desire to avoid it. But the way to avoid this is to accept the offer of the gospel.

Let me intreat you to consider—

First. How entirely reasonable are the terms upon which eternal life is offered to you. It is offered to you upon the bare term of your acceptance; whosoever will let him take the water of life freely. To accept of eternal life is to return to G. in the way of the gospel or in and through Jesus Christ. But is it not a reasonable thing that we should thus return? What can we say in justification of our conduct, if we refuse to return? Was there of first any good reason why we should revolt from God? Had God treated us in a manner that justly provoked us to rebel against him. Had he exercised tyranny over us, or treated in us the last cruelly and unjustly. So that we could not endure his government? Were not all the requirement of the original constitution perfectly reasonable and just? If so, then it was perfectly reasonable that we should have continued in our allegiance to our heavenly sovereign. And for the same reason it is perfectly reasonable that we should return to our allegiance again. But especially is it thus reasonable considering that he hath done so much to prepare the way and to open a wide and effectual door for our return' and that upon such easy terms.

Second. Consider also how unreasonable your conduct will be in continuing to refuse an acceptance of eternal life upon the terms of the gospel. God does not require of you that you should perform some work which will put you to exceeding great experience and labour. You have not this excuse to make viz. Who shall ascend into heaven? that is to bring Christ down from above; or who shall descend into the deep? i.e. to bring up Christ again from the dead. But the word is nigh thee, even in thy mouth and in thy heart: i.e. the word of faith which we preach. You remember the foolish conduct of Naaman the leper. When he came to the prophet to be healed of his leprosy because the prophet prescribed so easy a remedy as to go and wash in Jordan seven times; he was wroth and went away and said, Behold I thought, he will surely come out to me and stand and call on the name of the Lord his God and strike his hand over the place and recover the leper. So he turned, and went away in a rage. But his servants, who appear to have been much more wise and prudent than himself came near and spake unto him and said, My Father, if the prophet had bid thee do some great thing wouldst thou not have done it? How much rather then, when he saith to thee wash and be clean? So also you, my dear friends. If God had prescribed some great thing as the term of salvation, such as the giving of all your goods to feed the poor or your body to be burned; or that you should give the fruit of your body for the sin of your soul; would you not have done it? How much more then when he saith, whosoever will? On the whole let me lay before you that gracious invitation of our Lord in Mat. 22:2. And again he sent forth other servants saying, tell them which are bidden, Behold I have prepared my dinner; my oxen and my fatlings are killed, and all things are: come unto the marriage.

Appendix 3

Two Sermons for Moses Paul

In 1772 Moses Paul, a Native American of Wampanoag descent had the unfortunate experience to be subject of a capital murder trial. Ava Chamberlain chronicles the events of the evening of his death and the possibility that the charge of murder probably should have been properly termed homicide. The first sermon was used a second time by Edwards Jr. in another capital case involving a free black man named Joseph Mountain who had been charged with rape. Mountain, like Moses Paul, maintained that he had not committed the crimes for which he would be executed. These sermons provide a window into the spiritual concern of Jonathan Edwards Jr. that justice be fairly applied regardless of race. While the first sermon was written for the expected execution in June, the second sermon was designed to minister comfort to Moses Paul when after a temporary stay was issued. Over the next few months when the expectation of review came to naught, a sermon from John 3:16 was drafted in early September to encourage Paul to rest by faith in the benevolence of a just God. Both of these sermons are transcribed with permission from the original manuscripts located in the Hartford Seminary Library, 77 Sherman St., Hartford, CT 06105–9509. The second sermon from John 3:16 is originally in note form and thus needs some reconstruction by inserting ideas based on the context.

Jonathan Edwards Jr., "Volume 225," *Jonathan Edwards Jr. Papers (Sermons)*, Hartford Seminary Library (Box 166, Folder 2732)

Vol. 225. Preached New Haven June 7. 1772. at the desire of Moses Paul a Mohegan Indian, under sentence of death for the murder of Moses Cook of Waterbury. Again to Joseph Mountain, a Negro condemned for a rape, September 26, 1790.[1]

Psalm 55:23. But thou, O God, shall bring them down into the pit of destruction: bloody and deceitful men shall not live out half their days; but I will trust in thee.

DOCTRINE

The psalms of David were all generally composed upon some particular occasions either of mercy or affliction and had a primary reference to David's own particular affairs; but on ultimate reference to the affairs of the church in all ages. So, when in any psalm mention is made of the sufferings of David, the cruelty, malice, and perfidy of his enemies in persecuting him; as also of the wonderful deliverance which he obtained and the great mercy of God towards him therein, a reference is had either to the sufferings, [the] suffering [and] reward of Christ, or to those of the church in all ages of the world. David's sufferings therefore are frequently to be understood as the sufferings of the church; his friends and his deliverance, friends and the salvation of the church.

With regard to this psalm in particular from which our text is taken, it manifestly was written on some occasion when David was most bitterly persecuted and that by his friends who were under great obligations to him, and had made pretenses of unfeigned benevolence. (See vs. 1–4 and vs. 12–15) What occasion this was, to which the psalm refers is not absolutely certain. Commentators direct us to two. One when he had marched his few men out of the wilderness out of where they were obliged to hide the city of Keilah which was besieged by the Philistines. After he had delivered this city some gave information to Saul that David and his men were at Keilah; and Saul was preparing to come down thither in order to surprise

---

[1] Originally, single square brackets were inserted to indicate a section he would adapt for Joseph Mountain's situation. In this transcript, I have set them in double square brackets.

him and his men, and to cut them off. David hearing of this purpose of Saul, made inquired of the Lord whether the men of Keilah would deliver him into Saul's hands; and was answered that they would. Now on occasion of these perjurious and ungrateful returns from the men of Keilah for all his kindness towards them, it is supposed by some, that David wrote this psalm. But others, think with more probability, suppose it was written upon occasion of Absalom's conspiracy; in which Ahithophel formerly very intimate friend of David joined. And to him he seems to refer in the 12 and 13 verses upon which ever of these occasions the psalm was written, it is observable that in the text, David speaks of his enemies as blood thirsty and treacherous men who by fraud and deceit sought his life. And as he herein calls those bloody men, who had engaged in a design of unrighteously taking away his life; so much more do those deserve this appellation who have actually been guilty of shedding man's blood. It is further observable that it is plainly taught us in the text that such men shall not escape punishment. For however they may escape punishment from men, yet they shall not from God. For Thou, O God, shalt bring them down into the pit of destruction. Thus the text teaches that they in general shall fall under the divine vengeance. But it more particularly specifies the punishment which they shall suffer. Bloody and deceitful men shall not live out half their days.

Further our text teaches the ground of hope that there is with God. But I will trust in thee. It is indeed wonderful and astonishing that there should be any ground of hope for sinners before that God whom they have so grieved. Yet so offended it is: Such is the infinite grace of God through Christ.

In further speaking upon this subject, to which I have been led by the desire of the unhappy prisoner now in chains before us, as not unsuitable to his case; I shall briefly enlarge on these hints given us in the text in several particulars and thence make the application.

IMPROVEMENT

First. [[*Bloody and deceitful men*]] shall not go unpunished. This is what they perhaps generally expect, when they are perpetrating their wickedness of shedding blood and using deceit. They Never lay out to themselves to be discovered by men; and so entertain no expectation of being brought to punishment by them. And as to God they have no fear of him before their eyes, nor is he in all their thoughts. If they had but proper apprehension of God of his universal providence, of his hatred of every wicked work and that he will certainly bring them into judgment; these apprehensions would doubtless be sufficient to restrain them from such abominable sins [as] treachery and bloodshed. But these thoughts we may presume are far from their minds. And as to man, they flatter themselves that they shall escape his knowledge, and consequently his wrath.

But these imaginations are utterly vain. Indeed it is not impossible but they may, even in such abominable wickedness, escape the knowledge and wrath of man; but the knowledge and wrath of God which is infinitely more dreadful they can by no means escape. As to his knowledge it is infinite comprehending all things to us visible and invisible; all things secret and open; all things past, present and things to come; all things done under the covert of darkness, and even the secrets of the heart. Thus they cannot escape his knowledge and observation. And as impossible is it yet they should escape his wrath and judgments. For he will, they continuing in impenitency bring them down, as [[our text]] expresses it, to the pit of destruction. God is angry with all sinners, with all the wicked, and that every day. He is of purer eyes, than to behold evil and cannot look on iniquity of any kind even in those instances which we call smaller sins every thought, [every] idle word. [For this we will have to] give an account. How much more therefore may we expect that his wrath will burn and his indignation be inflamed against sinners of so gross a character as those who are guilty of deceit and blood? Doubtless for these things in a particular manner will bring into judgment.

Second. As [[bloody and deceitful]] men shall not go unpunished on the whole so sometimes wrath and punishment overtake them even in this world. The apostle Paul, (1 Tim. 5:24) says, some men's sins are open beforehand, going before to judgment; and some men they follow after: i.e. that the judgments of God come upon them before the usual time, viz. in this life. Whereas with regard to the generality of the wicked their punishment is deferred till they arrive in the world to come. And this is that to which the psalmist has more immediate reference [[in the text,]] when he says that bloody and deceitful men shall not live out half their days. The wise man also teaches the same doctrine in Prov. 10:27. "The fear of the Lord prolongeth days; but the years of the wicked shall be shortened." And in Eccl. 7:17. "Be not over much wicked, neither be thou foolish: why shouldest thou die before they time? The same thing is held up to our view in the fifth commandment in which we are commanded to honour our father and mother that our days may be long upon the land which the Lord our God giveth us. In all these perhaps you see, an untimely death is spoken of as the consequence and expressly threatened to those, who are guilty of wickedness; especially of the grosser kinds.

However there is a difference between our state and the state of the church under the law, [that is,] the Mosaic dispensation. Under that dispensation from the beginning, even to the end, sin was threatened with temporal punishment. He that was guilty of any sin of ignorance was to bring his sacrifice, to confess his sin and so to obtain pardon. But he that was guilty of any sin wilfully and knowingly, was to be cut off from his people and suffer death. Num. 15:30–31. Deut. 17:12.

And in general in case of disobedience and rebellion, they were to be cursed in the city and in the field, in their basket, and in their store; in the fruit of their body, of their land and their flocks: but no express mention was made of eternal torments. Those were typically and virtually threatened under temporal judgments. So we must understand the threatenings of that dispensation, unless we will wholly exclude the threatening of eternal torments.—But what I have said, the difference which mentioned between that dispensation and that of the gospel is manifest: it is this, that though under that dispensation temporal punishments were certainly to follow a wicked life on an apostacy from the true religion. But now they do not certainly follow. Then it was more that certain [[bloody and deceitful men]] should not live out half their days, or if they did not come to an untimely death, yet that they should meet with temporal curses of one kind or another. But now God more frequently suffers sinners to go on in sin and enjoy their good things in this life, reserving their punishment till time with them be no more.

However, sometimes even now, God punishes men in this world as well as the world to come. Sometimes even now, the sins of some men are open beforehand, going before to judgment and bringing down upon them on untimely death; whereby they are prevented from living out half their days. As to these things God acts as a sovereign, ordaining them according to his ow infinite wisdom. And when an untimely death or any punishment overtakes sinners in this world however they may seem to be inflicted upon them by men as all agree to punish bloody and murderous men with death; yet in reality they are ultimately to be referred to God. He has the heart of judges and of all in his hands as the rivers of waters and turneth whithersoever he will. He overrules all the affairs of the world insomuch that not a sparrow falleth to the ground without our heavenly father. Much more therefore do not so much more important events as the life and death of men, the condemnation and execution of criminals come to pass without the overruling and directing providence of God.

Third. However [[bloody and deceitful]] men may escape punishment in this world, yet continuing such they can by no means escape the world to come. This is intimated in [[that part of our text]] Now, O God shall bring them down to the pit of destruction. Yea it is intimated even in this, they shall not live out half their days. We have as much reason to understand this as referring to spiritual and eternal punishment threatened in the Old Testament. Beside it evidently intends some punishment peculiar to the wicked and is spoken of them in distinction from the righteous. But an early temporal death, or even death by the civil sword cannot be pretended to be peculiar to the wicked as distinguished from the saints. For immeasurable multitudes of the latter have suffered death in the early part of life, but the cruel hand of persecution. And therefore, our text and many others, such as that the memory of the wicked shall perish, his name shall not, he shall not be gathered or have any burial, etc. are by the best commentators understood to refer to eternal punishments in the world to come.

And these punishments [[bloody and deceitful]] men dying such can by no means escape. There is no discharge in this warning. The irrevocable sentence is already gone forth against them, and not only against them, but against all who die in a state of alienation to God and the gospel of his Son. He that believeth and is baptized shall be saved but he that believeth not shall be damned: and he that believeth not shall is condemned already, because he hath not believed on the name of the only begotten Son of God. And the apostle John, who had a clear vision of the eternal and invisible world, tells that without (i.e. without the gates of heaven) are dogs, and sorcerers, and whoremongers and murderers, and idolaters, and whosoever loveth and maketh a lie. And again; but the fearful and unbelieving, and the abominable, and murderers, and whoremongers and sorcerers and idolaters and all liars shall have their part in the lake that burneth with fire and brimstone which is the second death.

Now the nature of this death will appear from a few considerations.

First. In that state of death they will forever shut out of the presence and enjoyment of God his Son Jesus Christ and all holy and happy beings. They will indeed See Abraham afar off and Lazarus in his bosom, they will see the glorified saints and angels rejoicing and praising God in complete happiness: but they themselves shall be forever excluded. For between that world of torment into which they shall be plunged and that world of complete glory and happiness in which they shall see the saints, there will be a great gulf fixed, so that there will be no possibility of their passing from one to the other, however eagerly they may desire it. Thus they shall be forever deprived of all good.

Second. They will be made the subjects of the most exquisite torments. Their lusts and corruptions will then be left without restraint they being given up to a reprobate mind. And even this will create an intolerable misery. But further their conscience will become their brutest enemy and will prove a worm within them which dieth not. How will their guilty conscience then remind them of their past sins. Whether more gross, such as deceit, injustice, murder and bloodshed; or more common and surest impenitency, unbelief, hardness of heart and contempt of the service of God. It will then tell them how they had been told of these sins, warned against them: How the judgments of God against such sins how been set before them, and that they had been told the issue of these things would be death, eternal death, that very death which they shall then feel, and suffer. It will also remind them of the many gracious invitations of the gospel which had been set before them; how Christ and salvation had been offered to them on the condition of their repentance and acceptance of Christ and how they had been urged and pressed to enter on a life of true religion; but that they had obstinately persisted in their sins, in their hardness of heart, impenitency and inattention to the business of religion. All these sins and innumerable more with their aggravations will their consciences in that state of death bring to their remembrance. The torment attending those bitter reflections I have to yourselves to imagine. It must doubtless be exquisite and altogether inexpressible.

Third. Another part of the sufferings will proceed from the immediate hand of almighty God, doubtless by giving a very clear and striking sense of his awful and terrible majesty and of his infinite wrath against sin and against them in particular; and perhaps by many other ways, to us at present altogether inconceivable. Yea God will make bare his arm for their destruction. He will as it were exert himself to the uttermost, to make them miserable, and thus to give a most striking display in the view of the whole universe, of his hatred against sin and of what an awful and terrible thing it is to fall into the hands of the living God.

The dread fulness of this death further appears from the expression made use of with respect it in the Scriptures There it is spoken of as the worm that never dieth and as the fire that is never quenched; And wicked are said to be plunged in a lake that burneth with fire and brimstone. What more awful and striking representation could have been give of it? Tophet is said to be ordained of old, the pile thereof is fine and much wood, and the breathe of the Lord like a stream of brimstone doth kindle it. Now as this second death is so much infinitely more dreadful than the first, therefore we are commanded to fear, not them that kill the body and after that have no more that they can do. But to fear him that after he doth killed, hath power also to cast into hell; yea we are commanded to fear him.

Fourth. I would say some things to show the justice of inflicting this punishment on bloody and deceitful men and all who live and die in sin. So sin against God is to rise in rebellion against him; it is to say by our conduct that God is not worthy to feared and obeyed, and therefore to treat with him with contempt. And an impenitent sinner is one who goes on in this treatment and practically still justifies it. But is it not just to punish such conduct as this towards G? If the sinner rises up against and casts off God, is it unjust in G. to cast off the sinner? If he refuses to continue in his allegiance to God is it not just that God should refuse to admit him to the enjoyment of the benefit of his faithful subjects? If he despises the happiness of heaven, as every impenitent sinner under the gospel does, where is the injustice in suffering him to remain without it? and never to taste of the rich supper which he has provided and serves up in the heavenly state. If they despise the blessings of the gospel, walk[ing towards][2] death as all impenitent sinners under the gospel do, certainly it is no more than just that they should be suffered to have their own choice, and enjoy the death which they choose.

[[*Fifth.* If any person scruples the justice of God's conduct in punishing the sinner which eternal death, let him show wherein, let him come forth and plead his own cause against the Lord. Let him convince the Lord that he hath hitherto dealt too handy with sinners, that henceforth he ought in all justice to reform, and enter on quite a new dispensation towards them; and particularly towards him. Is there anyone who will dare to undertake this? I trough not.]]

Sixth. Although sinners are liable the punishment before mentioned; and although it be entirely just that this punishment should be inflicted upon them; yet there is a foundation for hope of an escape, even for the greatest sinners. It is indeed far beyond what we had any reason to expect. Not one sinner has the least reason on the footing of justice to expect an escape from eternal wrath. It is justly due to all. The ways of sin is death. And especially are these wages due to those who are guilty of aggravated sins. And the

---

[2]The words "walk" and "death" were inserted here and need some supplemental words to assist with understanding.

mouths of all shall be stopped and all sinners shall become guilty before God. So will this be the case in a very particular moment with regard to [[bloody and deceitful]] men. Yet there is a foundation for hope with regard to those. This foundation is the Lord Jesus Christ he is the only foundation other than which no man can lay. Nor is there any other name given under heaven among men, whereby we can be saved. And he is a foundation that is abundantly sufficient. For it is contained in the Scripture behold I lay in Zion a chief cornerstone, elect, precious: and he that believeth on him, shall not be confounded. And he came to save even the chief of sinners; for says he, It is a faithful saying, and worthy of all acceptation, that Jesus Christ came into the world to save sinners, of whom I am chief. And therefore the invitation is given to all; Whosoever will, let him take of the water of life; and ho everyone that thirsteth come ye to the waters, and yea come by wine and milk without money and without price. This, may be is the very glory of the gospel, that the blessings of it are freely offered to sinners who have nothing to pay for themselves. Thus is spoken by our Lord himself in this view, when he sent word to John the Baptist that the poor, those who cannot purchase the blessings of it, have the gospel preached to them. And agreeable to this is the presentation given in the parable of the great supper, the servants are sent not only to those who were bidden; but also into the streets and lanes of the city, to bring in the poor, the maimed, the halt and the blind: and not only so, but they were sent out into the highways and hedge to as many as they found, to compel them to come in. What more free, generous, and abundantly gracious offers and invitation could be desired, or indeed could possibly be given? I think it manifest that there could be none.

Thus, I have endeavoured to discuss the truths suggested by the text under several heads—as that [[bloody and deceitful]] men shall not go unpunished—that sometimes God orders it so that punishment overtakes them in this world—that however that may be, it will certainly overtake them in the world to come—that the eternal punishment of the world to come are justly due to them—and yet that there is a foundation for hope of an escape even with respect to them.

I come now to make the proper application. This shall be done in an address to the unhappy prisoner at whose desire, I preach this sermon.

APPLICATION

Moses Paul! as you have desired me to preach a sermon particularly applied to your case so I shall use that freedom of address, which becomes a minister of Christ preaching to a condemned malefactor. I hope you have been attentive to my discourse while I have been enlarging and inculcating the several truths of the text. And have in some measure anticipated me in making the application to yours. How far in reality the character of a [[bloody]] man belongs to you, God, and your own conscience best know. But this we all know that you have legally convicted of this character; and therefore it is to be presumed that this is your true character. Now you see how awful an affect our text bears upon you and such as you are: it declares that God will [[bring you, remaining of this character, down to the pit of destruction and that you shall not be suffered to live out half your days.]] And this sentence as it seems, he is about to execute upon you in its literal sense. For by the [[blood shed]] which you have committed, the sentence of the judge is gone forth against you, that you shall die and not live. And as you have not arrived to [age of 30 years], so you have not yet lived out half your days. And happy will it be for you if this is all the punishment which shall be laid upon you. Happy, if you escape the second death, a death infinitely more to be dreadful than that which was lately denounced against you and which you must ere long[3] suffer.

In this your miserable and lamentable condition, let me intreat you to consider how you have been brought into this misery. Reflect on your past life: how you have lived without God and have cast off his fear. For if you had lived in the fear of God you could never have arrived to that pitch of wickedness, which is like to cut you off in the midst of your days. Upon reflection you will doubtless find that you not arrived to this pitch of wickedness all at once. But that you began at first with small beginnings and proceeded by degrees, till at last you arrived at this this doleful spot. Reflect upon your particular sins, whatever they have been: your own conscience knows much better than I or any man upon earth. Reflect upon the contempt of God's. Sabbaths and proper use of his word the profanation of his holy name of which you have been guilty. [[Reflect upon your intemperance and abuse of yourself and the good creature of God by an inordinate use of spirituous liquors; and especially on this last as it seems to have been one cause of your present misery.]] And in the same view you have reason to reflect on yourself as you have not let a guard upon yourself with respect to the breaking of [[passionate anger and wrath.]] Reflect seriously and in the fear of God upon all these and all other particular sins in which you have lived; and particularly upon that gross and abominable sin [[of blood shed]] for which you are now condemned to death.

---

[3] The word *shortly* was struck out and ere long inserted because of the appeal and reschedule of the execution.

And besides these particular sins, reflect upon your general impenitency and unbelief, and upon all the aggravations of your sins. Your sins are attended with many aggravations which have not attended the sins of many others. You have been brought up in a Christian land, have been taught both to read [[and write]]. You understand the English language well. You have been capable therefore of learning your duty both by a perusal of the Scriptures and by an attendance upon the teaching of the ministers of the gospel. Herein you have been distinguished from the greater part of [[the original natives of this land; yea doubtless for the greater of your own tribe.]] Now how have you improved these advantages? Have you not in a great measure neglected and observed them? Have you not at least continued in impenitency and unbelief? This, although you have read repeatedly the call of God's word to repent and turn and live; to cast away all your transgressions, whereby you have transgressed, and to return unto the Lord that he might have mercy on you and to our God for he would abundantly pardon and although you have had Christ Jesus set before you, and offered to you as your Saviour, ready and willing to love you and all to the uttermost that come to him? Have you not refused to comply these gracious invitations and declarations of your duty and interest; and so in comparison with others who have sinned on high? Doubtless it may justly be for more intolerable for you in day of judgment than for the [[Indians]] who have never heard of the gospel.

Now if this be your character, surely you cannot deny, that the threat of the text may justly be executed upon you. As a [[bloody]] man you are justly cut off in the midst of your days. For the command of God is, [[He that sheddeth man's blood, by man shall his blood be shed.] And as a sinner, an impenitent, unbelieving sinner you justly deserve to suffer the second death. If you have all your life time been an enemy to God (as all you certainly are unless you have been renewed by divine grace,) is it not just that God should now become an enemy to you? If you have for rejected Jesus Christ the Saviour and refused to receive him as your Saviour, to submit to and obey him accordingly, is it not just that he should now leave you destitute of his salvation? If you have against light and knowledge gone on presumptuously in various sins, is it not just that God should at lest avenge himself upon his enemies and punish you according to the sentence which you know to be provided in such a case, by casting you into the lake that burneth with fire and brimstone? This doom is certain your just due. Nor could you have the least to object, should it executed upon you. All heaven would adore it as just.

But adored be the riches of divine grace, there is ground of hope even for you. Christ hath purchased salvation. He hath made atonement. Sufficient for all. He hath obtained the Holy Spirit to renew and sanctify, to confirm and establish his people. This ground of hope is [[hinted in the text; But I will trust in the thee.]] If you therefore will trust in God. If you will fly to the mercy of God in Christ if you will accept of Christ as your Lord and Saviour, relying on his atonement and resurrection alone for acceptance with God in short if you will accept of the salvation which is by Christ you shall be saved. For he that believeth shall be saved. And him that cometh unto Christ he will in no wise cast out. And to excite you so to do, suggest a few things—for your life [and] soul [will surely be] escaping hell [and going to] heaven—By regard to these therefore [you will be saved.] Be exhorted! And if finally saved [you will be] happy! [You will] see [and] need not fear [those who] kill body—

But if not—your death only an entrance into [greater torment].

By the example of the thief [who was] a malefactor. [He had led a]wicked life. Yet even in last hour [he was saved]. Manasseh [,king of Judah, was] a great sinner, [and was] imprisoned. [He had made wrong] choices as you. Yet [his prayer was heard by God] (2 Chron. 33. 11–14.) Even in old age [one can repent and believe]. The prodigal son [is an example of one who chose] riotous living—yet as soon as returned [he was forgiven]! So you, if you [return as those [will be forgiven]. Therefore, be animated to repent and hear.[4] Repent and pray[to] God! Turn thee, turn thee,

Improve your time [as] space allowed [by an appeal]. [Do] not [be] like Jezebel!

Let all be warned! withstand the beginning! Fly [away from] the abominable! So [do] not [let sin be] your ruin! Ecc. 7:17[5]

---

[4]This word is not clear. Possible Latin *anotus:* without ear.

[5]Eccl. 7:17 "Be not over much wicked, neither be thou foolish: why shouldest thou die before thy time?"

Jonathan Edwards Jr., "Volume 242," *Jonathan Edwards Jr. Papers (Sermons),* Hartford Seminary Library (Box 166, Folder 2732)

Vol. 242. Aug. 1772. Preached [at] New Haven [on] Aug. 30, 1772. Composed with reference to and at the special desire of Moses Paul to be executed this week.

John 3:16 For God So loved the world, that he gave his only begotten son, that whosoever believeth in him, should not perish, but have everlasting life.

Christ's incarnation and death [was] the most wonderful event. [There are some] who pretend [that it could] not [happen and are skeptical]. So [wonderful] that God became man. [How is it possible]? [How could God] die?

Many reject [this truth]. [Many say it is] merely a cunningly devised fable. But if [they] believed [the rest of the] Scriptures [except the incarnation and resurrection]. [Then they] must assent [to the incarnation, death and resurrection]. But if [they] assent [in general to the Scriptures then arises] another question. Why? As to this also [part of] the Scriptures.

DOCTRINE

Particularly the text here teaches:[6] 1) The motive of God's giving his Son [is] love. God so loved. 2) The greatness of this love. 3) The End[7] [which is] the salvation of sinners, Whosoever.

FIRST. The motive of God's giving his Son. God's love to men. 1) Confirm.[8] 2) What kind of love? 1) Confirm. 1. Abundantly declared in Scripture: our text

---

[6] The original word is "taught."

[7] That is, the *intended outcome* of God's love.

[8] The repeated word *Confirm,* here and below, refers to Petrus van Mastricht's method of creating a certainty in the hearers the "irrefutable consequence, so that the preacher does not say just any word of God, but precisely the particular word that is in his text." This is *confirmed* or *proven* "in parallel or equivalent passages, for the reason that the hearer may be all the more persuaded that this is the constant and perpetual thought of God." Petrus van Mastricht, "The Best Method of Preaching," in *Theoretical-Practical Theology,* Vol. 1 (Grand Rapids, MI: Reformation Heritage Books, 2018), 12–13.

1 John 4:9 [*In this was manifested the love of God toward us, because that God sent his only begotten Son into the world, that we might live through him.*]

1 John 3:16 [*Hereby perceive we the love of God, because he laid down his life for us: and we ought to lay down our lives for the brethren.*]

John 3:15 [*That whosoever believeth in him should not perish, but have eternal life.*]

Rom. 5:6, 8 [*For when we were yet without strength, in due time Christ died for the ungodly. . . . But God commendeth his love toward us, in that, while we were yet sinners, Christ died for us.*]

First. Could be no other [kind of love because] mankind [is] quite otherwise. – [Man's love is characterized as] generally from private profit. [That is from one's] own private interest, or honour. Few from [pure] love. But could be no such motive with God. [Can] not [be out of] private profit [because it is] impossible to be profitable to him.

Job 22:2 [*Can a man be profitable unto God, as he that is wise may be profitable unto himself?*]

Job 35:6–9 [*If thou sinnest, what doest thou against him? Or if thy transgressions be multiplied, what doest thou unto him? If thou be righteous, what givest thou him? Or what receiveth he of thine hand? Thy wickedness may hurt a man as thou art; And thy righteousness may profit the son of man.*]

Psalm 16:2 [*O my soul, thou hast said unto the Lord, Thou art my Lord: My goodness extendeth not to thee.*]

[Man seeks profit, but God has] no prospect of profit [because God is] independent. [He only] answers his designs. [His designs alone] glorify himself. If not by Salvation [then] by damnation. Therefore, [God is] love only.
  Second. What kind of love? that which is grace and mercy. Often read of those [gifts of love]

[Eph. 2:8].[*For*] *by grace* [*are ye*] *saved through faith;* [*and that not of yourselves: it is the gift of God*]

Tit. 3:5 [*Not by works of righteousness which we have done, but according to his mercy he saved us, by the washing of regeneration, and renewing of the Holy Ghost*]

These [are] exercises of love to the indigent. [They have] nothing to pay. [This is] implied in grace. Yea to the wretched mercy respects such.

Rev. 3:17 [*Because thou sayest, I am rich, and increased with goods, and have need of nothing; and knowest not that thou art wretched, and miserable, and poor, and blind, and naked.*]

Therefore when [the Scripture] said So loved [We are] not to imagine [God loves us] because [there is] something very amicable [or]attractive [in us]. [God] had no delight in us, but compassion. [No, there was] nothing worthy of delight. Or if – not [worthy, then it must be] grace [and] mercy – God loved therefore not because of our worthiness, [that is, from] any motive of our goodness – rather [apart] from our goodness. [This was our] misery. This [misery of ours] excited the divine compassion. Thus appears the motive: God's pure love, that is, compassion. [God's love was] excited by no goodness [, rather,] badness and wretchedness.

SECOND. The degree[9] of this love. *Gave [his] only begotten*. The degree of love [is]always measured by this: [that] good [which one is willing to] part with in order to [be gracous and merciful]. Some so love others [that they are] willing to part with much of [their] estate. [Some also to] labour much [for another]. So [also] parents [will give up the good of their lives] for [their] children. But rarely for others [they know. It is even] more rare for [people to give a good to] strangers. [It would be] surprising if [a parent were to] sacrifice a child [for a stranger. Even] more [if that child was] an only [child]. Most, if [any would not sacrifice their only child for a stranger.] God parted with his only begotten for those who are] not *only* strangers, but [we are] without all merit, [that is, people who are] all evil, even abominable characters, enemies. [We] had abused [his love]. If [then God's love must be] out of pure compassion. But [thus] so God has dealt towards men. We [are] not friendly, but [rather] enemies to God. [We] have abused [his love]. [We are] without good [and are] infinitely vile in ourselves. Yet for us [God gave] his Son, [his] only begotten. Such [is] the degree [of God's love].

---

[9]Edwards Jr. changes words for the second point from earlier stating it as *greatness*.

THIRD. The end of this gift [is] the Salvation of sinners.

[1 Tim 1:15 *This is] a faithful saying, [and worthy of all acceptation, that Christ Jesus came into the world to save sinners; of whom I am chief.*]

[Luke 19:10 *For the Son of Man is come to] seek and [to] save that which was lost.*

Herein God commends his love. See Rom. 5:6, 8. Even for the greatest [sinner] whosoever believeth [shall be saved.] All such assured. [There are] no exception of any class or individual. The door [is] open for all. Whosoever will. If any man thirst [let him come]. Come unto me all ye [who] labour [and I will give you rest.] Ho everyone that thirsteth. [There is] no price insisted on. [There is] no exception of thieves, liars, even murderers [like] David. Yea many of the murderers of Christ [came]. Observe the expression: *[shall] not perish, but – everlasting life.* [This means that] all who come to Christ [who] believe on [him will] not perish. [Instead you will be] saved from death [that is] the second death [where] soul and body [are] in hell. [Hell is] endless [a place where there is] no rest day or night. [It is a place of] torments [of one's spirit. [It is] inconceivable [and] more dreadful [because you are inflicted by God himself. [To not perish is to be] redeemed to eternal life and have everlasting life. [This is] not bare existence [rather, it is a] life of happiness. [The Holy] Spirit [is given] immediately from God [to his] chosen delights of his children.

IMPROVEMENT

FIRST. Hence the obligation we are under to God. To each person in the trinity distinctly. To the whole for contriving [the work of salvation].

To the Father for sending his son [who is] his only [and is] dear as himself, yet [he] spared [him] not. Such love the Father [had].
    To the Son for undertaking [and] freely offering up himself. Giving up all of heaven. [This would include the] tokens of father's love, ease, [and] life. Such love the Son [had]
    So [also] the Spirit for his readiness in comforting, etc. [Together] the Spirit and the bride say come.
    Love always infers obligation. So [it is] among men. But if common kindness [shows us this truth, then how much more should we have obligation to respond to God's love]?

SECOND. What aggravated [this shared love with mankind]? Sin. [We are under] condemnation if [we] reject all this love – these offers [of God's love]

The greater the love of God [then] the greater the sin of abusing [his love]. But [it is] impossible be greater [than what God ha demonstrated]. Greater love [hath] no man than this [that a man lay down his life for his friends.] Joh. 15:13. Now this love all those abuse [it are those] who comply not with the gospel.

God gave his Son to be received [to be believed on] as the Saviour. Not to receive is to reject [and] despise the greatest gift. [Is it] possible [one would consider him] not worth accepting, [or thinking they have] no necessity of, no [need of a] Saviour. How wroth must God be with such and what a condemnation for [such a person. It will be] more intolerable [for them] than for Sodom. If they that despised Moses's law [were stoned how much more, they that despise God's Son?]

THIRD. Let all be exhorted to receive Christ. God might have left [us] without a Saviour. [He was under] no obligation [to save us]. So most [would] have perished [with] no possibility. But [God] removed the obstacles. Now [we] only repent and believe the gospel. [You do] not need to make an atonement. Christ has done [everything]. Acquiesce in [the atonement of Christ]. Certainly this [is] reasonable. [This is] necessary or we will] perish unless [we believe].

[This is a very] profitable [to receive Christ]. [To receive Christ brings] eternal gains [You will] not perish, but [have] infinite riches, eternal honours [and] such happiness as eye hath not seen.

Mat. 11:28 [*Come unto me, all ye that labour and are heavy laden, and I will give you rest.*]

APPLICATION

Address to the prisoner: Unhappy man! You have heard [now about] the love of God [in] his giving his son. [You have heard about] what [he has] done to prepare the way. [The way] is prepared [and the] door of open to all even murderers. [You have heard] how ready God to forgive [you]. What think you? [Is this not] not good news [that there is] hope for you? [Is it not] a possibility? Should [you] not rejoice? [Should you not] leap in chains? With all eagerness humble [yourself and come]! Fly to the Saviour! [Will you not]? This [is your] reasonable service.

This the last Sabbath before another in eternity. [After this Sabbath will your eternal] state [be] fixed. [Then there will be] no hope. Now [you have] hope. Therefore, though often offered [he is] rejected. [Just now] once more God offers his Son [to you]. Christ himself [is offered] to wash [you,] to clothe [you], [and] present [you] without spot [or blemish]. Now [he] calls come unto me [you who are] weary [and heavy] laden with chains. [Come and] return, [oh] prisoner. [This is a day] of hope. [Right] here [believe in his love] and your soul [will] live. [Even] if but at the eleventh hour.

As you regard your eternal welfare [and] your immortal soul. Desire heaven [and] Dread hell. The wrath of that being whose eyes a flame of fire. That prison [is] infinitely stronger than that in which [you have] been confined [and] that death [is greater] than to [that] which [you have been] condemned. [You will experience] the company and tortures of devils. Therefore, obtain the favour of God [through] Christ [and you will experience the] company of saints and angels.

Be exhorted to fly to Christ! If [you do] not comply, [then expect] a savour of death unto death. [You will] think of [all] the calls [you have heard]. [You will] think of this offer in hell [and it will] add to your torment to eternity. Therefore, if [you respond for] no other motive, yet [respond to] this, now while [it is called] today. [Respond] before the night [and you are] in eternal darkness.

To others. When Christ [was] crucified [for all], [why] wait? [Do not say that it was] not for me. [Why not] for yourself? Though not the same reason [of murder] not for this [crime], yet [Christ died] for yourself. Many of you under the same condemnation [because the Scripture says that] he that believeth not [is condemned already]. Therefore, think of yourself. What [will] you [say] when [you] stand [before] the tribunal of God? [What will you say] when [your] sins [are] set in order before you? When [your] conscience condemn [you]. When the judge [remind you of your sin], [and] to the offer [of Christ's atonement]. [You will] not come out till [you have paid the last farthing]. But [there] is a way. But [just] one [way] of escaping all [condemnation]. [By] making sure of an interest in Christ. Therefore, come unto Christ. He that believeth [hath everlasting life].

APPENDIX 4

SERMON 412: FOR A FAST ON ACCOUNT OF OUR PRESENT DISPUTES WITH GREAT BRITAIN

Jonathan Edwards Jr., "Volume 412. Preached on occasion of a fast appointed by authority Feb. 1, 1775 on account of our present disputes with Great Britain," *Jonathan Edwards Jr. Papers (Sermons)*, Hartford Seminary Library. Box 166, Folder 2735, Item 75777. Transcript permission by the Hartford Seminary Library, 77 Sherman St., Hartford, CT 06105-9509.

412. "Volume 412. Preached on occasion of a fast appointed by authority Feb. 1, 1775 on account of our present disputes with Great Britain."

Ecclesiastes 4:1 "So I returned and considered all the oppressions that are done under the sun and behold the tears of such as were oppressed and *they* had no comforter. And on the side of their oppressors there was power, but they had no comforter."

Solomon the wisest of men was well acquainted with the affairs of human life; on this subject therefore he gives the most excellent and useful rules and instructions. But he was not only acquainted with the affaires of common life, affairs which concern men in general; he was as well acquainted with high life and with those things which especially concern the great and noble. Being himself a king, yea one of the greatest of kings, and having enjoyed a long and peaceful reign, he had much opportunity to make observations upon the various parts and modes of government and to note the various evils which attend public and civil affairs as well as the common, private concerns of men in general. This opportunity he did not let slip; he eagerly embraced it, and actually made observation upon these things, the result of which in many particulars he hath left upon record for the instruction of all who should come after him.

The remarks which he delivers us in the text are a part of the result of his observation and experience in national affairs. "So I returned [and considered all the oppressions that are done under the sun and behold the tears of such as were oppressed and they had no comforter. And on the side of their oppressors there was power, but *they had no comforter.*"] As these words are introduced in this manner, *So I returned and considered etc.* They seem to refer to something which preceded. It seems plainly to be suggested by them, that the wise man had been before considering the oppressions that are done under the sun; that his attention had been called off from them, and that now he had resumed the contemplation of them. And this if we examine the context, we shall find it to be fact. If we go no further back than the 16 verse of the preceding chapter we shall find that he was speaking upon the same subject. And moreover [I saw under the sun the place of judgment, that wickedness was there; and the place of righteousness, that iniquity was there.] We find here that he had in view a particular kind of oppression of that of perverting justice in judgment. His attention is then diverted to other subjects, especially to the common mortality of both men and beasts. At length in the text he informs us how [he has now] returned and resumed the same subject. "So I returned, etc."

DOCTRINE

In the text we may observe:

First. The object of the wise man's consideration, which was the oppressions which take place in the world, the oppressions in general of whatever kind, or proceeding from whatever source. "So I considered *all* the oppressions which are done under the sun." He had before taken into consideration some of them, viz. those which arise from the perversion of justice in courts of judicature. But now he returns to a more general and extensive consideration of [the] subject. *Second.* We may observe that the word *considered* seems to be emphatical. He doth not say that he occasionally thought upon these oppressions or that they transiently passed through his mind: Nor is this at all suggested in the expression. But it is naturally suggested that he fully and attentively considered them, or that he calmly and naturally deliberated upon them, viewing them on all sides. *Third.* We may observe the result of this full consideration of the subject. This consists in two things, (1) that the oppressors have power on their side, sufficient to support them in their oppressions; (2) that the oppressed, although really and sorely oppressed, so as to cause them to weep and shed tears under the cruel burdens laid upon them yet have none to comfort them. He repeats it twice: *And they had no comforter.... But they had no comforter.*

These three propositions seem evidently to be contained in the text:

1. That there are oppressions under the sun.

2. That on the side of the oppressors there is power.

3. That the oppressed, although they shed tears under their burdens, have no comforter.

Each of these propositions I would distinctly consider in the order in which I have not mentioned them.

FIRST. That there are oppressions in the world or under the sun. This is plainly supposed in what Solomon saith in the text; for could he consider the oppressions that are done under the sun, if there were none? The same thing is also supposed in [the] 8th verse of the 5th chapter. "If thou [seest the oppression of the poor, and violent perverting of judgment and justice in a province, marvel not at the matter: for he that is higher than the highest regardeth; and there be higher than they.] So he expressly mentioned on particular kind of oppression in chapter 3 verse 16, as we already observed.

And happy for us if all the evidence we have of the existence of oppression in the world were that of revelation! But this is a happy lot which when neither the world in general, nor we in particular, are blessed [with a personal knowledge of oppression]. It is manifest by observation of the world in general; and it is still now manifest by our own feelings that there are oppressions under the sun. Was not Israel anciently in Egypt oppressed, when they were kept to the hard drudgery of making bricks, and that without the necessary materials? Was not the same people afterwards oppressed when they were carried captive to Babylon being dragged out of their own country that land which flowed with milk and honey, deprived of all their estates and property, and held in a state of absolute servitude for the space of 70 years. Or without running so far back into antiquity, were not our ancestors the English oppressed when the country was invaded and subdued without even a tolerable pretense, first by the Romans, then by the Saxons, then by the Dans and afterward by the Normans, and they were treated in the most arbitrary and cruel manner, as to their property, their liberty, and even their lives themselves, by their sovereign victors? Were they not oppressed under Charles the first, when their money was distorted from them without their consent, given either in person, or by their representatives? When they were haled into the Star Chamber and into the high commissioned court, and tried for high crimes and misdemeanors, by the mere creatures of the crown, who they were sure would not dare; however innocent they might be to give judgment in their favor, to the offence of the crown, or its ministers?

But without further enlarging in this way or I might abundantly, I shall paint out some particular kinds or modes of oppressions, which have been and still are very prevalent in the world.

First. The first kind of oppression I would take notice of is in making laws. The legislative power in any state may be guilty of very great oppression in making bad laws. To be governed by good and wholesome laws is to enjoy the highest political liberty; but so far as the laws are bad, so for liberty is annihilated and slavery is introduced. Now in order that the laws be good, they must be such as are calculated to promote the good of the state for which they are enacted. So for they are adopted to this and so for they are good; on the other hand, so far as they are not adopted to this end, but one adapted to this end, but one adapted to the evil and confusion of the state, so for they are bad and ought either never to have existed or at last to be immediately repealed. The good of the state or what is the same thing, the general good of the individuals which compose the state is a very end, and the only just and of all law and of all government. If this end is not likely to be obtained, why should men enter into political society? or having entered into it, why should they continue in it? I presume no answer that will bear the light could ever be given to these plain questions.

Here then we have a plain and infallible touchstone, by which to try every law, by whatever corporation, assembly, parliament, king or emperor it be made. If now in question be for the general good of the state or kingdom, with respect to what it is enacted it is a good law, and by enacting it the legislative body is guilty of no oppression. But if it be not for the general good of the state it is a bad law, and in passing it, the legislature is guilty of oppression.

Laws may be oppressive [in] various ways. Some are oppressive immediately, as the good of the state is immediately obstructed, or as they bring upon the state immediate detriment. Thus should there be a law made to confiscate all the private property in the kingdom, this would be a law immediately oppressive. Again, other laws may be oppressive only by the consequence to which they lead: they are not directly detrimental to the community, yet they open such a door and afford such a precedent, as if followed may involve the state in the greatest damage, disorder and confusion. Thus a law made to restrain a particular branch of trade may really in itself be for the benefit of the state. Yet from such precedents, a corrupt legislature may take occasion to such restrictions upon trade as could soon bring the state to utter ruin. Again, some laws may be oppressive in both these senses at one and the same time.

I would further observe under this head, that the legislative power may be guilty of oppression not only by enacting bad laws, but also by not enacting those which are good and necessary for the good of the state. They are set to be the guardians of the rights and happiness of the people in all respects wherein they can be affected by the laws. They are therefore not only bound to abstain from making any unjust and hurtful laws, or to repeal them, whenever they are found to be hurtful; but they are also found positively to enact all those laws which appear to be necessary for conducive to the public good. A people may suffer as much through the want of good and wholesome laws, laws necessary to restrain violence, injustice or abuse, or to encourage peace, justice and virtue, as through laws which are positively had. Whenever therefore the legislative power in any state neglects to make such good and necessary laws, whatever the motive may be, it is really guilty of oppression. The laws must be adequate to maintain peace and justice and to punish the contrary, yea to punish everything which tendeth to disorder of the state, or the disquietude of its members.

Second. Another kind of oppression there may be in the execution of the laws. Let a state have ever so good and wholesome laws, this signifies nothing to guard it against oppression, unless they be executed. A law may as well not be made at all, as not be executed. It therefore often so happens that in a state where there are the most wholesome laws established, there is yet the greatest and most flagrant oppression. We have already observed that there are two ways wherein the legislative authority of a state may be guilty of oppression, either by making bad laws, or by neglecting to make those that are good and necessary. The like observation we may now make concerning the executive authority, that it may commit oppression either by obliging subjects to do or to submit to things which are contrary to things which are contrary to the established laws of the state or by neglecting to make them conform to the laws: Or in fewer words, the executive authority may commit oppression either by going beyond the law, or by falling short of it. These two things I would consider distinctly.

One. The executive authority may commit oppression in going beyond the law, and in making men do or suffer that which the law doth not in such cases require. This most manifest oppression, and thoroughly tends to the ruin of the state. For if the magistrate in the exercise of government do not proceed according [to] the laws and established principles of the constitution, we may as well have no laws, no constitution; for everything is suspended entirely upon his arbitrary will. If the law suit him, well: if not, he will proceed without it. So that in reality the arbitrary will of the magistrate or executive authority is upon this plan, the only law. And what security have we then for property, liberty, or even life? Most manifestly none at all.

Two. Oppression may as really and effectually be practiced by not executing or falling short of the law, as by going beyond it. And this is a much more common way of oppression than the former. But few magistrates, in a state whose constitution requires them to go according to certain fixed laws, are bold and hardy enough to proceed without and beyond the law. Whereas many, alas too many in all states fail of their duty in thoroughly putting the laws in execution. But this is as real oppression as the other. For what material adds to there between depriving the people of their rights by going beyond the law, and doing it by falling short of it? What great difference whether a man's property be wrested from him by the mere arbitrary will of a judge, or by the negligence of the same judge refusing to act according to law in adjudging him his right? In either case the man is equally injured, an equal door is opened for future iniquity, and the same foundation is laid for arbitrary government. The effect will be the same whatever the particular case be, whether it respect his property, his liberty, or his life. If the laws against any vice whatever are not executed, the magistrate is in this neglect guilty of oppression. He virtually gives his approbation to that vice yea he virtually practices it himself; and to be sure in refusing to execute the law, he condemns [the] law and practically calls out for the abolition of it. Such magistrates do really overturn all law, all justice, all good order in the state, all government, and in effect the very being of the state itself.

Indeed, every degree of neglect in executing the laws is not actually followed by this effect; yet it hath this tendency. What do we have laws but that they may be executed? Every neglect in the execution of the laws is like the letting out of water. When it first begins to run in a new channel it may run in such a small stream, that it may seem to be a mere trifle, not worthy of notice. But the longer it is suffered to run, the more it wears away the ground and the wider and deeper channel doth it make for itself, till at length it is impossible to put a stop to it. Therefore I scruple not to say that the magistrate who doth not strictly execute the laws of this country is as real an oppressor, as he that acts arbitrarily above and beyond law; yea that he virtually rises up in opposition and rebellion against those very laws which he was appointed to execute; and not only against the laws, but against the legislative authority; yea against the constitution and state itself.

This kind of oppression I before addressed, is much more common than that which consists in acting above and beyond law. There is this reason to be assigned for it, that it is not at first, so open and manifest. A positively arbitrary act is at once seen by everyone in a free state and the source for which it proceeds is also easily discerned. But this negatively oppression is not so easily seen. It sometimes puts on the guise of unity and mercy and under this is a pretense for a long while imposes upon people, especially the commonality. Sometimes it rises from mere sloth and want of activity in the man in authority. This being an habit of nature to some men is more readily excused, than designed wickedness. Sometimes it cloaks itself under former custom and rules. But what right pray had such a custom ever to be established, or such rules to be introduced? Who hatch a right to establish customs and may be contrary to the laws of the state?

I would further observe that sometimes this kind of oppression is practiced by really and finally not executing the laws; and sometimes by delaying and not executing them at the proper time and place. In whichever of these ways it be practiced it is still oppression. The delay of justice is a real injustice as the final refusal to grant it.

Give me leave further to add under this head, that the source of the most of this kind of oppression seems to be this, the appointment of improper and unfit men to civil authority. In order to be fit for an office in civil authority a man should doubtless in the first place be a man of some abilities. "Wo to thee, O land, when they king is a child, and thy prince eat in the morning." [Eccl. 10:16]. And "better is a poor and wise child, than an old & foolish king." [Eccl. 4:13] In the second place he ought to be a man of integrity. What a grand absurdity to appoint a man to civil authority, to distribute justice to all who apply to him, who cannot be solely trusted in [the] smallest matters? In the last place, he should be possessed of some degree of spirit and resolution. If either of these qualities be wanting in a civil magistrate, there will be wanting there will be the utmost danger of his practicing oppression. If he be not a man [of] some abilities, he may practice oppression, through mere ignorance. If he be not a man of integrity, he will do it from depravity and perversity of heart. If he be not a man of some activity and resolution, he may do through either sloth, or fearfulness.

Nor can the power which appointed such men to civil authority be entirely clear of the guilt of the oppression which they practice in consequence of their appointment. The cause of the cause in this case is doubtless to be considered as the cause of the effect.

Having somewhat particularly discussed the first proposition, we come at length to the second which is

SECOND. That on the side of the oppressors there is power. It is so in all cases whatever, otherwise, they would not be capable of practicing oppression. Are the legislators quietly of making unjust and oppressive laws? On their side is power; they can command the whole power of the nation or state. They can raise both men and money to carry their oppressive laws into execution. Or do they commit oppression by not making those laws which are necessary for wellbeing of the state? Still on their side is power; for during the time of their existence as legislators, they are, only so far as limited by the first principles of constitution absolute. Or even if they violate the constitution itself, they commonly have power enough to defend and support themselves in their iniquity. Of is the executive authority guilty of oppression either in actin without law, or in neglecting to put laws thereby into execution? They also have power on their side. They have the command of the public moneys in [the] bank; they have the standing army, if there be one, entirely under their control, and if this be not sufficient they can also raise the militia. Hence it is often dangerous even to speak against the proceedings of executive authority. they have such power that their resentment is often like the roaring of a lion. The wrath of a king, saith Solomon is like the roaring of a lion. [Prov. 19:10] This it is that makes it so difficult and dangerous for a people to seek relief from their oppressions; the reason is that on the side of their oppressors, there is power.

Beside the power of fire and sword, oppressors sometimes have the voice of a deluded or depraved people. Now this of itself implies or carries in it power. He that hath the voice of the people on his side, hath power on his side, and that whether he be vested with any other power or not. But when the unjust judge, the corrupt and designing civil magistrate is popular, or hath the voice of the people in his favor, especially in popular governments, this is a further addition to the power which he was incased by his office. Now sometimes it so happens, especially in times of degeneracy, that either the legislature or executive magistrate, or perhaps both, are guilty of injustice and wickedness in the exercise of their authority, and at the same time the people or a great part of them love to have it so. Some are benefited by it for the present and others do not immediately perceive of the oppressive and ruinous consequences which will follow; and so they acquiesces and implicitly gives their consent and even assist in binding and riveting the chains of slavery about their own necks. Thus much it may suffice for me to have said, in order to show in what sense on the side of the oppressors there is power. I come now to the

THIRD AND LAST proposition observed to be contained in the text, which is, that they shed many tears under their burdens, have no comforter. A person in prosperity can generally find friends enough. Even those who have no real friendship for him, but rather hate him, will, while prosperity continues, court his favor and pretend to be his friends. But no sooner are the scales of providence turned, and adversity takes place, then these friends drop off, like leaves in autumn. Now just so it is with respect to states and political bodies of men; so long as they remain powerful, so long they will be respected by neighboring states: but no sooner are they subdued, and rendered weak, than they are despised; and however greatly they may be oppressed by their conquerors, scarce anyone seems to regard them, or afford them the least pity or comfort. The same observation holds as to particular parts of states and distant bodies of men belonging to the same nation or kingdom. If for instance the people maintain their rights and privileges and have that share in government which of right belongs to them; they are considered by all men, as respectable body and their favor is courted. But let them once be deprived of these their rights, and therefore they are despised by all, and let them be abused and oppressed as much as they will and let them shed as many tears as they will, there is scarce a man found to comfort them. All their complaints are considered as the fruits of unreasonable petulance, if not a spirit of rebellion.

The same observation are applicable to the nobility and even to the king. So long as our king Charles I first retained his power, and was seated quietly upon his throne, his favor was courted both at home and abroad. The king of Spain was sufficiently fond of the proposal of marriage between Charles and his daughter, though afterwards it was broken off. And the ward of France actually gave him one of their infanta's. But no sooner were disturbances raised against Charles in his own kingdom, and his throne began to totter, than the friendship of state and all other foreign powers was cooled at once; insomuch that even his wife, who was sister to the French king, would not procure the smallest assistance for her husband, although she solicited it in person. And as the civil war proceeded and Charles fell entirely into the hands of his enemies, he seemed in the literal sense to be left without a comforter.

The Lords spiritual and temporal had been a powerful and respectable body but as soon as they were rejected from any part in government by the republicans, they were regulated and left without a comforter. The same thing happened to the republicans themselves. At the restoration they lost all their influence and fell a sacrifice to the revenge of their enemies, and the oppressions and cruelties which they all suffered and the deaths which many of them suffered were little or nothing noticed: under all these things they had no comforter.

I have now in some measures considered what was at first proposed. I next proceed to the

APPLICATION

of what we have said in general terms to the present state of our public affairs.

FIRST. We are naturally led by what hath been said to consider in what particulars we in this land, are oppressed. The present time is said to be a time of public calamities. Our rulers tell so, and therefore call upon us to celebrate a day of fasting and prayer to confess our sins, and to implore the divine favorable interposition, to deliver us from the calamities which threaten us. Now it becomes us to inquire, what are these calamities? For unless we know what they are, we cannot rationally humble ourselves because of them, or so rationally pray that they may be removed, or averted. To this inquiring then I answer that we complain of oppression from the court of Great Britain in several particulars. We complain that parliament assumes the right of making law to bind us in all cases whatsoever. So that

(1) They oppress us in their legislative capacity. For they have not only claimed the right of making laws to bind us, if had this been all, had they only claimed, but not acted upon their claim, we might have rested easy. But they have acted upon it, they have in fact made laws to bind us in cases, which immediately affect our interest; to tax us, to wrest our property

from us, without our consent. And they claim the right of doing it not only in those instances, in which they have done it, but in all other instances whatsoever, i.e., they claim a right of taking from us as much of our property as they please, and this without our consent and without even asking it.

Now this we call oppression. For it is undoubtedly the right of men to claim their property and to part with it only by their consent given either in person, by themselves immediately, or by their representatives, those whom they have chosen and authorized so to do. If this be not the right of all men, and so our right, there is no such thing as property in the world. Everything that a man possesses is liable to be arrested from him at any time, and he hath no right to say, why do ye so? But taking it for granted that there is such a thing as property in the world, and that every man hath a right to retain his property, till he consents and hath manifested his consent to part with it, either personally or by his representatives; I say taking these plain things for granted, it plainly follows that we Americans are oppressed by the court of Great Britain in the laws which they have lately made and assumed the right of making to tax us.

Again we suffer oppression from Great Britain not only as it claims the right of taxing us without our consent; but as it claims the right of making laws to bind us in all other cases. Now according to this, if the court of Great Britain shall be disposed to make a law that we shall be hand-cuffed, or that we shall wear an iron chain about our necks, or that we shall all have our noses cut off, or our eye plucked out, or in fine that we all shall be hanged; it hath a right to do it; should make any or all these laws, we have no right to complain. This part of their claim also, they have not only set up, but have acted upon it; they did so in making the law for transporting men from [the] province of the Massachusetts Bay to another colony, or even to Great Britain in order to [stand] their trial for crimes committed [in] the said Massachusetts Bay [Colony]. They did so in altering the constitution or charter of that province; and also in restoring and establishing the French laws and government, together with the popish religion in Canada. They that have a right and a power to alter one charter by a sovereign act, without so much as the form of a trail, or suffering the accused to speak for themselves have a right to do the same as to every other charter. They that have a right to order criminals from the Massachusetts Bay to another colony to Great Britain for trial for crimes committed in the said Massachusetts may make the same law or order with respect to any or every colony on the Continent. They that have a right to establish Popery and the French laws in Canada, have the same right to do it in any of the other colonies. Nor have we any security that they will not do these things to all the colonies.

Beside these tyrannical laws, the court of Great Britain has laid the most burdensome restrictions on our trade, whereby we are restrained from carrying on a free trade with those foreign ports where we could to the greatest advantage. They have also established a board of commissioners among are with a vast train of collectors, comptrollers, tidewaiters, etc., etc. all of whom have salaries which must be paid and are paid out of the duties they collect of the honest trader, which yet must finally come out of the consumer of the good. So that this vast train of commissioners, comptrollers, collectors, tidewaiters, etc., etc., do all live upon the people, they live on you, may be who buy and consume the goods, whether dry goods or West India.

Perhaps you have not been sensible of this, because you have never been particularly called upon for money to pay these salaries. But you have as really paid them, in paying for the goods which you have bought; for over and above the price of the goods was added the money which went to pay the salaries. If their salaries had been collected of you in the way of a rate and you had paid as much in that way as you now have in the way of duties on gods, I'll warrant you, you would have felt it, and complained of it most bitterly. Now all this we esteem oppressive. What might have they to respect our trade, more than we have to respect theirs? What right have they to impose upon us the burden of maintain so many of their four dependents? You have enough to do, to maintain our own poor; but beside this, they will make you maintain their dependents, not in the quality of poor maintained at the public expense but in the quality and state of the first gentry in the country.[1]

These are some of the instances wherein we are oppressed by the court of Great Britain acting as a legislative body. I proceed now to taking notice of some instances wherein we have suffered oppression from the same court or from its deputies acting as executive magistrates.

First. A standing army hath been kept in these colonies in time of profound peace, without the consent of our several assemblies. A standing army hath always been esteemed both a great grievance because it is so expensive, and because it tends so directly and greatly to deprave the morality of the people. It is dangerous to liberty, because it may be employed by only one who hath the command of it, and especially by the king of his

---

[1] At this point there are two marginal notes which indicate an extemporaneous incorporation of "restraining our trade" and "Fishery."

ministry, entirely to overturn the constitution and to support and carry into execution the most arbitrary and tyrannical edits. Now for these reasons we esteem the standing army kept among us to be an oppression laid upon us by the British ministry.

And it is an oppression most arbitrarily and wantonly perpetrated. For what need is there here of a standing army? The pretense is, that it is necessary for our defense. If so, why was it not necessary ever since the first settlement of the country? Ever since that period was no such thing known in the country. Yet the country was always more defenseless than it is at present. Truly if we were judged to be able to defend ourselves in those former times when we were fewer in number and in every respect more feeble, much more are we able to do it know, being so much more numerous, and every way so much stronger.

Second. Another grievance of this kind is, that this standing army and also a considerable naval armament have been employed to enforce the collection of those taxes which are leveed upon us without our consent. Thereby keeping of a standing among us is doubtless no small oppression; but much more so, to employ this army together with a flee to enforce other acts of oppression. Yet this is done it is especially and notoriously done towards Boston and the province of the Massachusetts Bay.

Third. Another grievance of the like kind is this, that the various most humble and loyal petitions which we have performed to the parliament of Great Britain and especially to his majesty the king, have been fruitless. It is allowed on all hands that it is the right of the subject to petition his majesty. Upon this right we have acted, and have laid our humble and loyal petitions before the throne. And what hath been the fruit? Where is the instance on all our late difficulties wherein the favor asked hath been granted, or the grievance complained of, hath been removed? I presume none can be found.

Fourth. The agents of the colonies at the court of Great Britain have been discountenanced and obstructed in their duty. That court seems to have been unwilling that the colonies should have any agents there, to stand at all for their rights, or to plead their cause. Therefore it has endeavored to prevent payment of salaries necessary for the support of the agents. This certainly is very oppressive. One would have thought it had been enough, yet there are no representatives of the colonies in the parliament; and the court might have been well content that the colonies should have as many agents there as they should think proper to maintain. But such is the spirit of tyranny and oppression there prevalent, that they are unwilling even for this. And therefore have instructed their governors here to do what in his [power] to prevent there being any agents.

Five. Another grievance of the like nature is the frequent and unreasonable dissolutions of colonial assemblies. The representatives of the people are the guardians of the rights of the people, and being met in general assembly they have opportunity to do many things in order to preserve their liberties and to guard against oppression. But it hath very often been so, that as soon as these assemblies have undertaken some business which tended to promote or secure the liberties of their constituents, and that in a constitutional way, they have been dissolved, and thus incapacitated to proceed in the important work which they had begun. Yea they have been dissolved merely because they would not comply with some arbitrary mandate, or in other words because they would not betray the liberties of the people. Now surely this is a great instance of oppression. By this means, both the liberties of a people may be arrested from them, and the necessary public business may be entirely prevented. In short at this note, it seems to lie I the breasts of ministerial governors, whether there should be any assemblies or not.

These are some and only some of the instances wherein we suffer oppressive from the court of Great Britain. For only to mention and very briefly explain them all, would require a whole discourse by itself. Surely these are sufficient to arouse us, and to excite us to fasting and prayer, and other religious exercises.

(2)[2] Let us apply this subject more nearby home, and imagine whether there be not some instances of oppression which arise not from so remote a cause. We are apt enough to see the faults of others, and to feel the troubles which are brought upon us by others, while we are often very inattentive to our own faults, to those troubles in which we involved ourselves. Now if it is so, as is frequently said that every man carries a wallet on his shoulder, with his neighbor's faults in the forepart, and his own in the hinder part; it is reasonable that we at least sometimes shift the wallet, bring the hinder part forward, and take a fair view of ourselves. We complain most bitterly of the oppression brought upon us by the court of Great Britain and as I have already shown, we have just reason to complain. But at the same time it is but reasonable that we inquire how far we are guilty of the same things towards one another; and how far our own government which is entirely within ourselves is oppressive. By what we have said in the preceding

---

[2]This paragraph begins with a bracket and the finishing bracket is not identified but could be connected with the brackets below.

discourse I think it appears that all oppression is by no means confined to absolute monarchies; but that it may take place in the popular governments such as ours is.

Here without undertaking to determine wherein our government actually is oppressive, I shall mention some particulars with respect to what it is from its very form especially in danger of becoming oppressive. As in absolute governments all power is derived from the king, and he is supreme; so in our government all power is derived from the people and they are supreme: and as in monarchical governments most of the grievances proceed from a fear of offending the monarch; so in popular governments, most of the oppression and grievances proceed from a fear of offending the people. Thus our governor appellants and representatives who are chosen by the people, are in danger of being deterred from making many wholesome laws or regulations which yet may be unpopular for fear that if they should they would be clopped from their offices. From this source we are in great danger of being oppressed by our legislators. For however the whole body the people may approve of error and injustice, yet truth is truth, and justice is justice. However the greatest danger is by no means from the whole body of the people rightly informed; as it is rarely to them supposed that they should approve of error and injustice: but from some interested individuals who take occasion to raise groundless clamors among the people. There is great danger that the fear of these individuals and of the people deceived by them will restrain our rulers in many instances from doing their duty.

To illustrate this matter a little suppose I were sent a representative of some town in this colony; and in the assembly some man is nominated for a certain important post, whom I know to be a man of but mean, slender abilities, and consequently nowise fit for the post for which he is nominated; would it not in this case be my duty to speak plainly, and say boldly that the man is not fit for the office? Yet in such a popular government as this I should be in great danger of neglecting my duty, should fear that gentlemen and his friends would never consent in [the] future to promote me. So in a thousand other instances.[3]

The executive magistrate also is in danger on the same account. There is danger that he will through fear of losing his popularity, be deterred from a strait, punctual, and timely execution of law and justice. So I might descend to innumerable particulars; but these may be sufficient at present. I say, these and such like are the dangers to which we in this colony are especially

---

[3] This paragraph has brackets around it.

exposed and there is one fact now in my view, which seems plainly to argue that all our political affairs are right; that is the multiplicity of law suits.

But if the debtors are not careful to their duty, and so lay a necessity upon their creditors to such their rights in this way; then they are to blame. Here give me leave to add, it appears evident to me that the flow, the dilatory execution of law and justice among us, is one chief cause of this multiplicity of lawsuits. Because villains know it will be longtime ere they shall be obliged by law to do justice, hence they are encouraged to keep others out if there out of their dues. Whereas if the case were otherwise, if they knew that they must very speedily be obliged to do justice, and that which the additional expense of the law, they would have sufficient motive to be more honest and just of themselves, and not to endeavor to keep others out of their just dues.[4]

(3) These being our calamitous circumstances, especially in our disputes with Great Britain the question naturally arises what is to be done? How shall we avoid these calamities and oppressions? So this I answer it becomes us in the first place to consider the hand of God in these things. The providence of God is so universal that not a sparrow falleth to the ground without our heavenly Father, and the very hairs of our head are all numbered. Much more is it concerned in ordering the state and revelations, the prosperity or adversity of kingdoms, provinces and empires. It is not to be doubted therefore that God in his wise and holy providence hath ordered these events to take place with respect to us: and this dispensation of providence plainly shows that God hath a controversy with us.

Hosea 4:1 [Hear the word of the LORD, ye children of Israel: For the LORD hath a controversy with the inhabitants of the land, because there is no truth, nor mercy, nor knowledge of God in the land.]

Jeremiah 25:31 [A noise shall come even to the ends of the earth; For the LORD hath a controversy with the nations; He will plead with all flesh; He will give them that are wicked to the sword, saith the LORD.]

The first step then, I conceive, to be take in order to avoid these oppressions, is to confess our sins before God, & his righteousness in chastising us in the manner he does. Unless we be thus humbled for our sins, we cannot truly repent and reform; and unless we reform we have no reason to expect that God will be reconciled to us. And such a repentance and reformation is our next duty. At the same time it becomes us to look to God in the most humble and earnest manner, that he would graciously interpose

---

[4]This paragraph ends with one bracket; however, the first bracket is either missing or intended to be joined to the previously bracketed paragraph.

in our behalf. It is easy with him who hath brought these troubles upon us, to remove them: he can do it, merely by speaking the word.t is easy with him to save by few or by many, by those that are strong, or by them that have no might. He is utterly irresistible, and if he be for us, who shall be against us?[5]

(4) While we are so anxious for the preservation of our civil liberties, let us by no means forget the importance of the spiritual liberty of the children of God. We are very careful to guard against temporal slavery, and this with good reason. But let us remember we are all naturally enslaved by sin, and in bondage to Satan. Now this is infinitely more to be dreaded, than the worst kind of temporal or civil slavery. What will it profit us though we should live all our days in the possession of the most perfect civil liberty, if at the same time we be the bondmen of Satan here, and must continue in his bondage through out eternity. Hence arises another of just reproof to those who are so anxious to guard against civil slavery, and yet are no wise concerned to escape from the slavery of sin and Satan. Out of your mouth and by your own practice will you be condemned; and your own consciences will testify the inconsistency of your conduct. Let me therefore intreat you, as you would be consistent with yourself and act as true and real friends of liberty, to be as much, and as sincerely engaged after spiritual and eternal liberty as you are after civil and temporal and in this case scruple not you will find it. If thou seek her as silver [and searchest for her as for hid treasures; Then shalt thou understand the fear of the LORD, and find the knowledge of God. Prov. 2:4-5].

---

[5]Edwards Jr. adds an astrict and in an empty spot on his manuscript notes the following points of emphasis: "use all human means—no miracles—deny ourselves—no comforter—despised by all—But—"

Appendix 5

"Confession of Faith"

Below is a transcript of Jonathan Edwards's public "confession of faith"[1] to be read publicly at the Lord's Table the following day. He had been affected during an awakening at the College of New Jersey, and at the age of eighteen, he was now ready to enter a covenant with the Lord Jesus Christ.

> Nassau Hall September 17, 1763
>
> I Jonathan Edwards, Student of the College in New Jersey on this seventeenth Day of September 1763, being the Day before the first Time I Propose to draw near to the Lord's table; after much Thought and due consideration, as well as Prayer to almighty God, for his Assistance, resolved in the Grace of God, to enter into an express Act of Self Dedication to the Service of God; as being a thing highly reasonable in its own Nature, and that might be of eminent Service, to keep me steady in my Christian course, to rouse me out of Sloth, and Indolence, and uphold me in the Day of Temptation.
>
> Eternal and ever-blessed God! I desire with the deepest Humiliation and Abasement of Soul to come, in the Name and for the sake of Jesus Christ, and present myself before thee, especially on such an Occasion as this; to enter into a Covenant with thee. But notwithstanding my sins have made such a Separation

---

[1] Jonathan Edwards Jr., "Confession of Faith September 17, 1763," *Jonathan Edwards Papers, Series IV. Edwards Family Writings,* Beinecke Rare Book and Manuscript Library. GEN MSS 151, Box 24, Folder 1355.

between thee and my soul, I beseech thee thro' Christ thy Son to vouchsafe thy presence with me, and Acceptance of the best Sacrifice which I can make.

I do O Lord! In Hopes of thy assisting Grace, solemnly make an entire and perpetual Surrender, of all that I am and have unto thee, being determined in the Strength, to renounce all former Lords who have had Dominion over me, every Lust of the Eye, of the Flesh and of the Mind, and to live entirely devoted to thee, and thy Service. To thee do I consecrate the Powers of my Mind, with whatsoever Improvements thou hast already or shalt be pleased hereafter to grant me in the literary way, purposing if it be thy good Pleasure, to purse my Studies assiduously that I may be better prepared to act in any sphere of Life, in which thou shalt place me.

I do also solemnly dedicate all my Possessions, my Time, my influence over others, to be all used for thy Glory. To thy Direction I resign myself, and all that I have trusting all future Contingencies in thy Hands, and may they Will in all things, and not mine be done. Use me, O Lord! As an Instrument of thy Service! I beseech the[e] number me among thy People; may I be clothed with the Righteousness of thy Son; ever impart to me through him all needful Supplies of thy purifying and cheering spirit! I beseech thee O Lord! That thou wouldst enable me to live according [to] this my vow constantly avoiding all Sin, and when I shall come to die in that Solemn and awful hour may I remember this my covenant, and do thou O Lord remember it too, and give my departing Spirit an abundant Admittance into the Realm of Bliss! And if when I am laid in the Dust, and surviving Friend should meet with this my memorial [...] may it be of Good to him, and do thou admit him, to partake of all the Blessings of thy Covenant of Grace, thru Jesus the great Mediator, to whom, with thee O Father, and they Holy Spirit, be everlasting Praises ascribed by Saints and Angels!

APPENDIX 6

LIST OF THEOLOGICAL QUESTIONS OF EDWARDS SR. AND EDWARDS JR. RELEVANT TO THE HOLY SPIRIT

Edwards Sr.'s Questions Relevant to the Holy Spirit[1]

9. How do you prove the personality and divinity of the Holy Ghost?
10. How do you prove that the persons in the Trinity are one God?
11. Whence arose the Manichean notion of two Gods, and how is it confuted.
50. What is the office of the Holy Ghost in the work of Redemption?
51. What is regeneration?
52. Whence arises the necessity of it?
61. What is the sum of man's duty, and what the effect produced by the sanctifying influence of the Holy Spirit?
62. Can that holy volition in us, which is the effect of divine power be wholly our act or our duty?

Edwards Jr.'s Questions Relevant to the Holy Spirit

62. How do you prove the divinity of Christ?
63. If Christ were a creature could he atone for the sins of men?
67. Was Christ a son from eternity?
68. Was Christ necessarily or voluntarily begotten of the father?

---

[1] Jonathan Edwards and Jonathan Edwards Jr., "The Theological Questions of President Edwards, Senior, and Dr. Edwards, His Son (1822 Questions)," in *Church and Pastoral Documents, Works of Jonathan Edwards*, vol. 39 (New Haven, CT: Yale University Press, 2008).

69. Is there more absurdity in supposing that Christ was eternally begotten, than that he was eternally the second person in the Trinity?
71. How do you prove the personality of the Holy Ghost?
72. How do you prove that the three persons of the Trinity are one God?
73. Was the tripartite distinction of the Deity from eternity?
74. Was the subordination of the three persons in the Trinity, as first, second and third, from eternity?
75. How do you disprove the doctrine that those three persons are three distinct characters only?
76. Is it not a plain contradiction, that God should be one God and yet three persons?
77. What is the Arian scheme of the Trinity?
78. What is the Socinian scheme of the Trinity?
79. Whence arose the Manichean notion of two Gods? and how is it confuted?
177. What is the office of the Holy Ghost in the work of our salvation?
178. What is regeneration?
179. What is the difference between regeneration and conversion?
180. What is the native blindness of mankind?
181. Is the native blindness of mankind entirely criminal?
182. What is divine illumination?
183. Are spiritual beauty and glory seen by pure intellect?
184. Is the sight of beauty distinct from the love of beauty?
185. Is it a matter of duty to all men to see the spiritual glory of divine objects?
186. Does regeneration immediately affect any faculty of the mind beside the will?
187. Is regeneration effected by light?
188. What do you mean by the physical operation of the spirit in regeneration?
189. Is the subject of regeneration active or passive in it?
190. Whence arises the necessity of regeneration?
191. Is not the physical operation of the spirit, and the passivity of the subject under the operation of regeneration, inconsistent with the moral agency of the subject?
228. What is the sum of man's duty, and what the effect produced by the sanctifying influence of the Spirit?
229. Can that holy volition in us, which is wholly the effect of divine power, be wholly our act, and our duty?

Appendix 7

Oneida County, NY Church Documents

Confession of Faith

Article. *First.* I believe that there is one only living and true God, infinite, eternal and unchangeable in his being, wisdom, power, holiness, justice, goodness and truth; and that this God subsists in three persons The Father, The Son and The Holy Ghost, the Same in essence and equal in glory.

Second. That the Scriptures of the old and new testaments are a revelation from God and a perfect rule to direct us how we may glorify and enjoy him.

Third. That God hath foreordained and worketh all things according to his eternal purpose and the counsels of his own will. That he created all things and preserves and governs all creatures and all their actions in a manner consistent with man's free agency and the use of means; so that the sinfulness of actions is imputable to creatures, and not to God, who is holy in all his works.

Fourth. That God made man after his own Image in knowledge, righteousness and true holiness; but that mankind by transgression soon fell from this holy and happy state and are by nature the subjects of that propensity or disposition, which universally leads them to actual sin as soon as they are capable of moral action.

Fifth. That God of his mere good pleasure elected some of mankind to everlasting life, and gave his only begotten Son to assume human nature and die for sinners; that whosoever believeth in him should not perish, but have eternal life; and thereby hath laid a foundation for the offer of pardon and salvation to all mankind in the Gospel, and does by his special grace and Holy Spirit regenerate, sanctify and enable to persevere in holiness all who shall be saved.

Sixth. That Jesus Christ, who is God and Man in one divine person arose from the dead on the third day, and ever lives to make intercession for his people, and govern all things for their good; and by the virtue of his atonement as the only meritorious cause, procures their justification, adoption and final salvation in consequence of their repentance and faith in himself.

Seventh. That a Church is a congregation of Christians professing faith in Christ and obedience to him, and joined in covenant for ordinary Communion in all his ordinances; and that those, who are sincere in their profession are real Saints. That a Church hath power to choose its own officers, but to admit members and to exercise government and discipline according to the rules of the Gospel is the province of the Session of the church.

Eighth. That the Sacraments of the New Testament, Baptism and The Lord's Supper are holy ordinances instituted by Christ; that Baptism is a sign and seal of the believer's faith and union with Christ; and acceptance and participation of his benefits, and the obligation of the subjects to be the Lord's; and that the infants of members of the visible Church are to be baptized. That in the Lord's Supper Christ's death is shown forth and commemorated; and the worthy receivers are by faith made partakers of all his benefits to their growth in grace.

Nineth. That the souls of believers are at their death made perfectly holy and immediately taken to glory.

Tenth. That at the end of this world there will be a resurrection of the dead, and a final judgement of all mankind, when the righteous shall be publicly acquitted [sic] by Christ the judge, and admitted to everlasting life and glory; and the wicked shall be condemned to go away into everlasting punishment.

Covenant

I do this day publicly avouch the one only living and true God to be my God; and as far as I know my own heart I love him supremely, am pleased with his whole character and law, and with the way of Salvation by Jesus Christ revealed in the Gospel; and by the assistance of divine grace I resolve to make his law the rule of my life, and I hope I do sincerely repent of all my sins, and receive the Lord Jesus as my only Saviour, trusting in the mercy of God through his atonement as the only ground of my justification and salvation.

I also think I have a cordial love of benevolence to all mankind, sincerely wishing their best good and happiness and a special love of complacency in those, who appear to be real Christians – And through Christ's strengthening me, without whom I can do nothing, I resolve to deny all ungodliness and worldly lusts, and to give myself to the Lord Jesus Christ to be taught and governed by him in all things. I also bind myself in his strength to walk with this Church in all the ordinances of Christ, and with the members thereof as becometh a member according to the requirements of the Gospel.

Rules for the Admission of Members

First. It is agreed that the same qualifications are necessary for admitting persons to receive baptism for themselves or children as for admission to full communion; and that none ought to be admitted but those, who make a credible profession of real Christianity.

Second. That Candidates for admission known to the Pastor, or in case there be no Pastor, to the Moderator of the Church; and the Pastor or Moderator, besides private conversation with the Candidates shall call a meeting of the Church, and that in such meeting there by a free Christian conversation and communication of Sentiments, views and motives to Christian conduct between the brethren and Candidates; and when the brethren shall have obtained satisfaction, the Candidates shall be propounded to the congregation, and shall stand propounded for a fortnight at least before their admission.

Third. That persons, who are recommended to this Church from other Churches shall in like manner as is expressed in the preceding article afford the Church an opportunity of free Christian conversation and inquiry; and shall give their assent to the articles of faith, to the rules of admission and to the Church covenant of this Church.

APPENDIX 8

JONATHAN EDWARDS JR.'S SERMONS DERIVED FROM THE SERMON ON THE MOUNT

These sermons are organized in chronological order by date of preparation or deliver rather than by canonical or alphabetical order. At the beginning of his ministry, the head word on the manuscript was 'Sermon.' This lasted until about the end of his first year of preaching when the head word became 'Volume,' changing again in time to the word 'Number' (No.). In the 1790s his choice heading word changed again. This time, he classified them by date. To these unpublished sermons are added three published sermons from the Sermon on the Mount. These three were published in the two-volume set, titled *The Works of Jonathan Edwards, D.D., Late President of Union College. With a Memoir [...]*, edited by Tyron Edwards, the grandson of the author.

Edwards, Jonathan, Jr. "The Broad Way [circa 1768]," in *The Works of Jonathan Edwards, D.D., Late President of Union College. With a Memoir [...]*. Edited by Tyron Edwards, 412–427. Vol. 2. New York: Dayton and Newman, 1842.

———. "Sermon 24. Oct. 23. 1768. Matthew 5.5." *Jonathan Edwards and Calvin Chapin Papers*. Beinecke Rare Book and Manuscript Library. GEN MSS 781, Box 1, Folder 1: 1–28.

———. "Volume 59. May and June 1769. Mat. 7.14." *Jonathan Edwards and Calvin Chapin Papers*. Beinecke Rare Book and Manuscript Library. GEN MSS 781, Box 1, Folder 1: 1–88.

———. "Grace Evidenced by Its Fruits [circa 1769]," in *The Works of Jonathan Edwards, D.D., Late President of Union College. With a Memoir [...]*. Edited by Tyron Edwards, 387–400. Vol. 2. New York: Dayton and Newman, 1842.

———. "Volume 66. July 16. 1769 Mat. 5.8." *Jonathan Edwards Jr. Papers (Sermons)*, 1–12. Hartford Seminary Library. Box 165, Folder 2727.

———. "Volume 130. Oct. 1770 Mat. 5. 25, 26." *Jonathan Edwards and Calvin Chapin Papers*, 1–8. Beinecke Rare Book and Manuscript Library. GEN MSS 781, Box 1, Folder 1.

———. "Volume 124. Feb. 16. 1771. Mat. 5.20." *Jonathan Edwards and Calvin Chapin Papers*, 1–16. Beinecke Rare Book and Manuscript Library. GEN MSS 781, Box 1, Folder 1.

———. "Vol. 211. March 1. 1772. Mat. 6.10." *Jonathan Edwards and Calvin Chapin Papers*, 1–8. Beinecke Rare Book and Manuscript Library. GEN MSS 781, Box 1, Folder 2.

———. "Vol. 276. Feb. 28. 1773. Mat. 6. 19, 20, 21." *Jonathan Edwards and Calvin Chapin Papers*, 1–4. Beinecke Rare Book and Manuscript Library. GEN MSS 781, Box 1, Folder 2.

———. "Vol. 305. July 19 25, 1773. Mat. 6.11." *Jonathan Edwards and Calvin Chapin Papers*, 1–4. Beinecke Rare Book and Manuscript Library. GEN MSS 781, Box 1, Folder 2.

———. "Vol. 308 August 15. 1773 Mat. 6.33." *Jonathan Edwards Jr. Papers (Sermons)*, 1–8. Hartford Seminary Library. Box 166, Folder 2733.

———. "No. 352. Feb. 27. 1774. Mat. 5.6." *Jonathan Edwards and Calvin Chapin Papers*, 1–4. Beinecke Rare Book and Manuscript Library. GEN MSS 781, Box 1, Folder 2.

———. "No. 353. Feb. 27. 1774. Mat. 7.12." *Jonathan Edwards Jr. Papers (Sermons)*, 1–4. Hartford Seminary Library. Box 166, Folder 2734.

———. "Volume 379. July 17. 1774. Mat. 5. 21, 22." *Jonathan Edwards and Calvin Chapin Papers*, 1–12. Beinecke Rare Book and Manuscript Library. GEN MSS 781, Box 1, Folder 2.

———. "No. 511 Jan. 19. 1777. Mat 5.6." *Jonathan Edwards and Calvin Chapin Papers*, 1–4. Beinecke Rare Book and Manuscript Library. GEN MSS 781, Box 1, Folder 2.

———. "No. 552. March 8.1778. Mat. 6.13." *Jonathan Edwards and Calvin Chapin Papers*, 1–8. Beinecke Rare Book and Manuscript Library. GEN MSS 781, Box 1, Folder 2.

———. "No. 769. July 7. 1782. Mat. 22.37, 38." *Jonathan Edwards Jr. Papers (Sermons)*, 1–4. Hartford Seminary Library. Box 167, Folder 2742.

_____. "No.753 March 3. 1782. Mat. 5, 17, 18." *Jonathan Edwards and Calvin Chapin Papers,* 1–4 and appendix. Beinecke Rare Book and Manuscript Library. GEN MSS 781, Box 1, Folder 3.

_____. "No. 803. March 9. 1783. Mat. 5.6" *Jonathan Edwards and Calvin Chapin Papers,* 1–6. Beinecke Rare Book and Manuscript Library. GEN MSS 781, Box 1, Folder 3.

_____. "No. 805. March 23, 1783. Mat. 5.46." *Jonathan Edwards and Calvin Chapin Papers,* 1–4. Beinecke Rare Book and Manuscript Library. GEN MSS 781, Box 1, Folder 3.

_____. "No. 839. Dec. 21. 1783. Mat. 5.13." *Jonathan Edwards Jr. Papers (Sermons),* 1–8. Hartford Seminary Library. Box 167, Folder 2743.

_____. "No. 870. Octr. 1784. Mat. 7. 21." *Jonathan Edwards and Calvin Chapin Papers,* 1–8. Beinecke Rare Book and Manuscript Library. GEN MSS 781, Box 1, Folder 3.

_____. "No. ___ Novr. 14, 1784. Mat. 5. 46." *Andover Newton Miscellaneous Personal Papers Collection,* 1–30. Yale Divinity Library. RG 295, Box 168, Folder 5.

_____. "No. 917 Oct. 23. 1785. Mat. 7.20." *Jonathan Edwards and Calvin Chapin Papers,* 1–4. Beinecke Rare Book and Manuscript Library. GEN MSS 781, Box 1, Folder 3.

_____. "No. 930. Jan. 22. 1786. Mat. 6.13." *Jonathan Edwards and Calvin Chapin Papers,* 1–4. Beinecke Rare Book and Manuscript Library. GEN MSS 781, Box 1, Folder 3.

_____. "No. 939. March 12. 1786. Mat. 5. 17, 18." *Jonathan Edwards and Calvin Chapin Papers,* 1–4. Beinecke Rare Book and Manuscript Library. GEN MSS 781, Box 1, Folder 3.

_____. "No. 988. April 15. 1787. Mat. VI. 20." *Jonathan Edwards and Calvin Chapin Papers,* 1–4. Beinecke Rare Book and Manuscript Library. GEN MSS 781, Box 1, Folder 3.

_____. "No. 1006. Sepr. 30. 1787 Mat. V. 8." *Jonathan Edwards Jr. Papers (Sermons),* 1–4. Hartford Seminary Library. Box 168, Folder 2746).

_____. "No. 1032. April 6. 1788. Mat. V.3." *Jonathan Edwards and Calvin Chapin Papers,* 1–4. Beinecke Rare Book and Manuscript Library. GEN MSS 781, Box 1, Folder 3.

_____. "No. 1095. July 19. 1789. Mat. 7.13, 14." *Jonathan Edwards and Calvin Chapin Papers,* 1–8. Beinecke Rare Book and Manuscript Library. GEN MSS 781, Box 1, Folder 4.

———. "No. 1113. Novr. 8. 1789. Mat. V.6." *Jonathan Edwards and Calvin Chapin Papers*, 1–4. Beinecke Rare Book and Manuscript Library. GEN MSS 781, Box 1, Folder 4.

———. "[Unnumbered] July 18. 1790 Mat. V. 43, 44." *Jonathan Edwards and Calvin Chapin Papers*, 1–4. Beinecke Rare Book and Manuscript Library. GEN MSS 781, Box 1, Folder 4.

———. "The Injustice and Impolicy of the Slave Trade, and of Slavery [circa 1791]," in *The Works of Jonathan Edwards. D.D., Late President of Union College. With a Memoir [...]. Edited by Tyron Edwards*, 75–97. Vol. 2. New York: Dayton and Newman, 1842.

———. "[Unnumbered] Feb. 6. 1791. Mat. VI.12." *Jonathan Edwards and Calvin Chapin Papers*, 1–6. Beinecke Rare Book and Manuscript Library. GEN MSS 781, Box 1, Folder 4.

———. "[Unnumbered] July 1. 1792 Mat. VI.10." *Jonathan Edwards and Calvin Chapin Papers*, Beinecke Rare Book and Manuscript Library. GEN MSS 781, Box 1, Folder 4.

———. "[Unnumbered] July 15. 1792. Mat. VII. 21." *Andover Newton Miscellaneous Personal Papers Collection, Jonathan Edwards, Jr.*, 1–4. Yale Divinity Library. Box 168, Folder 10.

———. "[Unnumbered] Aug. 4. 1793. Mat. V. 17." *Jonathan Edwards and Calvin Chapin Papers*, 1–4. Beinecke Rare Book and Manuscript Library. GEN MSS 781, Box 1, Folder 4.

———. "[Unnumbered] Octr. 2, 1793. Mat. V.20." *Jonathan Edwards and Calvin Chapin Papers*, 1–4. Beinecke Rare Book and Manuscript Library. GEN MSS 781, Box 1, Folder 4.

———. "[Unnumbered] June 1. 1794. Mat. VII. 13,14." *Jonathan Edwards and Calvin Chapin Papers*, 1–8. Beinecke Rare Book and Manuscript Library. GEN MSS 781, Box 1, Folder 4.

———. "[Unnumbered] June 29. 1794. At Colebrook March 31. 1797 Mat. V.13." *Jonathan Edwards Jr. Papers (Sermons)*, 1–4. Hartford Seminary Library. Box 169, Folder 2753.

———. "[Unnumbered] Augt. 3. 1794. Mat. V. 48." *Jonathan Edwards and Calvin Chapin Papers*, 1–4. Beinecke Rare Book and Manuscript Library. GEN MSS 781, Box 1, Folder 4.

———. "[Unnumbered] August 17, 1794, Mat. 5.20." *Jonathan Edwards and Calvin Chapin Papers*, 1–4. Beinecke Rare Book and Manuscript Library. GEN MSS 781, Box 1, Folder 4.

_____. "[Unnumbered] Augt. 24. 1794 Mat. V.3." *Jonathan Edwards and Calvin Chapin Papers,* 1–4. Beinecke Rare Book and Manuscript Library. GEN MSS 781, Box 1, Folder 4.

_____. "[Unnumbered] Augt 24. 1794 Mat. V. 25." *Andover Newton Miscellaneous Personal Papers Collection, Jonathan Edwards, Jr.,* 1–4. Yale Divinity Library. RG 295, Box 168, Folder 11.

_____. "[Unnumbered] March 1795. Mat. VI. 33." *Jonathan Edwards Jr. Papers (Sermons).* Hartford Seminary Library. Box 169, Folder 2753.

_____. "[Unnumbered] Augt. 28. 1796. Mat. VII. 21." *Jonathan Edwards and Calvin Chapin Papers,* 1–4. Beinecke Rare Book and Manuscript Library. GEN MSS 781, Box 1, Folder 4.

_____. "[Unnumbered] Octr. 10. 1798. Mat. VI. 33." *Andover Newton Miscellaneous Personal Papers Collection, Jonathan Edwards, Jr.,* 1–4. Yale Divinity Library. RG 295, Box 168, Folder 13.

_____. "[Unnumbered] Mat. V.6 [Undated Fragment]." *Andover Newton Miscellaneous Personal Papers Collection. Jonathan Edwards, Jr.,* 1. Yale Divinity Library. RG 295, Box 168, Folder 15.

_____. "[Unnumbered] Mat. V. 46. [Undated fragments]." *Jonathan Edwards and Calvin Chapin Papers,* 1–4 and leaf. Beinecke Rare Book and Manuscript Library. GEN MSS 781, Box 1, Folder 3.

BIBLIOGRAPHY

Primary Sources

Primary Published

Alleine, Joseph, *An Admonition to Unconverted Sinners; in a Serious Treatise.* London: Millar, Law and Cater; and Wilson, Spense, and Mawman, 1793.

Bacon, Leonard. *Thirteen Historical Discourses, on the Completion of Two Hundred Years: From the Beginning of the First Church in New Haven, with an Appendix.* New Haven, CT: Durrie and Peck, 1839.

Baldwin, Ebenezer and Jonathan Edwards Jr. "Some Observations upon the Slavery of Negroes." *Connecticut Journal, and the New-Haven Post-Boy* (October–December 1773). In *Am I Not a Man and a Brother: The Antislavery Crusade of Revolutionary America 1688–1788,* ed. Roger Burns. New York: Chelsea House, 1977.

Bellamy, Joseph. *True Religion Delineated; or, Experimental Religion, A Distinguishing from Formality on the One Hand, and Enthusiasm on the Other, Set in a Scriptural and Rational Light.* Boston: S. Kneeland, 1750.

———. *The Works of Joseph Bellamy.* Vol. 1. Boston: Doctrinal Tract and Book Society, 1850.

Brown, John. *John Brown Liberator of Kansas and Martyr of Virginia: Life and Letters.* 4th ed. Edited by F. B. Sanborn. Cedar Rapids, IA: The Torch Press, 1910.

Burr, Esther Edwards. *The Journal of Esther Edwards Burr 1754–1757.* Edited by Carol F. Karlsen and Laurie Crumpacker. New Haven, CT: Yale University Press, 1984.

Chauncy, Charles. *Seasonable Thoughts on the State of Religion in New England.* Boston: Rogers and Fowle, 1743.

Clark, Joseph S., ed. "Timothy Mather Cooley." In *The Congregational Quarterly,* vol. 2. Boston: Edward L. Balch, 1860.

Dana, James. *The intent of capital punishment. A discourse delivered in the city of New Haven, October 20, 1790. Being the day of the execution of Joseph Mountain, for a rape.* New Haven, CT: T. and S. Green, 1790. In *Early English Books Online Text Creation Partnership,* 2011. Accessed September 5, 2020. https://quod.lib.umich.edu/e/evans/N17366.0001.001.

Dean, Benjamin A. *History of the Colebrook Congregational Church 1795–1895: Centennial Address Delivered December 31, 1895.* Hartford: Connecticut State Library, 1913.

Dictionary of the English Language [...]. Edited by Samuel Johnson. London: A. Millar, 1766.

Dutton, Samuel William Southmayd. *The History of the North Church in New Haven: From Its Formation in May 1742, During the Great Awakening, to the Completion of the Century in May 1842: in Three Sermons.* New Haven, CT: A. H. Maltby, 1842.

Edwards, B.B., ed. *The American Quarterly Register,* vol. 3. Boston: American Education Society, 1836.

Edwards, Jonathan, Jr. "Remarks on the Improvements Made in Theology by His Father, President Edwards." In *The Works of Jonathan Edwards, D.D., Late President of Union College. With a Memoir [...].* Vol. 1. Edited by Tyron Edwards, 481–492. New York: Dayton and Newman, 1842.

———. "Thoughts on the Atonement." In *The Works of Jonathan Edwards, D.D., Late President of Union College. With a Memoir [...].* Vol. 1. Edited by Tyron Edwards, 493–508. New York: Dayton and Newman, 1842.

———. "Three sermons on the Atonement." In *The Works of Jonathan Edwards, D.D., Late President of Union College. With a Memoir [...].* Vol. 2. Edited by Tyron Edwards, 11–52. New York: Dayton and Newman, 1842.

Edwards, Jonathan, Sr. "Discourse on the Trinity." In *Writings on the Trinity, Grace, and Faith, Works of Jonathan Edwards.* Vol. 21. Edited by Sang Hyun Lee. New Haven, CT: Yale University Press, 1957–2008.

———. *Dissertation Concerning the Nature of True Religion.* In *Ethical Writings, Works of Jonathan Edwards.* Vol. 8. Edited by Paul Ramsey. New Haven, CT: Yale University Press, 1970.

———. "A Divine and Supernatural Light." In *Sermons and Discourses, 1730–1733, The Works of Jonathan Edwards.* Vol. 17. Edited by Mark Valeri. New Haven, CT: Yale University Press, 1957–2008.

———. *Faith*. In *Writings on the Trinity, Grace, and Faith*, in *The Works of Jonathan Edwards*. Vol. 21. Edited by Sang Hyun Lee. New Haven, CT: Yale University Press, 1957–2008.

———. *A Faithful Narrative, The Great Awakening*. In *The Works of Jonathan Edwards Online*, Vol. 4. Edited by C. C. Goen. New Haven, CT: Yale University Press, 1957–2008.

———. "Family and Descendants of President Jonathan Edwards (1891)." Jonathan Edwards Collection. Beinecke Rare Book and Manuscript Library. GEN MSS 151, Box 29, Folder 1586.

———. "418. Matt. 5:6." In *Sermons, Series II 1737, The Works of Jonathan Edwards, Sermons and Discourses*. Vol. 52. Edited by Jonathan Edwards Center at Yale University, 2008.

———. *Freedom of the Will*. In *The Works of Jonathan Edwards*. Vol. 1. Edited by Paul Ramsey. New Haven, CT: Yale University Press, 1970.

———. "Jonathan Edwards to Joseph Bellamy, January 15, 1746/7." In *Letters and Personal Writings, The Works of Jonathan Edwards Online*. Vol. 16. Edited by George S. Claghorn. New Haven, CT: Yale University Press, 1957–2008.

———. *An Humble Attempt*. In *Apocalyptic Writings, The Works of Jonathan Edwards*. Vol. 5. Edited by Stephen J. Stein. New Haven, CT: Yale University Press, 1957–2008.

———. *The Life of David Brainerd*. In *The Works of Jonathan Edwards*. Vol. 7. Edited by Norman Pettit. New Haven, CT: Yale University Press, 1957–2008.

———. "The Nature of True Religion." In *The Works of Jonathan Edwards*, Vol. 8. Edited by Paul Ramsey. New Haven, CT: Yale University Press, 1989.

———. "No. 435." In *Miscellanies, The Works of Jonathan Edwards*, Vol. 13. Edited by Harry S. Stout. New Haven, CT: Yale University Press, 1970.

———. "On the Equality of the Persons of the Trinity." In *Writings on the Trinity, Grace, and Faith, The Works of Jonathan Edwards*. Vol. 21. Edited by Sang Hyun Lee. New Haven, CT: Yale University, 1957–2008.

———. *Original Sin*. In *The Works of Jonathan Edwards*. Vol. 3. Edited by Clyde A. Holbrook. New Haven, CT: Yale University Press, 1970.

———. "Part II: Motives to a Compliance with What Is Proposed in the Memorial." In *An Humble Attempt*, in *Apocalyptic Writings, The Works of Jonathan Edwards*. Vol. 5. Edited by Stephen J. Stein. New Haven, CT: Yale University Press, 1957–2008.

———. *Religious Affections*. In *The Works of Jonathan Edwards*. Vol. 2. Edited by Paul Ramsey. New Haven, CT: Yale University Press, 1957–2008.

_____. *Some thoughts Concerning the Present Revival of Religion in New England*. In *The Works of Jonathan Edwards*, Vol. 4. Edited by C.C. Goen. New Haven, CT: Yale University Press, 1972.

_____. "A Spiritual Understanding of Divine Things Denied to the Unregenerate." In *Sermons and Discourses: 1723–1729, The Works of Jonathan Edwards*. Vol. 14. Edited by Kenneth P. Minkema. New Haven, CT: Yale University Press, 1957–2008.

_____. "The Threefold Work of the Holy Ghost." *Sermons and Discourses: 1723–1729, The Works of Jonathan Edwards Online*. Vol. 14. Edited by Kenneth P. Minkema. New Haven, CT: Yale University Press, 1957–2008.

_____. "284. Conversion." In *The "Miscellanies." The Works of Jonathan Edwards*. Vol. 13. Edited by Harry S. Stout. New Haven, CT: Yale University Press, 1957–2008.

_____. "The Value of Salvation." In *Sermons and Discourses 1720–23, The Works of Jonathan Edwards*. Vol. 10. Edited by Wilson H. Kimnach. New Haven, CT: Yale University Press, 1970.

Edwards, Jonathan and Jonathan Edwards Jr., "The Theological Questions of President Edwards, Senior, and Dr. Edwards, His Son (1822 Questions)." In *Church and Pastoral Documents, The Works of Jonathan Edwards Online*. Vol. 39. Jonathan Edwards Center: Yale University Press, 2008.

Edwards, Tyron. "Memoir." In *The Works of Jonathan Edwards, D.D., Late President of Union College. With a Memoir [...]*. Edited by Tyron Edwards, ix–xl. Vol. 2. New York: Dayton and Newman, 1842.

Emmons, Nathanael. "Duty of Sinners to Make Themselves a New Heart." *The Works of Nathanael Emmons*. Vol. 5. Edited by Jacob Ide. Boston: Crocker and Brewster, 1842.

Finney, Charles G. *Lectures on Systematic Theology, Embracing Lectures on Moral Government, The Atonement, Moral and Physical Depravity, Natural, Moral, and Gracious Ability, Repentance, Faith, Justification, Sanctification, andc.* Oberlin: James M. Fitch, 1846.

_____. "Sinners Bound to Change Their Own Hearts." *Sermon on Various Subjects*. New York: Benedict and Co. Printers, 1834.

Flavel, John. "Sermon V: Opening that Work of the Spirit more particularly, by which the Soul is enabled to apply Christ." *The Whole Works of the Reverend Mr. John Flavel, Late Minister of the Gospel at Dartmouth in Devon, in Two Volumes*. Glasgow, Scotland: John Orr, 1754.

Hageman, John Frelinghuysen. *History of Princeton and Its Institutions*, 2nd ed. Vol. 2. Philadelphia: J. B. Lippincott, 1879.

Harnack, Adolf von. *What Is Christianity?: Lectures Delivered in the University of Berlin during the Winter-Term, 1899–1900.* 2nd ed., rev. New York: G. P. Putnam, 1902.

Hodge, Charles. "The New Divinity Tried." In *Princeton V. The New Divinity: The Meaning of Sin, Grace, Salvation, and Revival,* 141–70. Cambridge, UK: The Banner of Truth Trust, 2001.

———. "Review of Remarks on the Princeton Review, Vol. 22. No. 4. Art. 7 by Edwards A. Park." *The Biblical Repertory and Princeton Review* 23, no. 2 (1851): 306–347.

———. "Review of The Theology of the Intellect and that of the Feelings. A Discourse before the Convention of the Congregational Ministers of New England, in Brattle Street Meeting House, Boston, May 30th, 1850 by Edwards A. Park." *The Biblical Repertory and Princeton Review* 22, no. 4 (1850): 642–647.

———. "Unity and Diversity of Belief even on Imputed and Involuntary Sin; with Comments on a Second Article in the Princeton Review relating to a Convention Sermon." *The Biblical Repertory and Princeton Review,* vol. 23, no. 4 (1851): 674–695.

Hopkins, Samuel. *The Life of President Edwards.* 1764. Reprint in *The Works of President Edwards.* Vol. 1. New York: S. Converse, 1829.

Hunter, David G., ed. *St. Hilary of Poitiers Commentary on Matthew.* Translated by D. H. Williams. Washington, DC: The Catholic University of America Press, 2012.

Mitchell, *Donald Grant. Doctor Johns: Being a Narrative of Certain Events in the Life of an Orthodox Minister of Connecticut.* In *The Works of Donald G. Mitchell.* Vol. 8. New York: Charles Scribner's Sons, 1907.

Mountain, Joseph. *Sketches of the life of Joseph Mountain, a Negro, who was executed at New-Haven [. . .].* Edited by David Daggett. New Haven, CT: T and S Green, 1790. In *Early English Books Online Text Creation Partnership,* 2011. https://quod.lib.umich.edu/e/evans/N17364.0001.001. Accessed 5 September 2020.

Occom, Samson. *A Sermon at the Execution of Moses Paul, an Indian [. . .].* Edited by Jonathan Edwards Jr., 1788; reprint in London: Buckland, 1789.

Paine, Thomas. "The Age of Reason." In *The Writings of Thomas Paine.* Vol. 4. New York: G. P. Putnam's Sons, 1896.

Park, Edwards Amasa. "Remarks on the Biblical Repertory and Princeton Review. Vol. 22. No. 4. Art. 7." *Bibliotheca Sacra* 8 (January 1851): 135–168.

———. "The New England Theology." *Bibliotheca Sacra* 9 (January 1852): 170–220.

———. *The Theology of the Intellect and that of the Feelings: A Discourse Delivered Before the Convention of the Congregational Ministers of Massachusetts, in Brattle Street Meeting House, Boston, May 30, 1850.* Andover, MA: Warren F. Draper, 1950.

Perkins, Nathan, ed. *The Constitution of the Missionary Society of Connecticut: with an Address from the Board of Trustees, to the Peoples of the State, and a Narrative on the Subject of Missions [...].* Hartford, CT: Hudson and Goodwin, 1800.

Perrin, Lavalette, William DeL. Love Jr., and Charles H. Clark, eds. *The Records of the General Association of Ye Colony of Connecticut: June 20, 1738–June 19, 1799.* Hartford, CT: The Case, Lockwood and Brainard Co., 1888.

Records of the Presbyterian Church in the United States of America: Embracing the Minutes of the General Presbytery and General Synod 1706–1788, Together with an Index and the Minutes of the General Convention for Religious Liberty, 1766–1775. Philadelphia: Presbyterian Board of Publication, 1904.

Sprague, William B. *Annals of the American Pulpit [...].* Vols 1–3. New York: Robert Carter and Brothers, 1857.

Stiles, Ezra, Benjamin Trumbull, and Jonathan Edwards Jr. "Letter to the Editor." *The Connecticut Courant,* vol. 24, no. 1512. Hartford, CT: Hudson and Goodwin, January 13, 1794.

Stiles, Ezra. *The Literary Diary of Ezra Stiles: January 1, 1769–March 13, 1776.* Edited by Franklin Bowditch Dexter. Vol. 1. New York: Charles Scribner's Sons, 1901.

———. *The Literary Diary of Ezra Stiles: March 14, 1776–December 31, 1781.* Edited by Franklin Bowditch Dexter. Vol. 2, New York: Charles Scribner's Sons, 1901.

———. *The Literary Diary of Ezra Stiles: January 1, 1782–May 6, 1795.* Edited by Franklin Bowditch Dexter. Vol. 3. New York: Charles Scribner's Sons, 1901.

Stowe, Harriet Beecher. *The Minister's Wooing.* New York: Derby and Jackson, 1859.

Van Mastricht, Peter. *Theoretical-Practical Theology: Prolegomena.* Vol. 1. Translated by Todd M. Rester. Edited by Joel R. Beeke. Grand Rapids: Reformation Heritage Books, 2018.

———. *Theoretical-Practical Theology: Prolegomena*. Vol. 2. Translated by Todd M. Rester. Edited by Joel R. Beeke. Grand Rapids: Reformation Heritage Books, 2019.

———. *A Treatise on Regeneration*, 1769; reprint. Morgan, PA: Soli Deo Gloria, 2002.

Wetmore, James Carnahan. *Wetmore Family of America, It's Collateral Branches: Genealogical, Biographical, and Historical Notices*. Albany, NY: Munsell and Rowland, 1861.

Willard, Samuel. *A Compleat [sic] Body of Divinity in Two Hundred and Fifty Expository Lectures on the Assembly's Shorter Catechism*. Boston: Green, Kneeland, and Elliot, 1726.

Williams, Nathan, John Smalley, and Benjamin Trumbull, eds., *The Connecticut Evangelical Magazine*, vol. 2. Harford: Hudson and Goodwin, 1801.

Primary Unpublished Manuscripts

Edwards, Jonathan, Jr. "[No number] At Schenectady, Wednesday at The Hill, June 1800, John III.7." *Andover Newton Miscellaneous Personal Papers Collection, Johnathan Edwards, Jr.* Yale Divinity Library. RG 295, Box 168, Folder 4.

———. "Commencement Address." *Jonathan Edwards and Calvin Chapin Papers Collection*. Beinecke Rare Book and Manuscript Library. GEN MSS 781, Box 1, Folder 5.

———. "Confession of Faith September 17, 1763," *Jonathan Edwards Papers, Series IV Edwards Family Writings*. Beinecke Rare Book and Manuscript Library. GEN MSS 151, Box 24, Folder 1355.

———. "Corrigenda, n.d." *Shephard Family Collection*. Beinecke Rare Book and Manuscript Library. Uncategorized.

———. "Diary." *Jonathan Edwards Papers, Series IV Edwards Family Writings*. Beinecke Rare Book and Manuscript Library. GEN MSS 151, Box 24, Folder 1357.

———. "454. Decr. 22. 1775. Delivered by at the desire of the officers of several companies in belonging to the town, to them and their companies." *Jonathan Edwards Jr. Papers (Sermons)*. Hartford Seminary Library. Box 166, Folder 2736.

———. "400. Novr. 24. 1774. Thanksgiving." *Jonathan Edwards Jr. Papers (Sermons)*. Hartford Seminary Library. Box 166, Folder 2735.

_____. "417. April 2. 1775. John 14.1." *Jonathan Edwards Jr. Papers (Sermons)*. Hartford Seminary Library. Box 166, Folder 2735.

_____. "No. 478. May 17, 1776. Isa. 45.7." *Jonathan Edwards and Calvin Chapin Papers*. Beinecke Rare Book and Manuscript Library. GEN MSS 781, Box 1, Folder 2.

_____. "No. 537. Novr. 20.1777. On a Thanksgiving soon after the defeat capture of Genl. Burgoyne and his whole army." *Jonathan Edwards Jr. Papers (Sermons)*. Hartford Seminary Library. Box 167, Folder 2738.

_____. "No. 624. Aug. 12.1779. On a fast kept by the town on account of the late invasion and present danger." *Jonathan Edwards Jr. Papers (Sermons)*. Hartford Seminary Library. Box 167, Folder 2739.

_____. "No. 648. Jan. 2. 1780. Prov. 3.17." *Andover Newton Miscellaneous Personal Papers Collection, Johnathan Edwards, Jr.* Yale Divinity Library. RG 295, Box 168, Folder 4.

_____. "No. 651. Jan. 23. 1780. Rom. 3.24." *Jonathan Edwards, Jr. Papers (Sermons)*. Hartford Seminary Library. Box 167, Folder 2740.

_____. "No. 659. March 19. 1780. 1 Pet. 1.12." *Jonathan Edwards, Jr. Papers (Sermons)*. Hartford Seminary Library. Box 167, Folder 2740.

_____. "No. 710 June 3. 1781. Psal. 73.28." *Jonathan Edwards Jr. Papers (Sermons)*. Hartford Seminary Library. Box 167, Folder 2741.

_____. "No. 770 July 7. 1782. Job. 14.1." *Jonathan Edwards Jr. Papers (Sermons)*. Hartford Seminary Library. Box 167, Folder 2742.

_____. "No. 793. Jan. 19. 1783. Eph. 4.24." *Jonathan Edwards, Jr. Papers (Sermons)*. Hartford Seminary Library. Box 167, Folder 2742.

_____. "Observations and Rules" (n.d.), *Jonathan Edwards Papers, Series IV Edwards Family Writings*. Beinecke Rare Book and Manuscript Library. GEN MSS 151 Box 24, Folder 1359.

_____. "Prayer in Mahican May 27, 1765." Translated by Carl Masthay. *Jonathan Edwards Papers, Series IV Edwards Family Writings*. Beinecke Rare Book and Manuscript Library. Gen MSS 151, Box 29, Folder 1596.

_____. "Sermon 3. August 1766. 2 Pet. 2.22." *Jonathan Edwards, Jr. Papers (Sermons)*. Hartford Seminary Library. Box 165, Folder 2725.

_____. "Sermon 5. Phil. 1.18 Composed at Princeton, Jan. 1767." *Jonathan Edwards Jr. Papers (Sermons)*. Hartford Seminary Library. Box 165, Folder 2725.

_____. "Sermon 74. August 31, 1769." *Jonathan Edwards Jr. Papers (Sermons)*. Hartford Seminary Library. Box 165, Folder 2727.

_____. "390. Preached on a fast appointed by authority on occasion of the late acts of the British Legislature relating to Boston, the Massachusets

[sic], Quebec, and America in general. Aug. 31. 1774." *Jonathan Edwards Jr. Papers (Sermons)*. Hartford Seminary Library. Box 166, Folder 2735.

———. "Volume 79. Rev. 22:17 [Last Clause] Oct. 15, 1769." *Jonathan Edwards Jr. Papers (Sermons)*. Hartford Seminary Library. Box 165, Folder 2728.

———. "Volume 95. Joh. 3.6., Feb. 18, 1770." *Jonathan Edwards Jr. Papers (Sermons)*. Hartford Seminary Library. Box 165, Folder 2728.

———. "Volume 147. Joh. 3.5., Feb. 3, 1771." *Jonathan Edwards Jr. Papers (Sermons)*. Hartford Seminary Library. Box 165, Folder 2730.

———. "Vol. 170., Ezek. 18.21., June 30, 1771." *Jonathan Edwards and Calvin Chapin Papers*. Beinecke Rare Book and Manuscript Library. Box 1, Folder 1.

———. "Vol. 189., Joh. 3.8., Sepr. 22. 1771." *Jonathan Edwards Jr. Papers (Sermons)*. Hartford Seminary Library. Box 166, Folder 2731.

———. "Volume 225." *Jonathan Edwards Jr. Papers (Sermons)*, Hartford Seminary Library. Box 166, Folder 2732.

———. "Volume 242." *Jonathan Edwards Jr. Papers (Sermons)*. Hartford Seminary Library (Box 166, Folder 2732).

Gelston, Maltby. *A Systematic Collection of Questions and Answers in Divinity*. Yale University Manuscript and Archives Division. Miscellaneous MSS Collection. MS 354, Series III. E–G, box 5, f. 499.

Primary Letters and Church Records

A Book Containing an Account of the Formation and Proceedings of the First Church in Whitestown. Transcribed by Harry Young. New Hartford, NY: New Hartford Presbyterian Church, n.d.

Austin, David. "Communications and Actions of the White Haven Society Regarding the Discipline of Church Members: Joseph Adams, 1780." *White Haven Church Records, Series 1*. New Haven Museum, CT. MSS 9, Box 1, Folder U.

"Broadside, New Haven, May 19, 1795." *Jonathan Edwards, 1745–1801, Edwards Family Collection*. Princeton University Library. AM 13472, Box 1, Folder 24.

"Committee Report on Enquiry of Several Brethren August 20, 1789." *White Haven Church Records, Series 1*. New Haven Museum, CT. MSS 9, Box 1, Folder U1.

"Committee Report of the Resignation of Samuel Bird December 30, 1767." *White Haven Church Records, Series 1.* New Haven Museum, CT. MSS 9, Box 1, Folder Q.

"Conciliatory Propositions in White Haven Between Dr. Edwards and Others, April 3, 1790." *Connecticut Miscellaneous Manuscripts Collection.* Manuscripts and Archives, Yale University Library. MS 149, Series III, Box 20, Folder 215.

Cornwell, John. Letter sent to White Haven Church and Jonathan Edwards [Jr.], May 27, 1782. *White Haven Church Records, Series 1.* New Haven Museum, CT. MSS 9, Box 1, Folder U1.

Edwards, Jonathan, Jr. Letter sent to David Austin April 3, 1790. *Connecticut Miscellaneous Manuscripts Collection.* Manuscripts and Archives, Yale University Library. MS 149, Series III, Box 20, Folder 215.

_____. Letter sent to Esther Stoddard Edwards 1765 April 12. *Shepard Family Collection.* Beinecke Rare Book and Manuscript Library. Uncategorized.

_____. Letter sent to John Ryland Jr. March 16, 1787. *Edwards Family Correspondence, Jonathan Edwards 1745–1801 Outgoing Letters.* Beinecke Rare Book and Manuscript Library. GEN MSS 152, Box 1, Folder 3.

_____. Letter sent to John Ryland Jr. October 2, 1787. *Edwards Family Correspondence, Jonathan Edwards 1745–1801 Outgoing Letters.* Beinecke Rare Book and Manuscript Library. GEN MSS 152, Box 1, Folder 3.

_____. Letter sent to Joseph Bellamy, November 31, 1768. *Jonathan Edwards Papers, Series V Edwards Family Correspondence, Jonathan Edwards 1745–1801 Outgoing Letters.* Beinecke Rare Book and Manuscript Library. GEN MSS 151, Box 26, folder 1414.

_____. Letter sent to Samuel Hopkins, October 29, 1793. *Park Family Papers Collection.* Sterling Memorial Library, Yale University. MS 384 Box 1.

_____. Letter sent to the Society of White Haven, January 31, 1786. *Connecticut Miscellaneous Manuscripts Collection.* Manuscripts and Archives, Yale University Library. MS 149 Series III. Box 20. Folder 215.

_____. Letter sent to Timothy Dwight, July 18, 1782. *Jonathan Edwards Jr., Correspondence, Andover Newton Miscellaneous Personal Papers Collection.* Yale Divinity Library. RG 295, Box 168, Folder 1.

_____. Letter sent to Timothy Edwards December 18, 1777. *Edwards Family Correspondence, Jonathan Edwards 1745–1801 Outgoing Letters.* Beinecke Rare Book and Manuscript Library. Gen MSS 151, Box 26, Folder 1424.

_____. Letter sent to unknown recipient July 8, 1773. *Jonathan Edwards Jr., Correspondence, Andover-Newton Miscellaneous Personal Papers Collection.* Yale Divinity Library. RG 295, Box 168, Folder 1.

Edwards, Jonathan, Sr. Letter sent to John Erskine, October 14, 1748. *Letters and Personal Writings,* in *The Works of Jonathan Edwards.* Vol. 16. New Haven, CT: Yale University Press, 1970.

———. Letter sent to Jonathan Edwards Jr. on May 27, 1755. *Jonathan Edwards Collection.* Beinecke Rare Book and Manuscript Library. Gen MSS 151, Box 22, Folder 1284.

Edwards, Timothy. Letter sent to Jonathan Edwards Jr. July 23, 1782. *Jonathan Edwards Papers, Series V Edwards Family Correspondence, Jonathan Edwards 1745–1801 Outgoing Letters.* Beinecke Rare Book and Manuscript Library. Box 26, Folder 1440.

———. Letter sent to Jonathan Edwards Jr. May 18, 1795. *Series V. Edwards Family Correspondence.* Beinecke Rare Book and Manuscript Library. GEN MSS 151, Box 26, Folder 1440.

Caldwell, James. Letter sent to Joseph Bellamy March 16, 1767. *Joseph Bellamy Letters.* Hartford Seminary Library. Box 188, Folder 2935, Item 81332.

Gelston, Maltby. *A Systematic Collection of Questions and Answers in Divinity.* Yale University Manuscript and Archives Division, Miscellaneous MSS Collection. MS 354, Series III. E–G, box 5, folder 499.

Gordon, William. Letter sent to Joseph Bellamy July 14, 1769. *Bellamy Papers.* Hartford Seminary Library. Box 188, Folder 2936, Item 81349.

Hawley, Gideon. Letter sent to Jonathan Walter Edwards June 10, 1802. *Jonathan Edwards Papers, Series V Edwards Family Correspondence, Jonathan Edwards 1745–1801 Incoming Letters.* Beinecke Rare Book and Manuscript Library. Gen MSS 151, Box 27, Folder 1487.

———. Letter sent to Jonathan Walter Edwards March 14, 1803. *Jonathan Edwards Papers, Series V Edwards Family Correspondence, Jonathan Edwards 1745–1801 Incoming Letters.* Beinecke Rare Book and Manuscript Library. Gen MSS 151, Box 27, Folder 1487.

———. Letter sent to Joseph Bellamy February 3, 1755, *Joseph Bellamy Letters.* Hartford Seminary Library. Box 190, Folder 2955.

———. Letter sent to Joseph Bellamy April 18, 1755, *Jonathan Edwards Papers, Series V Edwards Family Correspondence, Jonathan Edwards 1745–1801 Incoming Letters.* Beinecke Rare Book and Manuscript Library. Box 28, Folder 1535.

Litchfield Association Records, 1752–1852. In *General Association of Connecticut Collection.* Boston: Congregational Library and Archives.

"Miscellaneous Records of the Fair Haven Society." *White Haven Church Records, Series 1.* New Haven Museum, CT. MSS 9, Box 2, Folder A1.

"Narrative Recording the Formation of the Fair Haven Society, 1769–1772." *White Haven Church Records, Series 1.* New Haven Museum, CT. MSS 9, Box 2, Folder B.

"Petition Requesting the Calling of Mr. Fisk." *White Haven Church Records, Series 1.* New Haven Museum, CT. MSS 9, Box 1, Folder Q.

"The Result of the Council at Ordination of Mr. Edwards January 3, 1769." *Connecticut Miscellaneous Manuscripts Collection.* Manuscripts and Archives, Yale University Library. MS 149, Series III, Box 20, Folder 215.

Ryland Jr., John. Letter sent to Jonathan Edwards Jr. June 29, 1787. *Jonathan Edwards Papers, Series V Edwards Family Correspondence, Jonathan Edwards 1745–1801 Incoming Letters.* Beinecke Rare Book and Manuscript Library. Box 26, Folder 1458.

"Signers Against Mr. Edwards Ordination, Dec. 16th, 1768." *Connecticut Miscellaneous Manuscripts Collection.* Manuscripts and Archives, Yale University. MS 149, Series III, Box 20, Folder 215.

Washington, George. Letter sent to Jonathan Edwards Jr. August 28, 1788, in *Jonathan Edwards Jr. and Calvin Chapin Papers.* Beinecke Rare Book and Manuscript Library. MSS 151, Box 26, Folder 1461.

West, Stephen. Letter sent to Jonathan Edwards Jr. July 16, 1782, *Jonathan Edwards Papers, Series V. Edwards Family Correspondence, Jonathan Edwards 1745–1801 Incoming Letters.* Beinecke Rare Book and Manuscript Library. GEN MSS 151, Box 1, Folder 5.

White Haven Church. Letter sent to Joseph Bellamy December 20, 1768. *Joseph Bellamy 1719–1790 Correspondence.* Beinecke Rare Book and Manuscript Library. GEN MSS 151, Box 28, Folder 1531.

"White Haven Society's School Accounts Committed to the Care of Jeremiah Atwater, 1770–1802." *The United Church Papers, Series 1.* New Haven Museum, CT. MSS 9, Box 1, Folder K.

Secondary Sources

Belcher, Joseph. *George Whitefield: A Biography, with Special Reference to His Labors in America.* New York: American Trust Society, 1857.

Bezzant, Rhys S. *Edwards the Mentor.* New York: Oxford University Press, 2019.

"Biographical Sketch of Thomas Spencer." Mary King Research Library, Madison County NY Historical Society (File X00884).

Boardman, George Nye. *A History of New England Theology.* New York: A. D. F. Randolph, 1899.

Boss, Robert L., Joshua R. Farris, and S. Mark Hamilton, eds. *New England Dogmatics: A Systematic Collection of Questions and Answers in Divinity by Maltby Gelston (1766–1865).* Eugene, OR: Pickwick Publishers, 2019.

Bowden, Henry Warner. *Dictionary of American Religious Biography.* Edited by Edwin S. Gaustad. Westport, CT: Greenwood Press, 1977.

Breitenbach, William. *New Divinity Theology and the Idea of Moral Accountability.* Dissertation Series. New Haven, CT: Yale University Press, 1978.

_____. "Piety and Moralism: Edwards and the New Divinity." In *Jonathan Edwards and the American Experience.* Edited by Nathan O. Hatch and Harry S. Stout, 177–204. New York: Oxford University Press, 1988.

Caldwell, Robert W. *Communion in the Spirit: The Holy Spirit as the Bond of Union in the Theology of Jonathan Edwards.* Eugene, OR: Wipf and Stock, 2006.

"Capital Punishment in Connecticut." *Connecticut State Library.* Accessed August 22, 2020. https://libguides.ctstatelibrary.org/law/capitalpunishment/personsexecuted.

Carrick, John. *The Preaching of Jonathan Edwards.* Edinburgh: The Banner of Truth Trust, 2008.

Carver, Benjamin T. "The Development of the Redemptive Role of the Holy Spirit in the Reformed Trinitarian Theology of Jonathan Edwards." ThM Thesis. South Hamilton, MA: Gordon Conwell Theological Seminary, 2010.

Chamberlain, Ava. "The Execution of Moses Paul: A Story of Crime and Contact in Eighteenth-Century Connecticut." *The New England Quarterly Journal* 77, no. 3 (Sept. 2004): 414–450.

Cherry, Conrad. *The Theology of Jonathan Edwards: A Reappraisal.* Garden City, NJ: Anchor Books, 1966.

Conforti, Joseph A. *Jonathan Edwards, Religious Tradition, and American Culture.* Chapel Hill, NC: University of North Carolina Press, 1995.

_____. *Samuel Hopkins and The New Divinity Movement: Calvinism, the Congregational Ministry, and Reform in New England Between the Great Awakenings.* Grand Rapids: Christian University Press, 1981.

Collections of the Connecticut Historical Society. Vol. 10. Hartford, CT: Connecticut Historical Society, 1905.

Cookinham, Henry J. *History of Oneida County New York: From 1700 to the Present Time.* Vol. 1. Chicago: S. J. Clarke Publishing Co., 1912.

Cooley, Daniel W. and Douglas A. Sweeney. "The Edwardseans and the Atonement." *A New Divinity: Transatlantic Reformed Evangelical Debates during the Long Eighteenth Century.* Edited by Mark Jones and Michael

A. G. Haykin, 109–125. Reformed Historical Theology Series. Vol. 49. Edited by Herman J. Selderhuis. Gottigen, Germany: Vandenhoeck and Ruprecht Verlage, 2018.

Craun, Joy. "We Are Them: The Golden Rule as a Theological Impetus in the AntiSlavery and Abolitionist Movement." *Online Journal* 9, no. 1 (April 4, 2019): 25– 48.

Crisp, Oliver D., and Douglas A. Sweeney, eds. *After Jonathan Edwards: The Courses of the New England Theology*. New York: Oxford University Press, 2012.

Crisp, Oliver D. and Kyle C. Stobel. *Jonathan Edwards: An Introduction to His Thought*. Grand Rapids, MI: Eerdmans, 2018.

Crisp, Oliver D. "The Moral Government of God: Jonathan Edwards and Joseph Bellamy on the Atonement." 78–90. In *After Jonathan Edwards: The Courses of the New England Theology*. Edited by Oliver D. Crisp and Douglas A. Sweeney. New York: Oxford University Press, 2012.

_____. "Non-Penal Substitution." *International Journal of Systematic Theology* 9. No. 4: 415–433.

_____. "Penal Non-Substitution." *Journal of Theological Studies* 59, no. 1 (April 2008), 140–168.

Danaher Jr., William J. *The Trinitarian Ethics of Jonathan Edwards*. Louisville: John Knox Press, 2004.

Dixon, Philip. *Nice and Hot Disputes: The Doctrine of the Trinity in the Seventeenth Century*. London: T&T Clark, 2003.

Dodds, Elisabeth D. *Marriage to a Difficult Man: The "Uncommon Union" of Jonathan and Sarah Edwards*. Philadelphia: The Westminster Press, 1971.

Doyle, Peter Reese. *Jonathan Edwards on the New Birth in the Spirit: The Life, Times, and Thought of America's Greatest Theologian*. Durham, England: Torchflame Books, 2017.

Ewert, Wesley Carl. *Jonathan Edwards The Younger: A Biographical Essay*. Vol. 1. PhD diss., Hartford Theological Seminary, 1953.

_____. *Jonathan Edwards The Younger: Theological Questions and Answers of Maltby Gelston*. Vol. 2. PhD diss., Hartford Theological Seminary, 1953.

Fife, John and A. Taylor, eds. "On Diseases of the Eye (Continued)." In *Provincial Medical and Surgical Journal (1844–1852)* 10, no. 17 (1846).

_____. "On Diseases of the Eye (Continued)." In *Provincial Medical and Surgical Journal (1844–1852)* 10, no. 20 (1846).

Ford, George Hare. "The Defense of New Haven and Resistance Made Against Invading Troops Along the West Shore, July 1779." In *Revolutionary*

Characters of New Haven [. . .]. New Haven, CT: Sons of the American Revolution, 1911.

Foster, Frank Hugh. *A Genetic History of New England Theology.* Chicago: University of Chicago Press, 1907.

Gambrell, Mary Latimer. *Ministerial Training in 18th-Century New England.* New York: Columbia University Press, 1937.

Gerstner, Edna. *Jonathan and Sarah: An Uncommon Union: A Novel Based on Jonathan and Sarah Edwards (The Stockbridge Years, 1750–1758).* Morgan, PA: Soli Deo Gloria Publishers, 1995.

German, James D. "The Social Utility of Wicked Self-Love: Calvinism, Capitalism, and Public Policy in Revolutionary New England." *The Journal of American History* 82, no. 3 (December 1995): 965–998.

Goen, C. C. "Jonathan Edwards: A New Departure in Eschatology." *Church History* 28, no. 1 (1959): 25–40.

———. *Revivalism and Separatism in New England, 1740–1800: Strict Congregationalists and Separate Baptists in the Great Awakening.* Hamden, CT: Archon Books, 1969.

Grubb, Farley. "State Redemption of the Continental Dollar, 1779–90." *The William and Mary Quarterly* 69, no. 1 (2012): 147–80.

Gura, Philip F. *Jonathan Edwards: America's Evangelical.* New York: Hill and Wang, 2005.

Hall, David D. *Worlds of Wonder, Days of Judgment.* New York: Alfred A. Knopf, Inc, 1989.

Hamilton, S. Mark. "Jonathan Edwards on the Atonement." In *International Journal of Systematic Theology* 15, no. 4 (Oct. 2013), 394–415.

———. "Jonathan Edwards on the Election of Christ." In *Neue Zeitschrift für Systematische Theologie und Religionsphilosophie* 58, no. 4 (2016), 525–548.

———. "Jonathan Edwards, Anselmic Satisfaction and God's Moral Government." In *International Journal of Systematic Theology* 17, no. 1 (Jan. 2015), 46–67.

———. "Re-thinking Atonement in Jonathan Edwards and New England Theology." In *Perichoresis* 15, no. 1 (2017), 85–99.

———. "Jonathan Edwards, Anselmic Satisfaction and God's Moral Government." *International Journal of Systematic Theology* 17, no. 1 (Jan. 2015), 46–67.

Haroutunian, Joseph. *Piety versus Moralism: The Passing of the New England Theology.* New York: Henry Holt and Company, 1932.

Hastings, W. Ross. *Jonathan Edwards and the Life of God: Toward an Evangelical Theology of Participation*. Minneapolis: Fortress Press, 2015.

Hatch, Nathan O. *The Democratization of American Christianity*. New Haven, CT: Yale University Press, 1989.

Hatch, Nathan O. and Harry S. Stout., eds. *Jonathan Edwards and the American Experience*. New York: Oxford University Press, 1988.

Haykin, Michael A. G. "Andrew Fuller and the Sandemanian Controversy." In *'At the Pure Fountain of Thy Word': Andrew Fuller as an Apologist*. Edited by Michael A. G. Haykin. Carlisle, England: Paternoster Press, 2004.

———. "'The Sum of All Good': John Ryland, Jr. and the Doctrine of the Holy Spirit." *Churchman* 103, no. 4: 332–353.

Holmes, Stephen. *God of Grace and God of Glory: An Account of the Theology of Jonathan Edwards*. Edinburgh, Scotland: TandT Clark Ltd, 2000.

Howell, George R. and John H. Munsell. *History of the County of Schenectady, N.Y., from 1662–1886*. Schenectady, NY: Munsell and Company, 1886.

Jacobus, Donald Lines, ed. "Rev. Peter Buckley." In *The Buckley Genealogy*. New Haven, CT: Tuttle, Morehouse, and Taylor, 1933.

Last, Kathy, ed. "New Hartford Presbyterian Church Baptisms." Transcribed by the Daughters of the American Revolution. n.d. Accessed July 5, 2020. http://oneida. nygenweb.net/towns/newhartford/NHbaptisms.htm.

———. "New Hartford Presbyterian Church Marriages." Transcribed by the Daughters of the American Revolution. n.d. Accessed July 5, 2020. http://oneida.nygenweb. net/towns/newhartford/NHmarriages.htm.

Lee, Sang Hyun and Allen C., eds. Guelzo *Edwards in Our Time: Jonathan Edwards and the Shaping of American Religion*. Grand Rapids: Eerdmans, 1999.

Maclean, John. *History of the College of New Jersey, from Its Origin in 1746 to the Commencement of 1854*. Philadelphia: J. B. Lippincott, 1877.

Marsden, George M. *Jonathan Edwards: A Life*. New Haven, CT: Yale University Press, 2003.

Masur, Louis P. *Rites of Execution: Capital Punishment and the Transformation of American Culture, 1776–1865*. New York: Oxford University Press, 1989.

McClymond, Michael J. and Gerald R. McDermott. *The Theology of Jonathan Edwards*. New York: Oxford University Press, 2012.

McLachlan, James. *Princetonians: A Biographical Dictionary 1748–1768*. Princeton, NJ: Princeton University Press, 1976.

McPherson, James. *Battle Cry of Freedom: The Civil War Era*. New York: Oxford University Press, 1988.

Minkema, Kenneth P. *The Edwardses: A Ministerial Family in Eighteenth-century New England.* PhD diss., The University of Connecticut, 1988.

———. "Jonathan Edwards's Defense of Slavery." *Massachusetts Historical Review* 4 (2002): 23–59.

Mitchell, Mary Hewitt. *History of the United Church of New Haven.* New Haven, CT: The United Church, 1942.

Neele, Adriaan C. *Petrus Van Mastrict (1630–1706), Reformed Orthodoxy: Method and Piety.* Brill's Series in Church History. Vol. 35. Edited by Wim Janse. Leiden, Netherlands: Brill, 2009.

Patten, William. *Reminiscences of the late Rev. Samuel Hopkins, D. D., of Newport, R. I.: Illustrative of his character and doctrines, with incidental subjects: From an intimacy with him of twenty-one years, while pastor of a sister church in said town.* Providence, RI: I. H. Cady, 1843.

Paul, Roy M. *Jonathan Edwards and the Stockbridge Mohican Indians.* Peterborough, Canada: H&E Publishing, 2020.

Pauw, Amy Plantinga. *The Supreme Harmony of All: The Trinitarian Theology of Jonathan Edwards.* Grand Rapids: Eerdmans, 2002.

Post, Stephen. "Disinterested Benevolence: An American Debate Over the Nature of Christian Love." *Journal of Religious Ethics* 14, no. 2 (Fall 1986): 356–368.

Ramsey, Paul, ed. "Appendix One: Joseph Bellamy's Copy of the Charity Sermons," *Ethical Writings.* In *The Works of Jonathan Edwards.* Vol. 8. New Haven, CT: Yale University Press, 1970.

Reynolds, David S. *John Brown, Abolitionist: The Man Who Killed Slavery, Sparked the Civil War, and Seeded Civil Rights.* New York: Vintage Books, 2005.

Rosenberry, Lois (Kimball) Mathews. *The Expansion of New England.* Boston: Houghton Mifflin Company, 1909.

Shiels, Richard D. "The Second Great Awakening in Connecticut: Critique of the Traditional Interpretation," *Church History* 49, no. 4 (December 1980): 403–406.

Smith, Daniel Scott. "Child-Naming Practice, Kinship Ties, and Change in Family Attitudes in Hingham, Massachusetts, 1641 to 1880." *Journal of Social History* 18, no. 4 (Summer 1985): 541–566.

Somers, Wayne. *Encyclopedia of Union College History.* Schenectady, NY: Union College Press, 2003.

Stephens, Bruce M. *The Holy Spirit in American Protestant Thought, 1750–1850.* Studies in American Religion Series. Vol. 59. Lewiston, NY: Edwin Mellen Press, 1992.

Strobel, Kyle. *Jonathan Edwards's Theology: A Reinterpretation.* T&T Clark Studies in Systematic Theology, Vol. 19. New York: Bloomsbury T&T Clark, 2013.

Stout, Harry S. *The New England Soul: Preaching and Religious Culture in Colonial New England.* New York: Oxford University Press, 1986.

Sweeney, Douglas A. and Allen C. Guelzo, eds. *New England Theology: From Jonathan Edwards to Edwards Amasa Park.* Grand Rapids: Baker Academic, 2006.

———. "Edwards and His Mantle: The Historiography of the New England Theology. *The New England Quarterly* 71, no. 1 (Mar. 1998): 97–119.

Todd, Obbie Tyler. "Purchasing the Spirit: A Trinitarian Hermeneutic for Jonathan Edwards's Doctrine of the Atonement." *Puritan Reformed Journal* 10, no. 2 (July 2018): 148–167.

———. "The Grammar of Revival: The Legacy of Jonathan Edwards's Teological Language in Religious Affections (1746)." *Calvin Theological Journal* 54, no. 1 (2019): 35–56.

Towner, Lawrence W. "True Confessions and Dying Warnings in Colonial New England." In *Sibley's Heir: A Volume in Memory of Clifford Kenyon Shipton.*, 523–539. Boston: Colonial Society of Massachusetts, 1982.

Townshend, Charles Hervey. *The British Invasion of New Haven, Connecticut [. . .].* New Haven, CT: Tuttle, Morehouse and Taylor: 1879.

Valeri, Mark. *Law and Providence in Joseph Bellamy's New England.* New York: Oxford University Press, 1994.

———. "The New Divinity and the American Revolution." *The William and Mary Quarterly.* Vol. 46, no. 4 (Oct. 1989): 741–769.

Vanhoozer, Kevin J. and Owen Strachan. *The Pastor as Public Theologian: Reclaiming a Lost Vision.* Grand Rapids: Baker Academic, 2015.

Warfield, Benjamin B. "Edwards and The New England Theology." In *Encyclopedia of Religion and Ethics.* Vol. 5. Edited by James Hastings. New York: Charles Schribner's Sons, 1914.

———. "John Calvin the Theologian." *Presbyterian Board of Education* (1909). Accessed January 25, 2020. http://www.graceonlinelibrary.org/ biographies/johncalvin-the-theologian-by-benjamin-b-warfield/.

Weber, Donald. "The Edwardsean Legacy: The Example of Jonathan Edwards, Jr. of White Haven." In *Rhetoric and History in Revolutionary New England,* 47–73. New York: Oxford University Press, 1988.

Wicks, Mary Head. *Historical Sketches of the Paris Congregational Church: 1791–1941.* Utica, NY: Paris Congregational, 1941.

Williams, Nathan, John Smalley, and Benjamin Trumbull, eds. *The Connecticut Evangelical Magazine.* Vol. 2. Hartford, CT: Hudson and Goodwin, 1801.

Wilson-Kastner, Patricia. *Coherence in a Fragmented World: Jonathan Edwards' Theology of the Holy Spirit.* Washington, DC: University Press of America, 1978.

INDEX

Below is a brief index of significant persons, doctrines, and topics.

abolition, 17, 45, 48, 63, 92
affections, 124
Alliene, Joseph, 138
analogies of the Trinity, 106
analogy of honey, 77
Anselm, 115
anticlericalism, 7
apprentices, 112
Arminianism, 147
Austin, David, 56, 63
awakening process, 74, 89

Bacon, Leonard, 59
Baldwin, Ebenezer, 47
Beardselee, Ebenezer, 56, 58, 59
Beardselee, Hezekiah, 83
beatific vision, 136
Bellam, Joseph, 30
Bellamy, Joseph, 2, 3, 5, 11, 21, 32, 33,
        67, 71, 74, 78, 81, 90, 96, 98,
        99, 145
    teaching methods, 31
Bezzant, Rhys, 112
Bird, Samuel, 32, 34
Bradley, Dan, 62, 128, 130
Brainerd, David, 21
Breitenbach, William, 101
Brown, John, 93, 145
Burr, Esther Edwards, 25

Caldwell, Robert W., 105, 108

Calvin, John, 119
Calvinism, 102
Carey, William, 145
Chamberlain, Ava, 41, 44
Chapin, Calvin, 4, 29
Chauncy, Charles, 9, 101, 102, 127
Christian perfection, 87
Christology, 115, 116
civil war with Britain, 51
Colebrook Congregational Church, 98,
    127
College of New Jersey, 25, 32
common and special grace, 124, 142
concept of proportion, 88
confession of salvation experience, 91
Connecticut Missionary Society, 61
Continental Congress, 48
conversion, a lifetime process, 119
Cooley, Timothy Mather, 4, 8
Cornwell, John, 57–59, 74
Crisp, Oliver, 69, 129

Daggett, Naphtali, 53
Dana, James, 40, 59, 76
death of Jerusha Edwards, 18
Declaration of Independence, 52
Delaware Indians, 22
disinterested benevolence, 45, 86
disinterested love, 77
divine illumination, 120
Doyle, Peter Reese, 107

Dutton, Samuel, 32
Dwight, Timothy, 26, 146

Edwards, Jerusha (daughter of Edwards Jr.), 35
Edwards, Jonathan Edwards Sr.
 Mastricht, Peter van, 119
Edwards, Jonathan Jr.
 fever and death, 65
 alienation from congregation, 58
 aptitude for philosophy, 23
 attacks on arguments for slavery, 93
 besetting infirmity, 4
 caricature of spiritless preaching, 11, 65
 Colebrook Congregational Church, installation, 63
 complaints against, 57
 concern for justice, 41
 consistent Calvinist, 15
 conversion, 22, 26
 death, 22
 dismissal from White Haven, 59, 60
 early aptitude for languages, 20, 21, 28
 eye malady in youth, 19
 handwritten sermon notes, 11
 impatient spirit, 4
 initial objection to his father's leading doctrines, 3
 ordination, 33
 poker-face, 20
 popularity as public speaker, 9
 practical preacher, 90
 preaching ministry, 4
 preaching style, 5, 6
 presidency of Union College, 61, 64
 private diary, 27, 30
 promotion of missions, 61, 65
 public theology, 47
 remarriage to Mercy Sabin, 36
 Resolutions, 3
 salary, 56
 views on capital punishment, 42
 wedding to Mary Porter, 35
Edwards, Jonathan Sr.
 affections, 107
 battle over his mantle, 68
 benevolence, 46
 church discipline incident, 19
 concept of proportion, 88
 confession of salvation experience, 91
 death, 67
 defense of Native American interests, 41, 42
 definition of neighbor, 94
 dismissal, 19
 free agency, 90
 governmental theory of atonement, 82
 Holy Spirit and communion and partaking with humanity, 108
 Holy Spirit as bond of union, 107
 infused grace and the will, 110
 legacy of the Spirit, 111, 121
 marks of true religion, 79
 mentoring conversations, 78
 missionary aspirations for Edwards Jr., 21
 models of Trinitarian relations, 111
 natural and moral ability, 102
 necessity of regenerate heart, 83
 on excesses, 101
 partakers of divine nature, 109
 penal atonement theory, 147
 Peter van Mastricht, 111
 pneumatological legacy, 104
 presidency at College of New Jersey, 25
 principle of love, 47
 pure acts of benevolence, 45
 regenerating work of the Holy Spirit, 107
 regeneration, 109–111
 revivals, 101
 role of the Holy Spirit, 106, 107, 110
 slavery, 41, 94
 spiritual beauty, 72
 taste and relish, 72
 theological lineage, 67
 theology of the Spirit, 111
 Trinitarian model, 104
 true church within visible church, 88
 union in his Trinitarianism, 105
Edwards, Jonathan Walter, 23, 35
Edwards, Mary, 35

Index

Edwards, Mary Porter, 35
    death, 36
Edwards, Timothy, 22, 25, 60
Edwards, Tryon, 1, 38, 146
Edwardsean pneumatology, 114, 127, 131, 144, 146, 147
Edwardsean principle of benevolence, 42, 45–47, 92, 136
Emmons, Nathanael, 104, 119
empiricism, 128
enthusiasm, 6, 101
Erskine, John, 145
evangelical humility, 79

Fairhaven Church, 53
Ferm, Robert L., 3, 14, 25, 33
Finley, Samuel, 25
Finney, Charles G., 7, 67, 104, 119, 121, 127, 141, 144
First Church, 32, 40, 59, 76
Flavel, John, 138, 141
Fuller, Andrew, 145

Gelston, Maltby, 114, 119, 121, 123, 125, 144
genuine spirituality, 101
Gerstner, Edna, 20
Goddard, Ives, 28
Goen, C. C., 6
golden rule, 47, 92
Gordon, William, 2, 9
governmental theory of atonement, 48, 82, 83, 112, 115, 130
Great Awakening, 32, 101
Griffin, Edward Dorr, 63

Half-way Covenant, 8, 19, 33, 34, 58, 65, 76
Haroutunian, Joseph, 8, 14, 70, 73, 84
Hastings, Ross, 105
hasty pudding incident, 26
Hatch, Nathan, 146
Hawley, Gideon, 21, 22
heart religion, 97, 121, 146
Hodge, Charles, 103, 107, 111, 119, 122, 125, 127, 141, 144
Holmes, Stephen, 91
Holy Spirit, 117
Holy Spirit as bond of union, 107, 109, 115, 128, 130

Hopkins, Samuel, 3, 7, 30, 35, 67, 71, 99, 104
hunger for personal holiness, 76

individualism, 7, 121
indivisualism, 146
infused grace, 128, 140
Intolerable Acts, 38, 49

justice, 46
    benevolent application of, 44
    misapplication of, 44

light of nature, 87
Locke, John, 141
Log College, 25

Mahican language, 28
marks of true religion, 79
Masthay, Carl, 28
Mastricht, Peter van, 106, 108, 109, 111, 119, 149–151
Masur, Louis P., 39
McClymond, Michael, 88, 106, 111
McDermott, Gerald, 88, 106, 111
meekness and Christian virtue, 75
Modalism, 131
mood towards clergy, 6
Mountain, Joseph, 39, 40, 42, 47
Murray, John, 83

native depravity, 96
natural and moral ability, 102
Neele, Adriaan, 107
new birth, 138
New Divinity theology, 9, 56, 65, 83, 86, 91, 102, 145
New England Theology, 67, 71, 103, 145
New Lights, 76, 150
New Side preachers, 26
Norton, Asahel S., 63

Occom, Samson, 40, 45
Old Lights, 76
Oneida Indians, 21
oppression and unjust taxation, 49

Paine, Thomas, 87
Palmer, Thomas, 64

Park, Edwards Amasa, 68, 103, 104, 125, 150
Park, Edwards Amase, 119
patriotism, 50
Patten, William, 3
Paul, Moses, 15, 38, 40–47
Paul, Roy M., 41
Pauw, Amy Plantiga, 105, 106
Perkins, Nathan, 61
perseverance of saints, 126
physical infusion, 109, 132, 133, 141
Pierrepoint, James, 32
Plan of Union, 65
postmillennialism, 96
prayer for the kingdom and common things, 89
Princeton University, 67

Ramsey, Paul, 141
regenerate church membership, 66, 75, 88
regeneration, 115, 118, 119, 126
    active or passive, 123
    by Holy Spirit, 6, 126, 127, 131, 138, 140
    by supernatural light of Holy Spirit, 140
    conversion, the difference, 123, 132, 133
    immediate, 140
    not gradual, 140
    volition and freedom, 133
    why necessary, 123, 143
religious freedom, 50
revival, 26, 52, 73, 101
revivalism, 101
revivalistic rhetoric, 83
revolution, 48
Revolutionary War, 91
romanticism, 121
Ryland, John, 145

Sabbath attendance, 90
Sabellianism, 131
Sabin, Hezekiah Jr., 53
sanctification, 125
Sandemanians, 140
Schneck, William E., 26
Second Great Awakening, 13, 61, 64, 98, 99, 146

separatists, 6
Sermon on the Mount, 71
Sherman, Roger, 33, 56, 63
Six Nations, 21
Smith, Robert, 17, 65
soteriology, 129
Spencer, Thomas, 22, 23
spiritual poverty and native blindness, 72, 79, 120, 122
spiritual sense, 77, 81
Stamp Act, 48
Stiles, Ezra, 9, 36, 53, 58
    diary, 11
Stiles, ezra, 35
Stoddard, Solomon, 19, 101
Stout, Harry, 11
Stowe, Harriet Beecher, 7, 68
Strachan, Owen, 149
Strobel, Kyle, 45, 105, 106, 108, 129
Strong, Nathan, 5, 8, 12
Sweeney, Douglas, 33, 69

taste for spiritual beauty, 72, 120, 121
taste, relish, enjoy prospect of heaven, 73
Tennent, William, 25
theologians of the "Standing Order", 9
theological liberalism, 70
theological questions, 113, 114
Todd, Obbie T., 72, 82, 84
total depravity, 131, 135
Towner, Lawrence, 39
Trinitarian theology, 105
Trinity's bond of union, 105
Trinity, doctrine of, 131
true happiness, 74

Universalism, 83, 127, 147
universalism, 57

Valeri, Mark, 11, 134
visible church, 88

Washington, George, 20
Weber, Donald, 12, 150
West, Samuel, 127
West, Stephen, 9, 11
Wetmore, Seth Judge, 26
White Haven Church, 10, 13, 32, 35, 38, 41, 48, 56–58, 63, 74, 81, 146
Whitefield, George, 18, 26

Willard, Samuel, 138–140

witness of the Spirit, 126

Wooster, David General, 51

Yates, Andrew, 64

www.ingramcontent.com/pod-product-compliance
Lightning Source LLC
Chambersburg PA
CBHW071834230426
43671CB00012B/1961